THE Microwave
KITCHEN BIBLE

THE Microwave
KITCHEN BIBLE

A complete guide to getting

the best out of your microwave

with over 160 recipes

carol bowen

southwater

This edition is published by Southwater

Distributed in the UK by
The Manning Partnership
251–253 London Road East
Batheaston
Bath BA1 7RL
UK
tel. (0044) 01225 852 727
fax (0044) 01225 852 852

Distributed in Australia by
Sandstone Publishing
Unit 1, 360 Norton Street
Leichhardt
New South Wales 2040
Australia
tel. (0061) 2 9560 7888
fax (0061) 2 9560 7488

Distributed in New Zealand by
Five Mile Press NZ
PO Box 33-1071
Glenfield
Auckland 10
New Zealand
tel. (0064) 9 4444 144
fax (0064) 9 4444 518

Southwater is an imprint of Anness Publishing Limited
© 1997, 2000 Anness Publishing Limited

1 3 5 7 9 10 8 6 4 2

Publisher: Joanna Lorenz
Senior Cookery Editor: Linda Fraser
Editor: Bridget Jones
Designer: William Mason
Illustrator: Madeleine David
Indexer: Hilary Bird

CONTENTS

Introduction

ndeniably, speed is the main advantage of microwave cooking; however, it is not this in isolation that has made microwaves the success story they are. Not only do microwaves make easy work of cooking many staple dishes and family favorites, but they also cook them to perfection. With a microwave oven, limp, soggy greens, over-sticky rice, nutritionally poor fruit-based desserts, and labor- and time-intensive meat, fish, and poultry dishes are things of the past; these emerge from the microwave fresh, colorful, nutritionally rich, and, moreover, most appetizing. The time-saving aspect may be great, as when cooking a baked potato in about 6 minutes, or minimal, for example in the case of rice and pasta, but the additional benefit is being able to cook foods with the minimum attention and to just the right degree, be it *al dente*, tender-crisp, fork-tender, or succulently moist.

ADVANTAGES OF MICROWAVE COOKING

Speed
You can reduce normal cooking times by up to 75 percent by using a microwave oven.

Nutrient Retention
Nutrient loss from food is often associated with other cooking methods. With microwave cooking, because timings are short and so precise, and additional cooking liquid is minimal, there is less likely to be a loss of nutrients during cooking or by seepage as occurs when boiling.

Economy
Because microwave cooking does not involve a lengthy preheating period and cooks for a shorter period of time, this method requires less energy and, therefore, saves money on energy bills.

Few Cooking Smells
Cooking odors are usually contained within the microwave oven cavity, so kitchen odors are kept to an absolute minimum.

Cool Kitchen
Because of the mechanics of microwave cooking, the microwave oven, dishes, and the kitchen all stay cool, while only the food becomes piping hot. Also, in kitchens where there is a problem with ventilation, the microwave is a great improvement on the conventional stovetop, which creates a lot of steam during boiling or other moist cooking methods.

Less Risk of Burns
Because dishes do not become red hot, but only heat up by the conduction of heat from the food, there is less risk of getting a nasty

burn from dishes or from the oven itself. This makes the microwave one of the safest cooking machines for the very young and for the elderly or infirm to use.

Less Cleaning and Washing
It is possible to cook and serve in the same container with microwave cooking, thereby reducing the amount of dishwashing. Cleaning the oven is also easier because food does not bake on or splatter as can happen in conventional ovens and on stovetops.

An End to Dried-Out Dinners
With a microwave oven, dried-out dinners can become a thing of the past. Individual members of the family can eat when they want and latecomers can have a meal reheated in minutes to just-cooked perfection.

SELECTING FOOD FOR MICROWAVE COOKING

Aside from a few restrictions, virtually any food can be cooked in the microwave, but there are some foods that cook better than others. When planning a meal or choosing a recipe consider the following:

Fish and Shellfish
Whether fresh or frozen, whole or filleted, plain or in a fancy sauce, microwave-cooked fish and shellfish are hard to beat for texture, flavor, appearance, and ease of preparation. With little danger of drying out, these delicate foods stay succulently moist. Often, the only additional ingredients required are a tablespoon or two of water, lemon juice, or stock, or a little butter, so microwaved fish and seafood are favorites with those following a healthy diet regime or watching their weight.
Whole Fish Slit the skin in two or three places on whole fish, such as salmon, trout, and mackerel, to prevent it from bursting during cooking. (Boil-in-the-bag prepared fish should also have the pouch pierced.) The narrow end of the tail may need protecting for half the cooking time by shielding with a little foil.
Fillets, Steaks, and Portions For best results when cooking fillets, roll them up into an even shape and secure each one with a wooden toothpick. Brush with lemon juice

or melted butter and cover tightly during cooking. Fish steaks and pieces should be cooked so the thickest portions are to the outer edge of the dish and the thinner pieces to the middle, where they receive the least microwave energy.
Coated Portions Bread-crumb-coated and battered fish can be cooked in the microwave, but the result will not be as crisp as when cooked conventionally. A microwave browning dish can help appreciably with these products.
Shellfish Shrimp, lobster, and scallops cook superbly, but always start with the minimum time when cooking these items because they cook very quickly. Also remember to take the standing time into account as part of the overall cooking process. Mussels and clams can also be steamed and cooked in the microwave with unbelievable ease.

Poultry and Game
Whole birds; quarters; breast, thigh, and drumstick portions; stir-fry strips; and medallions of poultry and game can be cooked in the microwave with good results. Those dishes that require little browning, with portions cooked in a sauce, are most successful.
Whole Birds Truss well to hold the wings and legs close to the body to give a neat, compact shape. The narrow wingtips and drumstick bone ends may have to be protected with small pieces of foil for part of the cooking time. Start cooking whole birds breast-side down and turn over halfway through cooking. Place on a special microwaveproof roasting rack or on an upturned saucer so the bird is lifted above the cooking juices.

With large birds that require longer cooking times, browning is usually sufficient, but smaller birds and portions may need a little help. In all cases, whether cooking a whole bird or portions, these can be browned under a hot broiler after microwave cooking—the time savings are still considerable and warrant microwave cooking.

When cooking birds that have been stuffed, add an extra 1 minute per 1 pound to the times recommended in cooking charts. After cooking, leave to stand, covered in a tent of foil, to make best use of the residual heat; you will also find that the bird is easier to carve.
Small Birds and Portions Small birds, chicken quarters, and small poultry joints should be cooked skin-side up, with the thickest parts toward the outside of the dish. Many will brown and crisp more readily if placed in a roasting bag.

If you are unsure of timings, then consider investing in a microwave thermometer, which takes the guesswork out of roasting and cooking times by indicating the internal temperature of the food.

Meat
With careful consideration of the quality and cut, meat cooked in the microwave is a great success. Cheaper, longer-cooking cuts can be microwaved with a measure of success, but the microwave performs best with prime-quality cuts. With the exception of roast pork, do not salt meat before microwave cooking because it draws out the moisture and toughens the meat.
Joints Ideally, choose joints that are symmetrically shaped; in other words, bone and roll joints like legs and shoulders for perfect results.

Ground Meat Ground beef, lamb, and pork cook magnificently, whether as burgers or in moist dishes, like chili con carne or spaghetti sauce. Meatloaves should be made in a ring mold for faster cooking.
Cubed Meat Cubes of meat for dishes such as casseroles, and curries should be cut into pieces of the same size to insure even cooking. Reduce the liquid required for such dishes by up to a third because very little evaporation occurs in microwave cooking. Vegetables in covered baking dishes tend to retain their shape and do not break down to thicken the liquid.
Sausages, Bacon, and Kabobs
Sausages, bacon, and other fatty meats cook quickly with some degree of browning, but cover them with a sheet of paper towels during cooking to prevent fat splattering on the oven walls. Wooden skewers should be used for kabobs, which should, ideally, be cooked on a microwave roasting rack or placed across a shallow microwaveproof dish for success.

Vegetables

Whether freshly harvested from your garden, bought in the market, plucked from the supermarket shelf, or taken from the freezer or cupboard, the microwave cooks your vegetable selection to perfection. Only the minimum amount of water is used for microwaving most vegetables, so results are temptingly colorful and tender-crisp. Season with salt after cooking, because salt sprinkled directly onto vegetables can cause them to dehydrate and toughen.

Whole Vegetables Potatoes, eggplants, and tomatoes need pricking before cooking to prevent them bursting. Baked potatoes will also have a crisper, drier skin if cooked on a sheet of paper towel. Whole vegetables or items which are not cut into small pieces should be positioned so the thickest parts are toward the outer edge of the dish, where they receive the most energy.

Cut Vegetables Most vegetables should be cut into uniformly size pieces and placed in a cooking bag or covered dish. Stir, rearrange, or shake the vegetables halfway through the cooking time to insure even results.

Fruit

From the basic apple to the exotic mango, fruit can be cooked in the microwave to retain its glorious characteristics. Most fruits can be prepared, sprinkled with sugar, and cooked in a roasting bag or dish in the same way as fresh vegetables. Other items can be baked whole, poached in wine, cider, or syrup, or stuffed with a sweetened filling.

Whole Fruit These must be scored or pricked if they are not peeled, so the skin does not burst during cooking. Careful timing is important because fruit cooks surprisingly quickly.

Dried Fruit Dried fruit mixtures can also be cooked quickly to make fruit salads, compotes, and crumbles. Try mixtures of dried apple, pear, mango, peach, apricot, and prune, and cook them in fruit juice and water for mouthwatering puddings at any time of the year.

Frozen Fruit The microwave is also useful for preparing fruit for the freezer when there is a glut, a good price at the market, or windfall of tree fruit. Use the microwave for cooking the fruit or for speedily making the sugar syrup in which to freeze fruit for long-term storage.

Pasta, Rice, Grains, and Legumes

Any healthy diet should have its fair share of pasta, rice, grains, and legumes; but, so often, it is the lengthy preparation of the latter that prevents us from serving them more often. The microwave makes light work of rehydrating beans and legumes, reducing what was once a long, overnight process of soaking to about $1\frac{1}{2}$ hours.

The time savings with cooking pasta, rice, grains, and legumes are virtually negligible, but the bonuses are that little or no attention is required during cooking; the results are superb; there is not a sticky, tacky saucepan to wash afterward; no steamy kitchen and boil-over spills; and the food can be cooked ahead and reheated to perfection later.

All About Microwaves

For centuries people have cooked food to make it more palatable, easier to digest, and safe to eat. From the smoky fire of prehistoric times through to today's high-tech microwave ovens, the principle of heating food to cook it has remained the same; the difference is in the speed of cooking and the methods employed. Traditional methods of cooking food in the fire, in the gas or electric stove, and under or over the charcoal grill or broiler use conduction as the prime method of introducing heat. But what are microwaves and how do they cook?

MICROWAVE COOKING MADE SIMPLE

The mechanics of microwave cooking are no more magical than a television or radio. Inside the microwave is a magnetron vacuum tube, the "heart" or "brains" of the microwave, which converts ordinary household electrical energy into high-frequency, electromagnetic waves, called microwaves. The microwaves are then directed into the oven cavity, through a wave guide, and stirred by a fan for even distribution.

MICROWAVES IN ACTION

The waves are either reflected, pass through some materials, or are absorbed by other materials. Metals reflect them (so cooking utensils must be nonmetallic); glass, pottery, china, paper, and most plastics allow them to pass through (so they make ideal cooking utensils); and foods absorb them.

The microwaves are absorbed by the moisture in food, causing the food molecules to vibrate rapidly, thus producing heat to cook food.

Imagine the Boy or Girl Scout rubbing two twigs together to light a fire and you have the general idea. However, the speed at which the microwaves cause the molecules to vibrate is millions of times per second, producing remarkably intense heat that cooks super fast.

This is completely different from conventional methods, where heat is passed along a chain from one molecule to the next until the whole becomes hot and cooked. It is especially different in that dishes remain cool, metals cannot be used and timings are fast, calling for different cooking procedures and techniques.

FACTORS WHICH AFFECT MICROWAVE COOKING

Starting Temperature of Food
Foods that are cooked from room temperature will take less time to cook than foods that are frozen or chilled. Cooking times in the recipes that follow are based on starting temperatures at which the foods are normally stored, unless otherwise stated.

Density of Food
The denser the food, the longer it takes to cook. Heavy, dense foods, like potatoes, take longer to cook than light porous foods, like cakes. For the same reason a solid, dense mass of food, like a whole cauliflower, will take longer to cook than the same food divided into pieces (in the case of cauliflower, cut into small flowerets) and spread out for cooking.

Composition of Food
Foods which are high in fats and sugars will cook faster than foods high in liquid because fats and sugars absorb microwave energy more readily. They also reach higher temperatures during the cooking process than water-based foods. It therefore takes longer to cook foods that are high in moisture, like vegetables, than it does to cook those with little moisture, such as breads and cakes.

Quantity of Food
As the volume or quantity of food being cooked in the microwave increases, the cooking time increases. If you double the amount of food, the time will increase by about half as much again.

Size and Shape of Food
Smaller pieces of food cook quicker than larger pieces, and uniformly shaped pieces cook more evenly than irregular-shaped items. Cutting foods into regular pieces, fingers, or slices and slicing meat across the grain prior to cooking will all help to guarantee even cooking. With unevenly shaped pieces that cannot be cut, the thinner parts cook faster than the thicker areas, so they should be placed toward the center of the dish where they can be grouped together to receive less energy. Ideally, portions of food that are of the same size and shape cook most evenly.

It is also important to remember that round and ring shapes cook more evenly than square, oval, or rectangular shapes. With the latter, there is a concentration of energy in the corners and at the ends that can cause charring; to avoid this, protect the corners with small pieces of smooth foil to shield them from the microwave energy.

Bones in Meat

Bones in meat conduct heat, therefore meat next to the bone in a joint cooks first. Wherever possible, it is wise to bone and roll meat for even cooking. If not, remember to shield thin areas of meat next to the bone halfway through the cooking time to prevent overcooking.

Height in the Oven

Areas that are closest to any source of energy cook faster than those farther away, and the microwave is no exception to this rule. Depending on its design, your microwave may cook faster near the floor or the roof, where the energy source is located. Rotating, turning over, and stirring foods minimize this effect.

THE MICROWAVE

All basic models are much the same in design. They consist of a cabinet, magnetron, wave guide, wave stirrer, power supply, power cord, and controls. Some have special extra features such as automatic defrost, variable power control, turntable, integral ther- mometer or temperature probe, browning or crisping elements, and stay-hot devices.

The microwaves are safely contained in the cavity by the metal lining inside the base and walls, which reflects the microwaves into the food. All cooker doors and frames are fitted with special seals as an extra safety measure to insure the microwaves stay in the oven. In addition, all microwave ovens have one or more cut-out devices so the flow of microwaves stops automatically whenever the door is opened, or if the door has not been shut properly or is damaged.

Many microwave ovens have a turntable, which means foods, such as fish, do not need turning during cooking.

Portable Microwave Ovens

These are undoubtedly the most popular. Being almost as light and certainly as portable as a television, such cooking machines are popular choices for students, apartment dwellers, and the elderly. They are also good for use in a boat, trailer, or second home.

A portable microwave oven may be sited conveniently on a worktop, cart, or other firm, stable surface. Some models, with very basic controls, have been developed for the "simplistic cooking and reheating" market, and are usually short in height, designed to fit under the countertop. Often budget priced, this type of microwave will accom-modate a chicken or a couple of stacked plated meals, but it is not suitable for those who require a flexible oven arrangement or sophisticated cooking.

Double Oven

Some microwave models are available in the same unit as a conventional oven, with the microwave acting as a second or double oven. Most models are built-in, but a few free-standing models are available.

Combination Ovens

This is an expanding section of the microwave market and one that is likely to attract second-time buyers. These ovens have the facility to cook by both microwave and conventional means in one single operation and in one unit. The conventional and microwave powers can operate separately, simultaneously, or in sequence, as required. Some models also offer additional choices, with fan-assisted ovens, broilers, or automatic cooking sequence controls for microwave, combination, and conventional cooking. In the chapters that follow, look for recipes that can be cooked using combination controls, but follow the timings given in your manufacturer's instruction manual.

INSTALLING THE MICROWAVE

All that is required to install a portable microwave cooker is a power socket. Manufacturers also recommend that you place the microwave on a stable surface and have adequate ventilation. It is therefore possible to site the microwave in a multitude of places—the kitchen countertop is typical, but also consider a cart that can be wheeled between rooms or even out onto the terrace or patio for outdoor dining, providing wonderful flexibility when preparing accompaniments for barbecues.

If you plan to build-in your microwave, then make sure you buy the correct fixing kit or housing unit, with adequate venting, and always check your microwave manual for any special instructions.

CLEANING THE MICROWAVE

This is something of a bonus! Because the walls in the microwave oven cavity remain cool during cooking, cleaning is often just a quick-wipe operation. Food does not have the opportunity to bake-on, so wiping the inside at regular intervals, or when spills occur, with a damp, soapy cloth is sufficient. Remember always to disconnect the oven from the electrical supply before wiping or cleaning. Remove and wash oven trays, shelving and bases according to the manufacturer's instructions.

Wipe the outside surfaces and door regularly, but do not allow water to seep into the vents. If necessary, also clean any air filters or the stirrer fan guard according to the manufacturer's directions.

Stale cooking smells can be removed by boiling a solution of 1 part lemon juice to 3 parts water in a microwaveproof bowl in the microwave for about 5 minutes on HIGH. Then wipe the oven cavity dry with a clean cloth.

SERVICING

Remember to have the microwave checked by a qualified engineer every 12 months, or as recommended by the manufacturer.

NOTE
Do not operate the microwave oven when it is empty. For safety, especially when young children are around, place a cup of water in the oven when it is not in use. If the oven is accidentally switched on, the water will absorb the energy. This way there is negligible risk of damaging the magnetron, something that can occur if the oven is operated when empty.

A sophisticated microwave oven with combination cooking facility.

Microwave Dishes and Utensils

Without doubt, the range of dishes and utensils that can be used in the microwave is wider than that for conventional cooking.

GLASS, POTTERY, AND CHINA

Ovenproof and plain glass, pottery, and china are all suitable for microwave cooking. Be sure to check that they do not have any metallic trim, screws, or handles, and, if using a pottery dish, that it is nonporous.

Clear glass dishes, such as Pyrex, are particularly useful because you can actually see the food being cooked and check its progress during cooking.

Glass measuring jugs are also superb and let you measure, mix, cook and, sometimes, serve from the same container. Ovenproof glass and glass-ceramic dishes are invaluable for use in one operation from the freezer to the microwave and vice versa (once the food has cooled completely).

The only type of glass to avoid for microwave cooking is the leaded type most often found as decorative drinking glassware.

PAPER

Paper is a good utensil for low-heat and short cooking times, such as thawing, reheating, or very short cooking, and for foods with a low fat, sugar, or water content. Napkins, paper towels, cups, cartons, freezer wrapping paper, and the paper pulp board often used for supermarket packaging are all suitable. Paper towels are especially useful for cooking fatty foods, because they absorb excess fats and oils and can be used to prevent splattering on the microwave's walls.

Avoid using metal in any form, including dishes wth metal decoration or trims; porous pottery and mugs or cups with glued handles; crystal glass; and polystyrene trays or nondishwashersafe plastics.

Wax-coated paper cups and plates should be avoided because the high temperature of the food will cause the wax to melt; they can be used for thawing items to be served cold, such as frozen cakes and desserts.

PLASTICS

Whether these are dishwasher safe or not provides a useful indication as to whether or not a plastic item is suitable for microwave use. Unless made of a thermoplastic material, plastic dishes and containers should not be used for cooking foods with a high fat or sugar content, because the heat of the food may cause the plastic to melt and lose its shape.

Plastic wrap for microwave use and items like bags suitable for boil-in-the-bag cooking work well.

Pierce a bag or plastic wrap before cooking to allow steam to escape or fold back a corner to vent the plastic wrap to prevent it ballooning during cooking. Also take extra special care when removing plastic wrap or opening plastic bags in case any trapped steam escapes and burns your hand or forearm.

Roasting bags provide a clean, convenient way of cooking many foods, from vegetables to roasts. Roast meats particularly benefit from their use because browning seems to take place more readily in a roasting bag. Either tie loosely with room for steam to escape or snip a couple of holes in the bag to aid the steam escape and replace the metal ties with elastic, string, or other nonmetallic tie.

Do not attempt to microwave in thin plastic bags because they will not withstand the heat of the food. Thicker storage or freezer bags are acceptable. Use elastic bands, string, or nonmetallic ties to secure the bags loosely before cooking.

Melamine is not recommended for microwave cooking because it absorbs enough microwave energy to cause charring.

COTTON AND LINEN

Napkins are ideal for short warming or reheating procedures, such as reheating bread rolls for serving. It is important to use only cotton or linen, because synthetic fibers, or fabrics containing a proportion of them, will be damaged.

WOODEN BOWLS AND BAKEWARE

These are suitable only for short periods of reheating, otherwise the wood or wicker will dry out, crack, or char.

SPECIAL MICROWAVE EQUIPMENT

With the increased popularity of microwave cooking, there are many specialist innovations in microwave cookware. Several ranges manufactured from polythene, polystyrene, and

A selection of everyday items that are useful for microwave cooking.

thermoplastics are widely available and come in a comprehensive range of shapes and sizes. If you are an enthusiastic microwave cook then you might consider investing in some of the more useful items, such as a microwave baking tray, roasting rack, muffin tray, ring mold, and whisk.

If the microwave is your only form of oven, you may well be interested in some other very special items of cookware, developed to broaden the options when cooking in a microwave. These include a special popcorn popper, a microwave pressure cooker, special kabob and burger or chop cooker, and a range of microwaveproof saucepans.

Thermometers

Thermometers made especially for microwave ovens are available but can be used in an oven only when specified by the oven's manufacturer. Their main use is for checking the internal temperature of a meat to make sure it is cooked to your requirements. They can also be used to check that, after cooking for the recommended time, the internal

temperature of prepared meals is sufficiently high to destroy microorganisms that may be present and can cause food poisoning. Some newer ovens have an automatic cooking control based on a temperature-sensing probe that can be inserted into the food while in the oven. When the food reaches a precise temperature, the oven turns itself off automatically.

Browning Dishes

Available from most microwave dealers and large kitchenware stores, these duplicate the browning and searing processes of conventional cooking. They are especially useful for browning burgers, chops, sausages, and steaks. They can also be used to "fry" eggs and sandwiches, and to brown vegetables.

The browning dish is made of a glass ceramic substance with a special coating that absorbs microwave energy. It is heated in the microwave until the bottom coating changes color, usually for about 8 minutes on HIGH. Always follow specific manufacturer's directions because dishes, coatings, and timings vary.

Examples of special microwave cookware.

The food is then placed on the dish to brown and turned to sear both sides. Heating times and browning or searing times differ according to the food being cooked and the power output of the oven. Always follow the manufacturer's directions for best results.

CHECKING SUITABILITY FOR MICROWAVE COOKING

If you intend to cook food in both the microwave and the conventional oven in a continuous operation, be sure to use a dish that is ovenproof as well as microwaveproof. The following is a simple test to check microwave suitability:

Fill a heatproof cup with cold water and stand it in the container being checked. Place the container in the microwave and microwave on HIGH for $1\frac{1}{4}$ minutes. If the water is warm in the cup and the container is cool, go ahead and use the container. If the container is warm or even hot and the water is still cool, or barely lukewarm, do not use the container for microwave cooking.

THE SHAPE AND SIZE OF DISH TO USE

After checking the material, consider the shape and size of the dish. Ideally, the more regular the shape the better for microwave cooking. For example, a round shape is much better than an oval; a straight-sided container is better than a curved one because the microwaves penetrate more evenly; and a large shallow dish is better than a small deep one because the food is spread over a greater surface area and therefore exposed to more microwave energy.

A Few Ideas
The following novel pieces of cookware can be used in the microwave successfully:
• scallop shells
• glass or plastic baby bottles for warming milk and juice
• wooden toothpicks for securing foods and wooden kabob skewers for brochettes and kabobs
• paper cup cake cases for muffins—support them in teacups or ramekins.

MATERIAL TO AVOID—METALS

Most manufacturers object to the use of metal. Even small amounts in the oven will reflect the microwaves so they do not penetrate the food to be cooked.

Therefore, avoid metal dishes, baking trays, and metal baking pans, foil dishes, cast-iron cookware, plates, and china trimmed with a metallic design, metal kabob skewers, any dish with a metal screw or attachment, and the paper-coated metal ties often used with freezer and cook bags.

Microwave Techniques

PREPARING INGREDIENTS

When cutting ingredients, prepare even-size pieces so they cook at the same rate.

• Slim strips of vegetables, such as carrots, cook quicker and more evenly than large, irregular pieces or different size whole vegetables.

• Even cubes or dice cook well. Large vegetables, such as turnip, potato, rutabaga or pumpkin, can all be cut into neat cubes to promote quick, even cooking.

• Slicing meat across the grain into thin pieces helps to tenderize it.

SCORING OR PRICKING FOODS

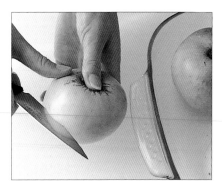

Foods with tight skins or membranes, such as sausages, kidneys, giblets, whole fish, baked potatoes, egg yolks, and apples must be lightly pricked or scored before cooking or they are liable to burst or explode. This is because of the tremendous amount of pressure that develops within foods when they cook very quickly.

STIRRING

Stirring is important when cooking conventionally, and it is also necessary when cooking by microwave. Conventionally, we stir to redistribute heat from the bottom of the pan to the top, but with a microwave the aim is to redistribute heat and cooked areas from the outside to the middle of a dish for even cooking. Precise stirring instructions will be given in a recipe if it is important; if not, stirring halfway through cooking is usually sufficient.

ROTATING

If your microwave has a turntable, this cooking technique becomes redundant. In models without a turntable, a quarter or half turn of the dish at regular intervals during the cooking period guarantees even results when food cannot be stirred or turned over.

TURNING OVER

Many large or dense items of food, such as potatoes or chicken drumsticks, should be turned over halfway through cooking to insure good results.

> ### COOK'S TIP
> ❧
> A pair of food tongs is useful for turning firm foods, such as chicken portions, chops, and sausages, for example.

ARRANGING FOOD

Arranging foods carefully in a dish for microwave cooking can mean an ingredient is perfectly cooked, rather than merely adequately cooked. For success, follow these guidelines:

• Try to cook foods of an even or similar size together and, if possible, arrange them in a ring pattern in a dish, leaving the middle empty.

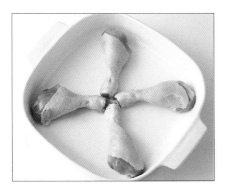

• If foods are not a regular shape, such as chicken drumsticks or spears of broccoli, arrange the thickest sections to the outside of the dish in a spokelike arrangement so the thick areas receive the most energy and cook more quickly than the thin areas that are grouped together.

• Arrange whole fish in pairs, head to tail, to form an even area that will cook uniformly. Thin areas cook quicker than thick or large areas, which are not penetrated as quickly by microwaves.

• When reheating plated meals, make sure the food is spread out evenly. Thicker vegetables should be arranged toward the edge to receive the most energy.

• When heating more than one plated meal at a time, special plastic microwave stacking rings can be placed between plates. These rings insure plates are positioned so they all receive an equal amount of energy and therefore the meals reheat at the same rate.

• Try to insure the depth of food is even; if it is not, stir or rearrange ingredients.

• Foods cooked in a ring pattern or mold make the most of the microwave. Cakes cook particularly well in a ring mold. If you don't have one, improvize. Place a glass tumbler in a round microwave-proof dish, and hold it in place while adding the batter.

REARRANGING FOODS

Even with a turntable, rearranging foods (usually once) guarantees even results. Move foods from the outside of the dish to the middle and vice versa.

• Rearrange foods cooking in a bag by gently shaking the bag. Remember scalding-hot steam can escape as the contents of the bag are shuffled, so protect your hand and forearm with a folded dishcloth or oven mitt.

SHIELDING

As with conventional cooking, some parts of foods are more vulnerable to overcooking than others. In such cases, it is acceptable to use small smooth strips of foil to protect thin or vulnerable areas.

This is the only time when metal may be introduced into a typical microwave oven, and it is important to make sure it does not touch the oven walls. Position the foil on the food for about half the cooking time, securing small patches with wooden toothpicks, if necessary.

Check the manufacturer's handbook to make sure this is permissible in your particular model of microwave oven.

• Fish heads and tails should be protected to prevent eyes from bursting and thin areas from overcooking.

• Wingtips on poultry and the thinner tail-ends on ducks should be shielded to prevent them from overcooking and drying out.

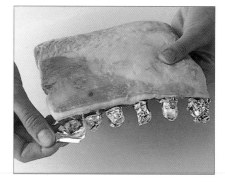

• Protruding bones, for example as on a rack of lamb, should be shielded to prevent scorching.

• Narrow ends of joints of meat, such as at the end of a leg of lamb or pork, should be shielded.

COVERING AND WRAPPING

Problems of surfaces drying out, splattering of food on the cavity walls, and slower-than-optimum cooking times can all be eliminated by covering or wrapping foods. This locks in moisture, retains juices, and speeds up cooking by trapping heat-retaining steam.

• Use double-strength plastic cooking bags, suitable for boiling

(sometimes referred to as "boil-in-the-bag" bags or "cook bags") or roasting bags for vegetables, meat, and poultry. Replace metal ties with elastic bands.

• Some bags come with special, microwaveproof plastic clips.

• String can be used to loosely tie bags closed.

> ### COOK'S TIP
> ❧
> Remember to check that a cooking bag is not too hot to hold before picking it up; protect your hand with a folded dishcloth, if necessary, and be aware that scalding-hot steam may escape from any small opening at the top of the bag as the contents move when lifted or as they are being rearranged.

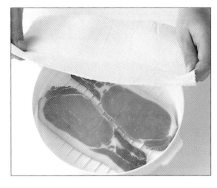

• Use a tight-fitting lid or improvize by using a saucer or plate instead.

• Waxed paper can be used to cover small bowls, such as when cooking steamed puddings. The paper can be secured with a large elastic band.

• Covering bacon with paper towels prevents spattering as well as absorbing any moisture that is given off.

• Paper towels are also invaluable for drying herbs.

• When dampened, paper towels can be used for reheating and steaming crepes and shellfish.

• Cover bowls with a tight membrane of microwavesafe plastic wrap. Puncture the top to let some steam escape during cooking.

• Use paper towels as a base on which to stand food.

• Turn back a small area of plastic wrap to make a vent to prevent a ballooning effect during cooking. Take care when removing the plastic wrap, because it will trap a significant amount of scalding-hot steam even when it is vented.

• Paper towels can also be used as a cover for some foods. They are especially good for absorbing excess moisture given off by foods like potatoes and bread while they cook.

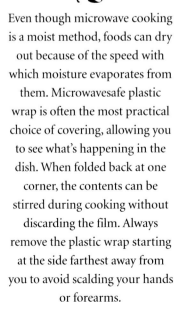

COOK'S TIP

Even though microwave cooking is a moist method, foods can dry out because of the speed with which moisture evaporates from them. Microwavesafe plastic wrap is often the most practical choice of covering, allowing you to see what's happening in the dish. When folded back at one corner, the contents can be stirred during cooking without discarding the film. Always remove the plastic wrap starting at the side farthest away from you to avoid scalding your hands or forearms.

REMOVING EXCESS COOKING JUICES

Any juices that seep from food will absorb microwave energy. If these juices are considerable, and the cooking time is longer than about 5 minutes on HIGH, it is advisable to remove some liquid regularly during cooking. Excess juices can prolong the cooking time appreciably. The juices can always be replaced toward the end of the cooking time if the food starts to dry out too much. Examples include cooking a chicken, duck, or turkey.

OBSERVING STANDING TIMES

Food continues to cook by conduction after the microwave's energy has been turned off. This is not solely a feature of microwave cooking—the same applies to a lesser degree with conventional cooking. With microwave cooking, however, there is greater residual heat, so it is important to err on the side of safety and undercook rather than overcook food. Whereas there is no rescue package for overcooked food, additional cooking time can always be given if the dish is still inadequately cooked after observing the standing time.

BROWNING FOODS

As a result of little applied surface heat during rapid cooking, foods cooked in the microwave do not readily brown. Try the following tips to encourage browning or disguise any pale results.

• Broil gratins and roasts before or after microwave cooking.

• Use a specialist microwave browning dish, especially for foods like chops, steaks, fried eggs, toasted sandwiches, stir-fries, and chicken portions.

• Buy or make a browning mix to coat foods—paprika, toasted bread crumbs, crushed potato chips, soy sauce, Worcestershire sauce, and soup mixes all work well.

• Due to its high fat content, bacon browns readily, so it can be laid over poultry or roast meat.

• Baked items, such as cakes, cookies, breads, and muffins, can be sprinkled or coated with toasted coconut, chocolate vermicelli, chopped nuts, chopped glacé fruits, poppy seeds, toasted seeds, and dark-colored spices.

• Glaze ham, poultry, or game with fruit preserve, particularly grape jelly or citrus marmalade, before cooking to add color.

• Add frosting to a pale cake or other baked items after cooking.

Herby Baked Tomatoes are cooked in the microwave, then browned under the broiler.

The Microwave and Freezer

During its introductory years, the domestic microwave was often referred to as "the unfreezer" due to its ability to thaw food both quickly and efficiently, and this is still one of the major advantages of microwave ownership.

Capitalizing on this effect, almost all microwave manufacturers have introduced a specific DEFROST control or button to insure optimum defrosting microwave action. This control programs the microwave to introduce just the right amount of energy to defrost food without cooking it. This is done by pulsing the power on and off at regular intervals over a specified period of time.

When a defrost setting is not built in, it is possible to simulate the action of the setting by turning the microwave on and off manually at regular intervals, allowing rest periods in between; but this is rarely as successful as using a pre-programed setting and it can be time-consuming.

DEFROSTING TIPS

Refer to your own manufacturer's manual for a guide to defrosting times, but always err on the side of safety by heating for too short a period, rather than too long, until you can readily judge the defrosting speed of your own particular microwave model.

• Open all cartons and remove any metal lids, ties, or fastenings before defrosting food.

• Defrost foods slowly. Never try to hurry the process because there is the danger of overcooking the food or drying it out unnecessarily.

• Frozen foods wrapped in foil or placed in foil containers should have all foil removed; they should be placed in a suitable dish for the microwave.

• Turn foods over during defrosting, about halfway through the recommended time.

• If it is not possible to turn food over during defrosting (for example, as with a decorated cake), then rotate the item or container regularly for even defrosting.

• Flex any pouches of food that cannot be broken up or stirred during the defrosting time and rotate on a regular basis.

• Place foods like cakes, rolls, and pastry items on a double sheet of paper towels to absorb excess moisture that can cause the food to become soggy.

• Blocks of frozen food should be broken up with a fork during defrosting so frozen chunks receive the maximum amount of microwave energy.

• Separate any blocks of frozen meat items, such as hamburgers, steaks, chops, and sausages, as they defrost.

• Remove any giblets from the cavity of a chicken and other poultry or game birds as soon as they have defrosted.

• Remove any juices or drips from frozen foods during the defrosting time with a bulb baster or spoon because these will only continue to absorb microwave energy, leaving less to defrost the main food.

• Items like meat joints, whole birds, and whole fish should be defrosted until icy, then left to defrost completely at room temperature before cooking.

• If any parts of the food start to defrost too fast (or even begin to become warm or cook), shield or protect these areas with small strips of smooth foil. These can be attached with wooden toothpicks if necessary. Check that this is acceptable for your model by reading the manufacturer's directions.

• Always observe standing times because foods will continue to defrost by means of conduction from the small level of internal heat that is produced. Leave foods to defrost until they are just icy.

• Before defrosting, prick, slash, or vent membranes and skins. Also, pierce plastic wrap, pouches, or similar wrappings in the same way as when cooking food in a skin.

• If you intend to defrost and cook in one operation, then follow all the guidelines on stirring, turning, rotating, and rearranging foods, not forgetting to allow standing time before serving.

COOK'S TIP

If a member of your household is not a confident cook, but has to reheat an occasional meal, freeze suitable portions with a label giving brief instructions for defrosting and reheating the food in the microwave.

FREEZER-TO-MICROWAVE REMINDERS

The microwave and freezer are a terrific twosome to ease the life of the regular home cook, working mother, busy hostess, and anyone with a prolific vegetable garden. When freezing homemade food that will later be defrosted or cooked in the microwave, the following hints are worth remembering.

• Freeze food in a microwaveproof container, so it can be defrosted, reheated, or cooked straight from the freezer.

• Single portions are very useful in the freezer, allowing any member of the family to quickly and easily defrost and cook an individual meal at any time.

• Before freezing a conventionally made pizza, pie, tart, or quiche, cut it into portions so the required number of servings can be removed from the freezer as required, rather than having to defrost the whole item.

• Completely cooked main courses can be plated on microwaveproof plates and frozen for almost instant dinners. Remember to follow the advice on arranging food for microwave cooking and reheating when preparing complete meals. Adding a sauce helps to keep the meal succulent and moist during defrosting and reheating.

• When cooking a main course, consider doubling the quantities and freezing the second meal for future use.

• Save time and effort in the future by freezing soups, casseroles, and hot-pots in freezerproof bags that are also suitable for microwave defrosting. Use large bags and knot the tops firmly to prevent the contents from leaking, and avoid using metal ties. The unopened bags can be placed in the microwave until the contents are slightly defrosted and free of the plastic, then the food is ready to be transferred to a suitable microwaveproof serving dish for the final reheating.

• Consider freezing homegrown or bargain vegetable produce in freezer and microwaveproof boil-in-the-bag bags. These will serve as freezing, defrosting, and cooking containers, without the need to transfer the contents before serving.

FREEZING FOOD TO FIT A DISH

1 If you do not want to lose the use of the dish while the food is in the freezer, line it with freezer wrap or foil, arrange the food in the dish and then freeze.

2 Once frozen, turn the food out of the container, wrap it tightly, label, and return to the freezer.

3 To defrost or reheat the food, remove the freezer wrap or foil and return the food to the original container before placing in the microwave.

| COOKING AND FREEZING IN ONE BAG | FREEZING AND DEFROSTING BABY FOOD | REHEATING FOODS IN THE MICROWAVE |

1 Fruits like apples and pears can be cooked in a roasting bag or boilable bag.

2 When cooked, the fruit can be crushed in the bag to make a purée and sealed while still hot. As the mixture cools it will form a vacuum pack that is ideal for freezing and ready for defrosting or reheating in the microwave.

COOK'S TIP

Make a note of the weight of vegetables or fruit on freezer labels so you can calculate the microwave cooking time easily for the whole bag.

• Leftovers from suitable meals can easily be puréed and frozen in ice-cube trays ready for baby and toddler meals. To defrost and reheat 2 cubes (about 4 tablespoons food), place in a microwaveproof bowl. Place a small glass or cup of water in the microwave at the same time to absorb some energy and prevent the baby food from overheating. Microwave on HIGH for 1 to $1\frac{1}{4}$ minutes until thawed and hot, stirring once to break up. Leave to stand and check the temperature before serving.

COOK'S TIP

Once the trays of baby food are frozen, release the hard cubes of purée and store them in an airtight freezer bag. This way you will not have all your ice-cube trays in use.

Most foods will reheat successfully in the microwave without loss of quality, flavor, and color, and with maximum nutrient retention compared to alternative reheating methods. For best results follow these guidelines:

• Arrange foods on a plate with the thicker portions to the outer edge where they will receive the most energy.

• When plating meals for reheating, arrange the food in an even layer.

• Cover foods with plastic wrap if a lid is not used to retain moisture.

• Observe the standing time to make maximum use of the microwave energy and to prevent the food overcooking.

• When reheating potatoes, pastry items, and other moist baked foods, place them on a double sheet of paper towels to absorb the excess moisture and prevent sogginess.

• If possible, stir foods regularly during reheating; if this is not possible, then turn foods over or rearrange them, or at least rotate the dish for even reheating.

Basic Recipes

The microwave is invaluable for cooking a host of dishes, as you will see from the recipes that follow in this book, and it is also indispensable for cooking a range of basic recipes that form the basis for more complicated dishes and meals. The following are a few of the most useful basic recipes.

GIBLET STOCK FOR GRAVY

1 Place the contents of a bag of giblets from a chicken, turkey, or duck in a microwaveproof bowl with $1\frac{1}{4}$ cups boiling water and a few sliced seasoning vegetables, such as carrots, celery, and onion.

2 Microwave on HIGH for 7 to 10 minutes. Strain and use the gravy as required.

WHITE POURING SAUCE

1 Place 2 tablespoons butter in a microwaveproof pitcher and microwave on HIGH for 30 to 60 seconds until melted.

2 Stir in 2 tablespoons all-purpose flour and $1\frac{1}{4}$ cups milk. Microwave on HIGH for $3\frac{1}{2}$ to 4 minutes, stirring or whisking once every minute, until smooth, boiling, and thick. Season to taste and serve. Makes $1\frac{1}{4}$ cups.

VARIATIONS

One-Stage Sauce: Place the flour and butter in a microwaveproof pitcher. Add the milk and whisk lightly. The ingredients will not combine thoroughly at this stage because the butter does not mix in, but it will break into small pieces. Continue as above.

Caper Sauce: Add 1 tablespoon drained capers and 1 teaspoon vinegar from the jar of capers or lemon juice to the cooked sauce. Good with cooked lamb.

Cheese Sauce: Add 2 to 4 ounces grated cheese, a pinch of dry mustard powder, and a pinch of cayenne pepper to the cooked sauce. Whisk or stir well. Serve with vegetables, eggs, fish, or pasta.

Parsley Sauce: Add 1 to 2 tablespoons chopped fresh parsley and a squeeze of lemon juice (optional) to the cooked sauce and whisk or stir well. Serve with fish, ham, and vegetables.

SCRAMBLED EGGS

1 Place 1 tablespoon butter in a microwaveproof pitcher or bowl and microwave on HIGH for about 30 seconds to melt.

2 Beat 4 eggs with 2 tablespoons milk and salt and pepper to taste. Add to the butter and microwave on HIGH for $1\frac{1}{4}$ minutes. Stir or whisk the set pieces of egg from the outside of the bowl or pitcher to the center.

3 Microwave on HIGH for $1\frac{1}{4}$ to $1\frac{3}{4}$ minutes longer, stirring or whisking twice. When about three-quarters cooked, there is still a significant amount of runny egg, as shown here. When cooked, the eggs are moist, not completely set. Leave to stand for 1 to 2 minutes, by which time the eggs will be set ready for serving. Serves 2.

BAKED POTATOES

1 Scrub and prick the potatoes. Place on a double thickness of paper towels. If cooking more than two potatoes, arrange them in a ring pattern.

2 Microwave on HIGH for the time given, turning over halfway through cooking. Leave to stand for 3 to 4 minutes before serving.

3 The potatoes may be cut in half and the flesh forked up or mashed, then replaced in the shells, topped with cheese or butter and heated for a few seconds in the microwave to melt the butter or cheese before serving.

COOKING TIMES FOR BAKED POTATOES

1 x 6-ounce potato	4 to 6 minutes
2 x 6-ounce potatoes	6 to 8 minutes
3 x 6-ounce potatoes	8 to 12 minutes
4 x 6-ounce potatoes	12 to 15 minutes

CORN-ON-THE-COB

These can either be cooked husked or unhusked.

1 For fresh unhusked corn-on-the-cob, fold back the husk and discard the silk.

2 Replace the husk to cover the corn and arrange the cobs, evenly spaced, on the bottom of the cooker or turntable. Microwave on HIGH for the time given, rotating and rearranging once halfway through cooking. Leave to stand for 5 minutes before removing the husk and cutting off the woody base with a sharp knife.

3 Alternatively, wrap fresh husked cobs individually in plastic wrap or place in a microwaveproof dish with 4 tablespoons water and cover. Microwave on HIGH for the time given, rotating and rearranging once halfway through cooking. Leave to stand for 3 to 5 minutes before serving.

COOKING TIMES FOR CORN-ON-THE-COB

Cooking Times for Corn Cobs in Husks

1 x 6- to 8-ounce cobs	3 to 5 minutes
2 x 6- to 8-ounce cobs	6 to 8 minutes
3 x 6- to 8-ounce cobs	8 to 10 minutes
4 x 6- to 8-ounce cobs	10 to 12 minutes

Cooking Times for Husked Corn Cobs

1 x 6- to 8-ounce cob	3 to 4 minutes
2 x 6- to 8-ounce cobs	5 to 6 minutes
3 x 6- to 8-ounce cobs	7 to 8 minutes
4 x 6- to 8-ounce cobs	9 to 10 minutes

HOLLANDAISE SAUCE

1 Place $\frac{1}{2}$ cup butter in a large microwaveproof pitcher and microwave on HIGH for $1\frac{1}{2}$ minutes until melted. Whisk in 3 tablespoons lemon juice, 2 egg yolks, a pinch of mustard powder, and salt and pepper to taste.

2 Microwave on MEDIUM for 1 minute, whisk and serve. This sauce is delicious with poached salmon or cooked asparagus. Serves 4 to 6.

RED LENTILS

1 Place 1 cup lentils in a large microwaveproof bowl. Add a little chopped onion, celery, and lemon juice, if liked. Cover with $3\frac{3}{4}$ cups boiling water or stock and add salt and pepper to taste.

2 Cover, leaving a gap for steam to escape, and microwave on HIGH for 15 to 25 minutes, stirring once halfway through cooking. Time the cooking according to requirements: If you want the lentils to retain some shape, use the shorter time; if you want soft lentils for a soup or dip, use the longer cooking time. Serves 4.

QUICK SOAKING OF DRIED BEANS

1 To shorten the soaking time for dried beans, place them in a microwaveproof bowl and cover with boiling water.

2 Cover and microwave on HIGH for 5 minutes. Leave to stand for $1\frac{1}{2}$ hours, then drain, rinse, and cook the beans.

VEGETABLE RICE

1 Place generous 1 cup long-grain white rice in a microwaveproof bowl with $2\frac{1}{4}$ cups boiling water, 1 teaspoon salt, and a knob of butter, if liked. Cover loosely with a lid or vented plastic wrap and microwave on HIGH for 3 minutes.

2 Reduce the power setting to MEDIUM and microwave for 12 minutes longer, stirring two or three times.

3 Add about 1 cup diced and softened vegetables (for example a single vegetable or selection from peas, beans, peppers, onion, and corn). Stir well to mix, cover, and microwave on HIGH for $1\frac{1}{2}$ minutes.

4 Leave to stand, tightly covered, for 5 minutes. Fluff the rice with a fork to separate the grains before serving. Serves 4.

OATMEAL

1 Traditional and quick-cook varieties of oatmeal can be prepared quickly and easily in the microwave. To make traditional oatmeal, place $\frac{1}{3}$ cup oatmeal in a microwaveproof bowl with $\frac{1}{4}$ teaspoon salt.

2 Stir in $\frac{3}{4}$ cup water or milk, making sure the oatmeal and liquid are thoroughly mixed.

3 Cover with vented plastic wrap and microwave on LOW for 10 to 12 minutes, stirring twice. Leave to stand, covered, for 2 minutes before serving.

4 Prepare quick-cook oatmeal as above, but microwave on LOW for 5 minutes. Serves 1.

GARLIC OR HERB BREAD

1 Cut a 4-ounce short, crusty French bread into diagonal slices about $1\frac{1}{2}$ inches thick, almost to the bottom of the loaf, but not quite through. Spread garlic or herb butter between the slices and reform the loaf into a neat shape.

2 Wrap loosely in paper towels and microwave on HIGH for $1\frac{1}{2}$ minutes. Serve at once, while still warm. Serves 4.

Making the Most of Your Microwave

Getting used to the speed of microwave cooking does take time, patience, and perseverance, so you are unlikely to become a microwave mastercook overnight. The golden rule is to become a constant clock-watcher until you know your microwave really well. Do not be afraid or intimidated by the microwave—open the door, peer in and poke food as much as you like to see if it is defrosting, cooking, or reheating adequately. You will soon be able to cook the recipes in this book successfully, adapt some of your own conventional favorites, and halve or double quantities with practiced ease.

The following are tips that provide amusing, useful tricks to make you wonder how you ever managed without a microwave!

PEELING TOMATOES

Place up to 6 tomatoes in a ring on paper towels. Microwave on HIGH for 10 to 15 seconds. Leave to stand for 15 minutes, then peel the tomatoes.

PEELING PEACHES AND APRICOTS

Place up to 4 peaches in a microwaveproof bowl with very little water. Cover and microwave on HIGH for 1 to $1\frac{1}{2}$ minutes. Leave the peaches to stand for 5 minutes, then drain and peel them.

TO SOFTEN CHILLED HARD CHEESES

Place about 8 ounces chilled hard cheese on a microwaveproof serving plate and microwave on LOW for 30 to 34 seconds, turning over after half the time. Leave to stand for 5 minutes before serving.

TO RIPEN SEMISOFT CHEESE

Place about 8 ounces semisoft cheese on a microwaveproof serving dish and microwave on LOW for 15 to 45 seconds, depending upon degree of ripeness, checking constantly and turning over after half of the time. Leave to stand for 5 minutes before serving.

SOFTENING BUTTER

Microwave on HIGH for 5 to 10 seconds, then leave to stand for 5 minutes before using.

BLANCHING ALMONDS

Place 1 cup water in a pitcher. Microwave on HIGH for $2\frac{1}{2}$ minutes or until boiling, add the almonds, and microwave for 30 seconds. Drain the nuts, then slip off their skins.

TOASTING NUTS

For a golden result, place in a browning dish and microwave on HIGH for 4 to 5 minutes, stirring each minute. Alternatively, for a lighter result, cook in an ordinary microwaveproof dish.

TOASTING COCONUT

Spread 1 cup shredded coconut on a microwaveproof plate. Microwave on HIGH for 5 to 6 minutes, stirring every 1 minute.

DRYING HERBS AND CITRUS PEELS

Place on a microwaveproof plate and microwave on HIGH until dry. Never leave unattended and check at 1 minute intervals to guarantee success.

SQUEEZING CITRUS JUICE

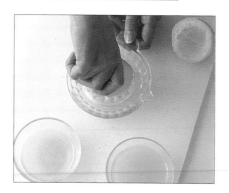

To extract the maximum juice from citrus fruit, prick the skins and microwave on HIGH for 5 to 10 seconds.

TO DRY BREAD FOR CRUMBS

1 Place a thick slice of bread on a microwaveproof plate and microwave on HIGH for $2\frac{1}{2}$ to $3\frac{1}{2}$ minutes until dry.

2 Allow the bread to cool completely before crumbling or grating it for use.

TO MAKE CROUTONS

1 To make dry, oil-free croutons, dice 6 ounces bread into cubes. Place on paper towels on a large, flat microwaveproof plate and microwave on HIGH for 3 to 4 minutes, stirring once every minute until dry.

2 To make butter-crisp croutons, place 2 tablespoons butter in a microwaveproof dish and microwave on HIGH for 30 seconds to melt.

3 Add 3 cups bread cubes and toss to coat them in the melted butter. Microwave on HIGH for 3 to 4 minutes, stirring every minute, until crisp and brown.

COOK'S TIP

Croutons can be flavored in a variety of ways to complement the dishes they garnish. A crushed garlic clove or a little dried oregano can be added to the butter for butter-crisp croutons. Chopped fresh herbs, such as tarragon or parsley, should be tossed with the cooked croutons. Grated Parmesan cheese or lemon peel can be added to cooked croutons.

PROVING YEAST DOUGH

1 To rise bread dough quickly, give a 2-pound piece of dough short bursts of microwave energy on HIGH for 5 to 10 second intervals, observing a 10 minute standing time between each heating period.

2 Repeat until the dough has risen to double its size.

DEFROSTING FROZEN PIECRUSTS OR PUFF PASTRY DOUGH

Place 14 ounces of dough on a microwaveproof plate and microwave on DEFROST for 4 to $4\frac{1}{2}$ minutes, turning over once during the time. Leave to stand for 5 minutes before using.

TO COOK POPPADOMS

1 Arrange two or three plain or spiced poppadoms on the bottom of the oven or on the turntable so they do not touch or overlap. Microwave on HIGH for 45 to 60 seconds until puffy and bubbling. Leave to stand on a wire rack for 15 seconds to crisp.

2 To make poppadom cases or cups (ideal for holding salad) position a poppadom over a small microwaveproof bowl and microwave on HIGH for 20 to 25 seconds. As it cooks, the poppadom will droop in folds over the bowl to make a cup shape. Leave to stand for about 15 seconds to crisp before removing from the bowl.

TO MAKE COOKIE CUPS

Cookies, such as brandy snaps and florentines, can be heated in the microwave over a microwaveproof bowl to form a cup shape that can later hold mousse, ice cream, or fruit salad for an almost-instant dessert. Position two biscuits over the top of two microwaveproof bowls and microwave on HIGH for 30 to 45 seconds until very warm and pliable. While hot, mold the cookies around the bowls to form cup shapes. Leave until completely cold and firm before removing from the bowls.

SOFTENING JAMS AND SPREADS

Remove any lids and any metal trims or transfer the jam or spread to a microwaveproof dish. Microwave on HIGH for 5 to 10 seconds per 1 pound.

DISSOLVING GELATIN

1 Sprinkle the gelatin over cold water, as usual, and leave to stand until spongy.

2 Microwave on HIGH for 30 seconds until clear and completely dissolved.

CLARIFYING CRYSTALLIZED HONEY

Remove the lid and any metal trims on the jar. Microwave on HIGH for 1 to 2 minutes. Stir well.

DISSOLVING JELLY TABLETS

1 Break up a $4\frac{1}{2}$-ounce jelly tablet and place in a microwaveproof bowl or pitcher with $\frac{2}{3}$ cup water.

2 Microwave on HIGH for 2 minutes.

3 Stir well to dissolve, then make up with cold water according to the package directions.

Melting Chocolate

Break chocolate into pieces and place in a microwaveproof bowl. Microwave on HIGH, for about 1 minute per 1 ounce.

Softening Ice Cream for Scooping

Microwave about 1 quart hard (not softscoop) ice cream on MEDIUM for 45 to 90 seconds. Leave to stand for 1 to 2 minutes before scooping.

Flambéing with Alcohol

Heat the alcohol, such as brandy, in a microwaveproof and flameproof pitcher on HIGH for 15 seconds. It will then ignite more easily, ready for pouring over plum pudding, crepes, or fresh fruit.

To Reheat Black Coffee

Place $2\frac{1}{2}$ cups cold coffee in a microwaveproof pitcher and microwave on HIGH for $4\frac{1}{2}$ to 5 minutes.

To Reheat a Mug of Tea or Coffee

Make sure the mug is microwaveproof. Heat on HIGH for 30 to 60 seconds and stir before tasting. Repeat if necessary, always stirring before tasting because hot spots in the liquid can burn the mouth.

Warming a Baby's Bottle

Invert the teat and microwave 1 cup prepared milk on HIGH for 1 minute to warm. Shake the bottle gently and test the milk to check the temperature before attempting to feed the baby. If in doubt check your baby milk formula directions for preparing in the microwave.

To Heat Milk for Drinks

Frothy hot milk for café au lait, hot chocolate, or other beverages can be heated very quickly. Place $1\frac{1}{4}$ cups cold milk in a microwaveproof pitcher and microwave on HIGH for 2 to $2\frac{1}{2}$ minutes. Whisk well until frothy, if liked, and serve at once.

To Make Mulled Wine

Mix 3 cups red wine, 12 cloves, 2 small cinnamon sticks, the grated peel and juice of 1 orange and 1 lemon, and 2 to 3 tablespoons brown sugar in a microwaveproof bowl or pitcher. Microwave on HIGH for 5 minutes, or until almost boiling. Add extra sugar to taste, if liked, and serve the wine warm. This serves about 6.

Before You Begin

MICROWAVE POWERS AND SETTINGS

• All the recipes and charts in this book were created and tested using microwave ovens with a maximum power output of 650 to 700 watts.

• The ovens had variable power and the descriptions used refer to the following power outputs.

HIGH = 650 to 750 watts or 100%
MEDIUM HIGH = 500 to 550 watts or 75%
MEDIUM = 400 watts or 55 to 60%
LOW = 250 watts or 40%
DEFROST = 200 watts or 30%

• The chart below gives the approximate power input in watts at these levels and relative cooking times.

• The microwave ovens used for testing had turntables—if yours does not and tends to have an irregular heating pattern with hot and cold spots, follow the rules on turning, rotating and rearranging foods.

UNLESS OTHERWISE STATED

• all spoon quantities are measured level
• flour is scooped into the cup

FOODS TO AVOID

The following foods do not cook well in the microwave and they are best avoided.

Eggs in Shells
These are liable to explode due to the buildup of pressure within the shell. Eggs can, however, be baked, scrambled, poached, and "fried" in the microwave with superb results.

Popcorn
This can prove to be too dry to attract microwave energy, although some manufacturers have produced microwave popcorn, sold in special bags with seasonings and flavorings, and this works superbly. A special microwave popcorn popper can also be purchased to cook ordinary popcorn in the microwave.

Batter-Based and Some Air-Incorporated Recipes
Dishes like Yorkshire pudding, soufflé, crepes, choux pastry, batter-coated fish, and whisked cake batters need conventional cooking to become crisp and firm. The microwave will, however, make the basic sauce for a soufflé and will reheat crepes perfectly.

Conventional Meringues
These should be baked in the conventional oven because they do not dry sufficiently and become crisp in the microwave.

Deep-Fat Frying
This is not recommended because it requires prolonged heating, it is difficult to control the temperature of the fat, and the food may burn.

Liquid in Bottles and Pots
Check that bottles do not have necks that are too narrow to allow sufficient escape because steam as built-up pressure may cause them to shatter. Similarly, tall coffee pots, with slim spouts, can break or cause coffee to spurt out.

GUIDE TO COMPARITIVE MICROWAVE OVEN CONTROL SETTINGS

Settings used in these recipes	Setting variations on popular microwave ovens				Approximate % power input	Approximate power outputs in watts	Cooking times in minutes—for times greater than 10 minutes simply add together the figures in the appropriate columns									
	1	keep warm	low	2	25%	150W	4	8	12	16	20	24	28	32	36	40
Defrost	2	simmer	simmer	3	30%	200W	$3\frac{1}{4}$	$6\frac{3}{4}$	10	$13\frac{1}{4}$	$16\frac{3}{4}$	20	$26\frac{1}{4}$	$26\frac{1}{4}$	30	$33\frac{1}{4}$
Low	3	stew	medium/low	4	40%	250W	$2\frac{1}{2}$	5	$7\frac{1}{2}$	10	$12\frac{1}{2}$	15	$17\frac{1}{2}$	20	$22\frac{1}{2}$	25
	4	defrost	medium	5	50%	300W	2	4	6	8	10	12	14	16	18	20
Medium	5	bake	medium	6	60%	400W	$1\frac{3}{4}$	$3\frac{3}{4}$	5	$6\frac{3}{4}$	$8\frac{1}{4}$	10	12	$13\frac{1}{4}$	15	$16\frac{1}{2}$
Medium High	6	roast	high	7–8	75%	500 to 600W	$1\frac{1}{4}$	$2\frac{3}{4}$	4	$5\frac{1}{4}$	$6\frac{3}{4}$	8	$9\frac{1}{4}$	$10\frac{1}{4}$	12	$13\frac{1}{4}$
High	7	full/high	normal	10	100%	700W	1	2	3	4	5	6	7	8	9	10

SOUPS AND APPETIZERS

Italian Fish Soup

INGREDIENTS

Serves 4

2 tablespoons olive oil

1 onion, thinly sliced

a few saffron threads

1 teaspoon dried thyme

large pinch of cayenne pepper

2 garlic cloves, finely chopped

2 x 14-ounce cans peeled tomatoes, drained and chopped

¾ cup dry white wine

8 cups hot fish stock

12 ounces white, skinless fish fillets, cut into pieces

1 pound monkfish, membrane removed, cut into pieces

1 pound mussels in the shell, thoroughly scrubbed

8 ounces small squid, cleaned and cut into rings

2 tablespoons chopped fresh parsley

salt and ground black pepper

thickly sliced bread, to serve

1 Place the oil in a large microwaveproof bowl. Stir in the onion, saffron, thyme, cayenne pepper, and salt to taste. Microwave on HIGH for 3 minutes, until soft. Add the garlic and microwave on HIGH for 1 minute.

2 Stir in the tomatoes, white wine, and fish stock. Cover and microwave on HIGH for 10 minutes, stirring halfway through the cooking time.

3 Add the fish fillet and monkfish pieces to the bowl. Cover and microwave on HIGH for 2 minutes, stirring once.

4 Stir in the mussels and squid. Cover and microwave on HIGH for 2 to 3 minutes, stirring once, until the mussels open. Stir in the parsley and season with salt and pepper.

5 Ladle into warmed soup bowls and serve immediately, with warm crusty bread.

Creamy Cod Chowder

Serves 4 to 6

12 ounces smoked cod fillet

1 small onion, finely chopped

1 bay leaf

4 black peppercorns

$3\frac{3}{4}$ cups skim milk

2 teaspoons cornstarch

2 teaspoons water

$1\frac{1}{2}$ cups canned corn kernels, drained

1 tablespoon chopped fresh parsley

1 Skin the fish fillet: Hold the tail firmly and cut the fish off its skin using a sharp knife. Cut at an acute angle, taking care not to cut the skin and folding back the fish fillet.

2 Place the fish in a large microwaveproof bowl with the onion, bay leaf, and peppercorns. Pour in the milk.

3 Cover and microwave on HIGH for 8 to 10 minutes, stirring twice, or until the fish is just cooked.

4 Using a perforated spoon, lift out the fish and flake it into large chunks. Remove and discard the bay leaf and peppercorns.

5 Blend the cornstarch with the water and add to the milk mixture. Microwave on HIGH for 2 to 3 minutes, stirring twice, until slightly thickened.

6 Drain the corn kernels and add to the milk mixture with the flaked fish and parsley.

7 To reheat the chowder, microwave on HIGH for 2 to 3 minutes until piping hot, stirring twice, but do not boil. Ladle the chowder into 4 or 6 soup bowls and serve straight away.

Beef Chili Soup

This hearty dish, based on a traditional chili recipe, is excellent with fresh crusty bread as a warming start to any meal.

INGREDIENTS

Serves 4

1 tablespoon oil

1 onion, chopped

6 ounces ground beef

2 garlic cloves, chopped

1 red chili, sliced

2 tablespoons all-purpose flour

14-ounce can crushed tomatoes

$2\frac{1}{2}$ cups hot beef stock

2 cups canned red kidney
   beans, drained

2 tablespoons chopped fresh parsley

salt and ground black pepper

1 Place the oil and onion in a microwaveproof bowl. Microwave on HIGH for 2 minutes, stirring once. Stir in the beef and microwave on HIGH for 4 to $4\frac{1}{2}$ minutes, stirring twice.

2 Add the garlic, chili, and flour. Microwave on HIGH for 1 minute, stirring once.

3 Add the tomatoes and stock, stirring well. Cover and microwave on HIGH for 8 minutes, stirring twice.

4 Stir in the red kidney beans and season well with salt and pepper. Cover and microwave on HIGH for 10 minutes, stirring halfway through cooking.

5 Add the chopped fresh parsley and check the seasoning, adjusting to taste. Serve the soup with crusty bread.

Chunky Bean and Vegetable Soup

A substantial soup, not unlike minestrone, using a selection of vegetables, with cannellini beans for extra protein and fiber. Serve with a hunk of wholegrain bread.

INGREDIENTS

Serves 4

2 tablespoons olive oil

2 celery stalks, chopped

2 leeks, sliced

3 carrots, sliced

2 garlic cloves, crushed

14-ounce can crushed tomatoes
   with basil

5 cups hot vegetable stock

15-ounce can cannellini beans (or mixed
   legumes), drained

1 tablespoon pesto sauce

salt and ground black pepper

shavings of Parmesan cheese,
   to serve

1 Place the olive oil in a large microwaveproof bowl with the celery, leeks, carrots, and garlic. Microwave on HIGH for 4 minutes, stirring halfway through cooking, until softened.

2 Stir in the tomatoes and the stock. Cover and microwave on HIGH for 10 minutes, stirring halfway through cooking.

3 Stir in the beans and pesto, with salt and pepper to taste. Microwave on HIGH for 3 to 5 minutes longer, stirring halfway through cooking. Serve in heated bowls, sprinkled with shavings of Parmesan cheese.

COOK'S TIP

Canned garbanzo beans give the soup a delicious nutty flavor. Flageolet beans are more delicate and borlotti beans are slightly more substantial.

Chilled Leek and Potato Soup

This creamy, chilled soup is a version of the classic Vichyssoise, originally created by a French chef at the Ritz Carlton Hotel in New York City to celebrate the opening of the roof gardens.

INGREDIENTS

Serves 4

2 tablespoons butter

1 tablespoon vegetable oil

1 small onion, chopped

3 leeks, sliced

2 potatoes, diced

2½ cups hot vegetable stock

1¼ cups milk

3 tablespoons light cream

a little extra milk (optional)

salt and ground black pepper

4 tablespoons plain yogurt and snipped chives, to garnish

1 Place the butter and oil in a large microwaveproof bowl. Add the onion, leeks, and potatoes. Cover and microwave on HIGH for 10 minutes, stirring halfway through cooking. Stir in the stock and milk. Microwave on HIGH for 5 to 8 minutes longer, until the potatoes are tender.

2 Puree the vegetables and liquid in a blender or food processor until smooth. Return the soup to the bowl, stir in the cream and season well.

3 Leave the soup to cool and then chill it for 3 to 4 hours, or until really cold. You may need to add a little extra milk to thin the soup down as it will thicken slightly on cooling.

4 Serve the chilled soup in individual bowls, each topped with 1 tablespoon of plain yogurt and a sprinkling of snipped fresh chives.

Curried Parsnip Soup

The spices impart a delicious, mild curry flavor to sweet parsnips.

INGREDIENTS

Serves 4

2 tablespoons butter

1 garlic clove, crushed

1 onion, chopped

1 teaspoon ground cumin

1 teaspoon ground coriander

3 cups sliced parsnips

2 teaspoons medium curry paste

2 cups hot chicken stock

2 cups milk

4 tablespoons sour cream

squeeze of lemon juice

salt and ground black pepper

chopped fresh cilantro, to garnish

store-bought garlic and cilantro naan bread, to serve

1 Place the butter in a large microwaveproof bowl with the garlic and onion. Cover the bowl and microwave on HIGH for 2 minutes. Stir in the spices and microwave on HIGH for 1 minute longer.

2 Add the parsnips and stir until well coated with butter. Then stir in the curry paste, followed by the stock. Cover and microwave on HIGH for 10 to 12 minutes, stirring halfway through cooking, until the parsnips are tender.

3 Puree the soup in a blender or food processor until smooth. Return the soup to the bowl and stir in the milk. Microwave on HIGH for 2 to 3 minutes, stirring halfway through cooking. Add 2 tablespoons of the sour cream, the lemon juice, and seasoning to taste.

4 Stir the fresh cilantro into the remaining sour cream and use to top each portion of soup. Serve with naan bread.

Creamy Cauliflower and Walnut Soup

Even though cream is not added to this soup, the cauliflower gives it a delicious, rich, creamy texture.

INGREDIENTS

Serves 4

1 medium cauliflower

1 onion, coarsely chopped

2 cups hot chicken or vegetable stock

2 cups skim milk

3 tablespoons walnut pieces

salt and ground black pepper

paprika and chopped walnuts,
    to garnish

1 Trim the cauliflower of outer leaves and break it into small flowerets. Place the cauliflower, onion, and stock in a large microwaveproof bowl.

2 Cover and microwave on HIGH for 8 to 10 minutes, stirring halfway through cooking, or until soft. Add the milk and walnuts, then puree in a food processor until smooth.

3 Return the soup to the bowl and season to taste. Microwave on HIGH for 2 minutes to reheat. Serve sprinkled with paprika and chopped walnuts.

VARIATIONS

To make Creamy Cauliflower and Almond Soup, use 3 tablespoons finely ground blanched almonds in place of the walnut pieces.

Curried Carrot and Apple Soup

INGREDIENTS

Serves 4

2 teaspoons sunflower oil

1 tablespoon mild curry powder

$3^1/_3$ cups chopped carrots

1 large onion, chopped

1 cooking apple, cored and chopped

3 cups hot chicken stock

salt and ground black pepper

low-fat plain yogurt and carrot curls,
    to garnish

COOK'S TIP

Choose an acidic apple that will soften and fluff up as it cooks. Chop it into small pieces before adding to the bowl.

1 Place the oil in a large microwaveproof bowl. Add the curry powder and microwave on HIGH for 1 minute, stirring halfway through cooking.

2 Add the carrots, onion, and apple, stir well, cover, and microwave on HIGH for 8 to 10 minutes, stirring halfway through cooking, until softened.

3 Spoon the vegetable mixture into a food processor or blender, then add half the stock and process until smooth.

4 Return the soup to the bowl and pour in the remaining stock. Microwave on HIGH for 3 to 4 minutes, stirring once, to reheat. Adjust the seasoning before serving in bowls, garnished with swirls of yogurt and a few curls of carrot.

Jerusalem Artichoke Soup

Topped with saffron cream, this soup is wonderful on a chilly day.

INGREDIENTS

Serves 4

4 tablespoons butter

1 onion, chopped

$3\frac{1}{2}$ cups peeled and chopped
  Jerusalem artichokes

$3\frac{3}{4}$ cups hot chicken stock

$\frac{2}{3}$ cup milk

$\frac{2}{3}$ cup heavy cream

good pinch of saffron powder

salt and ground black pepper

snipped fresh chives, to garnish

1 Place the butter and onion in a large microwaveproof bowl and microwave on HIGH for 2 to 3 minutes, until soft, stirring once.

2 Add the artichokes to the bowl and stir to coat them in the butter. Cover and microwave on HIGH for 8 to 10 minutes, stirring halfway through cooking. Pour in the stock and milk, then cover and microwave on HIGH for 5 to 8 minutes, stirring once. Cool slightly, then process in a blender or food processor until smooth.

3 Strain the soup back into the bowl. Add half the cream, season to taste, and microwave on HIGH for 2 to 3 minutes to reheat. Lightly whip the remaining cream with the saffron powder. Ladle the soup into warmed soup bowls and put a spoonful of saffron cream in the center of each. Scatter the snipped chives over and serve at once.

Broccoli and Stilton Soup

A really easy, but rich, soup—choose something simple to follow, such as plainly roasted or broiled meat, poultry, or fish.

INGREDIENTS

Serves 4

12 ounces broccoli

2 tablespoons butter

1 onion, chopped

1 leek, white part only, chopped

1 small potato, cut into chunks

$2\frac{1}{2}$ cups hot chicken stock

$1\frac{1}{4}$ cups milk

3 tablespoons heavy cream

4 ounces Stilton cheese, rind removed,
  crumbled

salt and ground black pepper

1 Break the broccoli into flowerets, discarding tough stems. Set aside 2 small flowerets for garnishing the soup.

2 Place the butter in a large microwaveproof bowl with the onion and leek. Microwave on HIGH for 3 minutes until soft. Add the broccoli and potato, then pour in the stock. Cover and microwave on HIGH for 12 to 15 minutes, stirring twice, until the vegetables are tender.

3 Cool slightly, then puree in a blender or food processor. Strain through a strainer back into the bowl.

4 Add the milk, cream, and seasoning to the bowl and microwave on HIGH for 3 to 4 minutes to reheat. At the last minute, add the cheese and stir until it just melts.

5 Place the reserved broccoli flowerets in a small microwaveproof bowl, cover, and microwave on HIGH for 30 seconds, then cut them vertically into thin slices. Ladle the soup into warm bowls. Garnish with the broccoli flowerets and serve with a generous grinding of black pepper.

Artichoke and Mushroom Soup

Delicate Jerusalem artichokes are perfectly matched with mushrooms in this simple soup. Select closed-cap mushrooms for good color and light flavor.

INGREDIENTS

Serves 4

2 to 4 tablespoons butter

2 cups sliced mushrooms

2 onions, chopped

$3\frac{1}{2}$ cups peeled and sliced
    Jerusalem artichokes

$1\frac{1}{4}$ cups hot vegetable stock

$1\frac{1}{4}$ cups milk

salt and ground black pepper

1 Place the butter and mushrooms in a large microwavesafe bowl. Cover and microwave on HIGH for 2 minutes. Using a perforated spoon, lift out the mushrooms and reserve them on a plate. Add the onions and artichokes to the bowl, stirring well. Cover and microwave on HIGH for 8 to 10 minutes, stirring halfway through cooking.

2 Add the vegetable stock to the bowl and microwave on HIGH for 5 minutes longer, until the artichokes are soft. Season to taste.

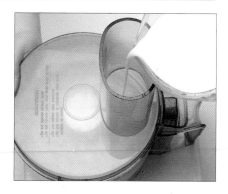

3 Process the soup in a blender or food processor, adding the milk slowly until smooth. Return the soup to the bowl. Stir in the mushrooms and microwave on HIGH for 2 to 3 minutes to reheat before serving.

Tomato and Red Pepper Soup

A late summer soup that can be served cold. Made using very ripe bell peppers and tomatoes, this tastes best when it is made with sun-ripened produce.

INGREDIENTS

Serves 4

5 large tomatoes

2 to 4 tablespoons olive oil

1 onion, chopped

$5\frac{1}{2}$ cups thinly sliced red or orange
    bell peppers

2 tablespoons tomato paste

a pinch of sugar

2 cups hot vegetable stock

4 tablespoons sour cream (optional)

salt and ground black pepper

chopped fresh dill, to garnish

1 Skin the tomatoes by plunging them into boiling water for 30 seconds. Chop the flesh and reserve any juice.

2 Place half the oil in a microwavesafe bowl with the onion. Microwave on HIGH for 2 minutes, stirring once. Add the bell peppers and the remaining oil, mixing well. Cover and microwave on HIGH for 5 minutes, stirring halfway through cooking.

3 Stir in the chopped tomatoes, tomato paste, seasoning, sugar and a few tablespoons of stock. Cover and microwave on HIGH for 4 minutes, stirring halfway through cooking, until the vegetables are tender.

4 Stir in the rest of the stock and puree in a blender or food processor until smooth. Strain the soup to remove the skins and season to taste.

5 Pour into bowls, swirl in the sour cream, if using, and garnish with dill.

Corn Soup

This is a simple-to-make, yet very flavorsome soup. It is also sometimes made with sour cream and cream cheese.

INGREDIENTS

Serves 4

2 tablespoons corn oil

1 onion, finely chopped

1 red bell pepper, seeded and chopped

3 cups corn kernels, thawed if frozen

3 cups hot chicken stock

1 cup light cream

salt and ground black pepper

$\frac{1}{2}$ red bell pepper, seeded and cut into small dice, to garnish

1 Place the oil, onion, and red bell pepper in a microwaveproof bowl. Cover and microwave on HIGH for 4 minutes, stirring once. Add the corn and microwave on HIGH for 4 minutes, stirring once during cooking.

2 Carefully tip the contents of the bowl into a food processor or blender. Process until smooth, scraping the mixture down the container occasionally and adding a little of the stock, if necessary.

3 Put the mixture into a microwaveproof bowl and stir in the stock. Season to taste, then microwave on HIGH for 4 minutes, stirring once.

4 Gently stir in the cream. Serve the soup hot or chilled, sprinkled with the diced red bell pepper. If serving hot, microwave on HIGH for 1 to 2 minutes after adding the cream, but do not allow the soup to boil.

Zucchini Soup

INGREDIENTS

Serves 4

2 tablespoons butter

1 onion, finely chopped

$2\frac{1}{2}$ cups trimmed and chopped young zucchini

3 cups hot chicken stock

$\frac{1}{2}$ cup light cream, plus extra to serve

salt and ground black pepper

COOK'S TIP

This simple soup is ideal for using up a glut of homegrown zucchini. Be sure to select young vegetables with fine skin because large, old zucchini tend to be watery, with a weaker flavor and coarse skin.

1 Place the butter and onion in a large microwaveproof bowl. Cover and microwave on HIGH for 2 minutes, stirring once. Add the zucchini and microwave on HIGH for 6 minutes, stirring once.

2 Pour in the chicken stock, cover, and microwave on HIGH for 3 minutes, stirring once.

3 Puree the mixture in a blender or food processor until smooth. Season to taste.

4 Stir the cream into the soup, return it to the bowl and microwave on HIGH for 1 minute to heat through without allowing it to boil. Serve hot, swirled with a little extra cream.

Chili Shrimp

This delightful, spicy combination makes a tempting light main course for a casual supper. Serve with rice, noodles, or freshly cooked pasta and a leafy salad.

INGREDIENTS

Serves 3 to 4

3 tablespoons olive oil

2 shallots, chopped

2 garlic cloves, chopped

1 fresh red chili, chopped

3 cups peeled, seeded, and chopped
   ripe tomatoes

1 tablespoon tomato paste

1 bay leaf

1 thyme sprig

6 tablespoons dry white wine

1 pound shelled cooked large shrimp

salt and ground black pepper

roughly torn basil leaves, to garnish

1 Place the oil, shallots, garlic, and chili in a microwaveproof bowl and microwave on HIGH for 2 minutes, stirring once.

2 Add the tomatoes, tomato paste, bay leaf, thyme, wine, and seasoning. Cover and microwave on HIGH for 6 to 7 minutes, stirring twice. Discard the herbs.

3 Stir the shrimp into the sauce and microwave on HIGH for 2 to 3 minutes, stirring once. Taste and adjust the seasoning. Garnish with torn basil leaves and serve at once.

COOK'S TIP

For a milder flavor, scrape and then rinse out all the seeds from the chili before chopping it.

Scallops with Ginger

Scallops cook very well in the microwave. Rich and creamy, this dish is very simple to make with delicious results.

INGREDIENTS

Serves 4

3 tablespoons butter

8 to 12 scallops, shelled

1-inch piece fresh ginger root,
   finely chopped

1 bunch scallions, diagonally sliced

2 tablespoons white vermouth

1 cup crème fraîche or sour cream

salt and ground black pepper

chopped fresh parsley, to garnish

1 Place the butter in a shallow microwaveproof dish. Microwave on HIGH for 30 seconds to melt.

2 Remove the tough muscle opposite the coral on each scallop. Separate the coral and cut the white part of the scallop in half horizontally. Add the scallops, including the corals, cover, and microwave on HIGH for 4 to 6 minutes, rearranging once.

3 Lift out the scallops with a perforated spoon and transfer them to a warm serving dish, keep warm.

4 Add the ginger and scallions to the juices in the bowl and microwave on HIGH for 1 minute. Pour in the vermouth and microwave on HIGH for 30 seconds. Stir in the crème fraîche and microwave on HIGH for 1 to $1\frac{1}{2}$ minutes, stirring twice. Taste and adjust the seasoning.

5 Pour the sauce over the scallops, sprinkle with parsley, and serve at once.

Chicken Liver Pâté with Marsala

This pâté is really quick and simple to make, yet it has a delicious—and sophisticated—flavor. It contains Marsala, a soft and pungent fortified wine from Sicily. Brandy or a medium-dry sherry can be used instead.

INGREDIENTS

Serves 4

12 ounces chicken livers, defrosted if frozen

1 cup butter, softened

2 garlic cloves, crushed

1 tablespoon Marsala

1 teaspoon chopped fresh sage

salt and ground black pepper

8 sage leaves, to garnish

Melba toast, to serve

1 Trim any membranes and sinew from the livers, then rinse and dry with paper towels. Place 2 tablespoons of the butter in a microwaveproof bowl with the chicken livers and the garlic. Cover loosely and microwave on HIGH for about 4 minutes, or until the livers are firm, but pink in the middle, stirring twice.

2 Use a perforated spoon to transfer the livers to a blender or food processor. Add the Marsala and chopped sage.

3 Place ⅔ cup of the remaining butter in a microwaveproof bowl and microwave on HIGH for 1½ minutes to melt. Pour it into the blender or processor and blend until smooth. Season well.

4 Spoon the pâté into four individual pots and smooth the surfaces. Place the remaining butter in a microwaveproof bowl and microwave on HIGH for 1 minute to melt and pour it over the pâtés. Garnish with sage leaves and chill until set. Serve with triangles of Melba toast.

COOK'S TIP

To make Melba toast, toast medium-thick bread. Cut off the crusts and slice the toast in half horizontally. Lightly brown the untoasted sides under a hot broiler. Cool on a wire rack.

Mushroom Pâté

This is a vegetarian alternative to liver-based pâtés. Cooking the onion in butter gives a rich flavor, but you can use oil instead, if preferred.

INGREDIENTS

Serves 4

2 tablespoons olive oil or butter

2 onions, chopped

$4\frac{1}{2}$ cups chopped or roughly sliced mushrooms

1 cup blanched almonds, finely ground

a handful of parsley, stems removed

salt and ground black pepper

flat-leaf parsley, to garnish

thin slices of toast, cucumber, endive, and celery stalks, to serve

1 Place the olive oil or butter in a microwaveproof bowl with the onions. Microwave on HIGH for 5 to 7 minutes, stirring twice.

2 Add the mushrooms and microwave on HIGH for 3 to $3\frac{1}{2}$ minutes, stirring halfway through cooking. Season well.

3 Transfer the cooked onion and mushrooms to a blender or food processor with their juices. Add the ground almonds and parsley, and process briefly. The pâté can either be smooth or you can leave it slightly chunky. Taste again for seasoning.

4 Spoon the pâté into individual pots. Garnish with flat-leaf parsley and serve with thin slices of toast and sticks of cucumber, endive, and celery.

Eggs en Cocotte

A classic appetizer, these baked eggs are cooked on a flavorsome base of ratatouille, making them ideal for microwave cooking. They are excellent served for lunch or supper, with plenty of warm crusty bread.

INGREDIENTS

Serves 4

4 eggs

4 teaspoons freshly grated
   Parmesan cheese

chopped fresh parsley, to garnish

For the ratatouille

1 small red bell pepper

1 tablespoon olive oil

1 onion, finely chopped

1 garlic clove, crushed

2 zucchini, diced

14-ounce can crushed tomatoes with basil

salt and ground black pepper

1 First prepare the vegetables: cut the red bell pepper in half and remove the seeds. Then dice the pepper flesh.

2 Place the oil in a microwave-proof bowl. Add the onion, garlic, zucchini and pepper and microwave on HIGH for 3 to 4 minutes, stirring once, until softened. Stir in the tomatoes, with salt and pepper to taste, and microwave on HIGH for 3 to 4 minutes, stirring once.

3 Divide the ratatouille between four individual microwave-proof dishes or large ramekins, each with a capacity of about $1\frac{1}{4}$ cups.

4 Make a small hollow in the middle of each portion of ratatouille and break in an egg.

5 Grind some black pepper over the top of each and sprinkle with the cheese. Gently prick each yolk with a needle or wooden toothpick. Microwave on HIGH for 4 to 6 minutes until the eggs are just set. Sprinkle with the fresh parsley and serve at once.

Leeks with Mustard Dressing

Pencil-slim baby leeks are increasingly available, and are beautifully tender. Use two or three of these smaller leeks per serving.

INGREDIENTS

Serves 4

8 slim leeks, each about 5 inches long

3 tablespoons water

1 to 2 teaspoons Dijon mustard

2 teaspoons white-wine vinegar

1 hard-cooked egg, halved lengthwise

5 tablespoons olive oil

2 teaspoons chopped fresh parsley

salt and ground black pepper

1 Place the leeks in a microwaveproof dish with the water. Cover and microwave on HIGH for 3 to 5 minutes, rearranging twice. Leave to stand for 2 minutes, then drain thoroughly.

2 Meanwhile, stir the mustard and vinegar together in a bowl. Scoop the egg yolk into the bowl and mash it thoroughly into the vinegar mixture using a fork.

3 Gradually work in the oil to make a smooth sauce. Season to taste with salt and pepper.

4 Place the leeks on several layers of paper towels, then pat them dry with several more layers of paper towels.

5 Transfer the leeks to a serving dish. While they are still warm, spoon the dressing over them and leave to cool. Finely chop the egg white, then mix it with the chopped fresh parsley and scatter this over the leeks. Cover and chill until ready to serve.

COOK'S TIP

Although this dish is served cold, make sure the leeks are still warm when you pour the dressing over so they absorb the mustard flavor.

Leek Terrine with Deli Meats

This attractive first course is simple to make, yet it looks spectacular. Make the terrine a day ahead and keep it covered in the refrigerator, if you like. For vegetarian guests offer chunks of feta cheese with the terrine, instead of the cooked meats.

INGREDIENTS

Serves 6

20 to 24 small young leeks

3 tablespoons water

4 tablespoons walnut oil

4 tablespoons olive oil

2 tablespoons white-wine vinegar

1 teaspoon wholegrain mustard

salt and ground black pepper

about $\frac{1}{2}$ pound mixed sliced meats,
　　such as prosciutto, coppa,
　　or pancetta

$\frac{2}{3}$ cup walnuts, toasted and chopped

1 Cut off the roots and most of the green parts from the leeks. Wash them thoroughly under cold running water to remove any grit or mud.

2 Place the leeks in a roasting bag with the water. Secure loosely with string or an elastic band and microwave on HIGH for 6 to 8 minutes, turning over and shaking to rearrange halfway through cooking. Leave to stand for 3 to 5 minutes; drain well.

3 Fill a microwaveproof $8\frac{1}{2}$- x $4\frac{1}{2}$-inch bread pan with the leeks, placing them alternately tops to root ends, and seasoning each layer.

4 Put another microwaveproof bread pan inside the first and press down on the leeks. Carefully invert both pans and drain out any water.

COOK'S TIP

It is important to use tender young leeks for this terrine. It is mainly the white part that is used in this recipe, but the green tops can be reserved for making soup. The terrine must be pressed for at least 4 hours—this makes it easier to cut into slices. You can vary the sliced meats as you like; try, for example, bresaola, salami, smoked venison, or roast ham.

5 Place one or two weights in the top pan and chill the terrine for at least 4 hours, or overnight.

6 Meanwhile, make the dressing. Whisk together the walnut and olive oils, vinegar, and wholegrain mustard in a small bowl. Add seasoning to taste.

7 Carefully turn out the terrine onto a board and cut it into slices using a large sharp knife. Lay the slices of leek terrine on serving plates and arrange the sliced meats alongside.

8 Spoon the dressing over the terrine and scatter with the chopped walnuts. Serve at once.

VARIATION

If you are short of time, serve the cooked leeks simply marinated in the walnut-and-mustard dressing.

Stuffed Grape Leaves

Based on the Greek dolmas (or dolmades), but with a wholegrain vegetarian stuffing, this makes an excellent low-fat, high-fiber first course, snack, or buffet dish. This is a quick version of the traditional specialty—the leaves and filling are cooked separately, rather than by long, slow cooking together for the authentic dish.

INGREDIENTS

Makes about 40

1 tablespoon sunflower oil

1 teaspoon sesame oil

1 onion, finely chopped

$1^1/_3$ cups brown rice

$2^1/_2$ cups hot vegetable stock

1 small yellow bell pepper, seeded and finely chopped

$^2/_3$ cup ready-to-eat dried apricots, finely chopped

2 lemons

$^1/_2$ cup pine nuts

3 tablespoons chopped fresh parsley

2 tablespoons chopped fresh mint

$^1/_2$ teaspoon apple-pie spice

8 ounces packaged grape leaves preserved in brine, drained

$^2/_3$ cup water

2 tablespoons olive oil

ground black pepper

lemon wedges, to garnish

To serve

$1^1/_4$ cups low-fat plain yogurt

2 tablespoons chopped fresh mixed herbs

cayenne pepper

1 Place the sunflower and sesame oils together in a large microwaveproof bowl. Microwave on HIGH for 30 seconds. Add the onion and microwave on HIGH for 2 minutes, stirring once.

2 Add the rice and stir to coat the grains in oil. Pour in the stock, cover loosely, and microwave on HIGH for 3 minutes. Reduce the power setting to MEDIUM and microwave for 25 minutes longer, stirring two or three times.

3 Stir in the chopped bell pepper and apricots. Replace the cover and leave to stand for 5 minutes.

4 Grate the peel off 1 lemon, then squeeze both lemons. Drain any stock that has not been absorbed by the rice. Stir in the pine nuts, herbs, apple-pie spice, lemon peel, and half the juice. Season with pepper; set aside.

5 Place the grape leaves in a bowl with the water, cover, and microwave on HIGH for 4 minutes. Drain the leaves well, then lay them shiny side down on a board. Cut out any coarse stems.

6 Place a heap of the rice mixture in the middle of a grape leaf. Fold over first the stem end, then the sides and finally the pointed end to make a neat roll. Repeat with the remaining leaves.

7 Pack the rolls closely together in a shallow serving dish. Mix the remaining lemon juice with the olive oil and pour over the grape leaves. Cover and chill before serving.

8 Serve the grape leaves, garnished with lemon wedges. Spoon the yogurt into a bowl, stir in the chopped herbs and sprinkle with a little cayenne. Offer this light sauce with the chilled stuffed grape leaves.

COOK'S TIP

If grape leaves are not available, the leaves of chard, young spinach, or cabbage can be used instead.

FISH AND SEAFOOD

Fisherman's Casserole

A perfect dish for microwaving because it's cooked in one container.

INGREDIENTS

Serves 4 to 6

1 pound mixed firm fish fillets, such as
    cod, haddock, and monkfish

4 tablespoons butter

1 onion, sliced

1 celery stalk, sliced

$2\frac{1}{2}$ cups chopped potatoes

3 cups hot fish stock

1 bouquet garni

1 cup frozen fava beans

$1\frac{1}{4}$ cups milk

4 ounces shelled cooked shrimp

8 mussels, shelled

salt and ground black pepper

chopped fresh parsley, to garnish

1 Skin the fish and cut the flesh into bite-size chunks using a large sharp knife. Place the butter in a microwaveproof dish and microwave on HIGH for 1 minute until melted. Add the onion, celery, and potatoes, cover, and microwave on HIGH for 4 minutes, stirring once during cooking.

2 Stir in the stock, bouquet garni, and beans. Cover and microwave on HIGH for 10 minutes, stirring twice.

3 Add the fish and milk, re-cover, and microwave on HIGH for 5 to 7 minutes until the fish flakes. Stir in the shrimp, mussels, and seasoning and microwave on HIGH for 1 to 2 minutes to warm through. Sprinkle with parsley and serve.

Potato-Topped Fish Pie

Cheese-topped potatoes enclose a creamy mixture of fish, shrimp, and hard-cooked eggs.

INGREDIENTS

Serves 4

$1\frac{3}{4}$ cups hot milk

1 bay leaf

$\frac{1}{4}$ onion, sliced

1 pound haddock or cod fillet

8 ounces smoked haddock fillet

3 hard-cooked eggs, chopped

5 tablespoons butter

2 tablespoons all-purpose flour

1 cup frozen peas

3 ounces shelled cooked shrimp

2 tablespoons chopped fresh parsley

lemon juice, to taste

$3\frac{1}{4}$ cups cooked diced potatoes, mashed

4 tablespoons grated Cheddar cheese

salt and ground black pepper

1 Place $\frac{1}{2}$ cup of the milk, the bay leaf and onion in a microwaveproof dish. Add the white and smoked fish, cover and microwave on HIGH for 7 to 8 minutes, rearranging once; strain and reserve the milk. Flake the fish into a microwaveproof baking dish, discarding the skin and any bones. Add the eggs.

2 Place 2 tablespoons of the butter, the flour and remaining milk in a microwave-proof pitcher. Whisk in the reserved cooking liquid from the fish. Microwave on HIGH for 5 to 7 minutes, stirring every 1 minute, until smooth, boiling, and thick. Stir in the peas and cooked shrimp.

3 Add the parsley, lemon juice, and seasoning to taste. Pour the sauce over the fish and eggs and carefully stir the ingredients.

4 Spoon the mashed potato evenly over the fish and fork up the surface. Dot with the remaining butter.

5 Sprinkle the cheese over the pie. Microwave on HIGH for 5 to 6 minutes. Brown under a heated hot broiler, if liked. Serve piping hot.

COMBINATION MICROWAVE

This recipe is suitable for cooking in a combination microwave. Follow your oven manufacturer's timing guide for best results.

Cod Creole

The lime or lemon juice and cayenne add piquancy to this dish.

INGREDIENTS

Serves 4

1 pound cod fillet, skinned

1 tablespoon lime or lemon juice

2 teaspoons olive oil

1 onion, finely chopped

1 green bell pepper, seeded and sliced

$\frac{1}{2}$ teaspoon cayenne pepper

$\frac{1}{2}$ teaspoon garlic salt

14-ounce can crushed tomatoes

1 Cut the cod fillet into bite-size chunks and sprinkle with the lime or lemon juice.

2 Place the olive oil, onion, and bell pepper in a large microwaveproof bowl. Cover and microwave on HIGH for 3 minutes, stirring once. Add the cayenne pepper and garlic salt.

COOK'S TIP
Be careful not to overcook the fish—or to let it bubble too vigorously in the sauce—because the chunks will break up.

3 Stir in the cod with the crushed tomatoes and cover. Microwave on HIGH for 8 to 10 minutes, stirring twice, until the fish is cooked and flakes easily. Serve with boiled rice or potatoes.

Five-Spice Fish

The Chinese mixtures of spicy and sweet-and-sour flavors are particularly successful with fish— and dinner is ready in minutes!

INGREDIENTS

Serves 4

1 teaspoon Chinese five-spice powder

4 teaspoons cornstarch

4 portions white fish fillet, such as cod, haddock, or hoki, about 6 ounces each

1 tablespoon sesame or sunflower oil

3 scallions, shredded

1 teaspoon finely chopped fresh ginger root

2 cups sliced button mushrooms

1 cup sliced baby corn

2 tablespoons soy sauce

3 tablespoons dry sherry or apple juice

1 teaspoon sugar

salt and ground black pepper

1 Mix the five-spice powder and cornstarch together and use to coat the fish portions.

2 Place the oil in a shallow microwaveproof dish with the scallions, ginger, mushrooms, and corn. Cover and microwave on HIGH for 2 minutes, stirring once. Add the fish and toss well to mix. Cover and microwave on HIGH for 4 to 6 minutes, stirring once.

3 Mix together the soy sauce, sherry or apple juice, and sugar, then pour this mixture over the fish. Cover and microwave on HIGH for 2 to 3 minutes, stirring once. Adjust the seasoning, then serve with noodles and stir-fried vegetables.

Monkfish with Mexican Salsa

INGREDIENTS

Serves 4

1½ pounds monkfish tail

3 tablespoons olive oil

2 tablespoons lime juice

1 garlic clove, crushed

1 tablespoon chopped fresh cilantro

salt and ground black pepper

cilantro sprigs and lime slices, to garnish

For the salsa

4 tomatoes, peeled, seeded, and diced

1 avocado, peeled, stoned, and diced

½ red onion, chopped

1 green chili, seeded and chopped

2 tablespoons chopped fresh cilantro

2 tablespoons olive oil

1 tablespoon lime juice

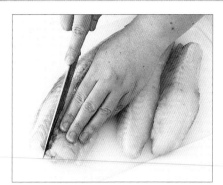

1 Prepare the monkfish. Using a sharp knife, remove the pink-gray membrane. Cut one fillet from each side of the backbone, then cut both fillets in half to make four steaks.

2 Mix together the oil, lime juice, garlic, cilantro, and seasoning in a shallow nonmetallic dish. Add the monkfish steaks and turn them several times to coat with the marinade. Cover the dish and leave the fish to marinate at cool room temperature, or in the refrigerator, for several hours.

3 About 30 minutes before cooking the fish, mix all the salsa ingredients together and leave to marinate at room temperature.

4 Remove the monkfish from the marinade and place in a shallow microwaveproof dish. Cover and microwave on HIGH for 4 to 6 minutes, turning once and brushing twice with the marinade, until cooked through.

5 Serve the monkfish garnished with cilantro sprigs and lime slices and accompanied by the salsa.

COOK'S TIP

It is important to remove the tough, pink-gray membrane covering the monkfish tail before cooking, otherwise it will shrink and toughen the flesh.

Spaghetti with Seafood Sauce

For speed, the sauce for this recipe is cooked in the microwave while the spaghetti is cooked on the stovetop.

INGREDIENTS

Serves 4

3 tablespoons olive oil

1 onion, chopped

1 garlic clove, finely chopped

8 ounces spaghetti

$2\frac{1}{2}$ cups pureed and strained tomatoes

1 tablespoon tomato paste

1 teaspoon dried oregano

1 bay leaf

1 teaspoon sugar

1 cup shelled cooked tiny shrimp, drained and well rinsed if canned

1 cup shelled cooked shrimp

$1\frac{1}{2}$ cups shelled cooked clams, drained and well rinsed if canned or bottled

1 tablespoon lemon juice

3 tablespoons chopped fresh parsley

2 tablespoons butter

salt and ground black pepper

4 whole cooked shrimp, to garnish (optional)

1 Place the oil in a microwave-proof bowl and add the onion and garlic. Microwave on HIGH for 3 minutes, stirring halfway through cooking.

2 Meanwhile, cook the spaghetti in a large saucepan of boiling salted water for 10 to 12 minutes until *al dente.*

3 Stir the tomatoes, tomato paste, oregano, bay leaf, and sugar into the onions and season well. Cover and microwave on HIGH for 4 minutes, stirring twice during cooking.

4 Add both shrimp, the clams, lemon juice, and 2 tablespoons of the parsley. Stir well, then cover and microwave on HIGH for 3 to 4 minutes, stirring once, until the shellfish are heated through.

5 Meanwhile, drain the cooked spaghetti and add the butter to the pan. Return the drained spaghetti to the pan and toss it in the butter. Season well with ground black pepper.

6 Divide the spaghetti between four warm plates and top with the seafood sauce. Sprinkle with the remaining parsley, garnish with whole shrimp, if using, and serve immediately.

Stuffed Flounder Rolls

Flounder fillets are a good choice because they are delicate in flavor, easy to cook, and free of bones.

INGREDIENTS

Serves 4

2 carrots, grated

1 zucchini, grated

4 tablespoons fresh whole wheat
   bread crumbs

1 tablespoon lime or lemon juice

4 flounder fillets

salt and ground black pepper

1 Mix together the grated carrots and zucchini. Stir in the bread crumbs, lime or lemon juice, and seasoning.

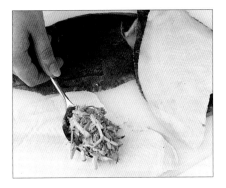

2 Lay the fish fillets skin side up and divide the stuffing between them, spreading it evenly.

3 Roll up the fillets to enclose the stuffing and place in a microwaveproof dish. Cover and microwave on HIGH for 4 to 6 minutes, rearranging once. Leave to stand, covered, for 3 minutes before serving. Serve hot with new potatoes.

COOK'S TIP

The flounder rolls create their own delicious juices, but for additional sauce, stir chopped fresh parsley into a little low-fat fromage blanc and serve this with the fish.

VARIATIONS

Lemon sole can be used instead of flounder. Alternatively, buy thick pieces of cod or salmon fillet and simply top them with the carrot and zucchini mixture. The microwave cooking times will be a little longer if cod steaks are used.

Mediterranean Flounder

Sun-dried tomatoes, toasted pine nuts, and anchovies make a flavorsome combination for the stuffing mixture.

INGREDIENTS

Serves 4

4 flounder fillets, about 8 ounces each, skinned

6 tablespoons butter

1 small onion, chopped

1 celery stalk, finely chopped

2 cups fresh white bread crumbs

3 tablespoons chopped fresh parsley

2 tablespoons pine nuts, toasted

3 or 4 pieces sun-dried tomatoes in oil, drained and chopped

2-ounce can anchovy fillets in oil, drained and chopped

5 tablespoons fish stock

ground black pepper

1 Using a sharp knife, cut the flounder fillets in half lengthwise to make eight smaller fillets.

2 Place the butter in a microwaveproof bowl and add the onion and celery. Cover and microwave on HIGH for 2 minutes, stirring halfway through cooking.

3 Mix together the bread crumbs, parsley, pine nuts, sun-dried tomatoes, and anchovies. Stir in the softened vegetables with their buttery juices and season with pepper.

4 Divide the stuffing into eight portions. Taking one portion at a time, form the stuffing into balls, then roll up each one inside a flounder fillet. Secure each roll with a wooden toothpick.

5 Place the rolled fillets in a buttered microwaveproof dish. Pour in the stock and cover the dish. Microwave on HIGH for 6 to 8 minutes, or until the fish flakes easily; remove the toothpicks. Serve with a little of the cooking juices drizzled over.

Halibut with Fennel and Orange

The fennel for this recipe can be cooked in a roasting bag, but remember to replace the metal tie with an elastic band or a piece of string.

INGREDIENTS

Serves 4

1 fennel bulb, thinly sliced

2 tablespoons water

grated peel and juice of 1 orange

$2/3$ cup dry white wine

4 halibut steaks, about 7 ounces each

4 tablespoons butter

salt and ground black pepper

fennel fronds, to garnish

1 Place the fennel in a microwaveproof bowl with the water. Cover and microwave on HIGH for 4 to 5 minutes, until just tender.

2 Place the orange peel, juice and wine in a microwaveproof jug and microwave on HIGH for 2 to 3 minutes until reduced by about half.

3 Drain the fennel well. Butter a shallow microwaveproof dish. Spread the fennel over the dish and season it to taste. Arrange the halibut on the fennel, season the fish and dot with butter. Pour the reduced orange and wine over.

4 Cover and microwave on HIGH for 7 to 8 minutes, rotating the dish twice, until the halibut flesh flakes. Serve garnished with fennel fronds.

Salmon with Cucumber Sauce

Cucumber and dill are classic accompaniments for delicate salmon; here they are used in a creamy sauce.

INGREDIENTS

Serves 6 to 8

4 pounds salmon, dressed and scaled

melted butter, for brushing

3 parsley or thyme sprigs

$1/2$ lemon, halved

1 large cucumber, peeled

2 tablespoons butter

$1/4$ cup dry white wine

3 tablespoons finely chopped fresh dill

4 tablespoons sour cream

salt and ground black pepper

1 Season the salmon and brush it inside and out with melted butter. Place the parsley or thyme and lemon in the body cavity.

2 Prick the salmon skin in several places to prevent bursting and place the fish in a shallow microwaveproof dish. Shield the head and tail with small pieces of smooth foil to prevent them from overcooking. Cover and microwave on HIGH for 20 to 22 minutes, rotating the dish three times during cooking. Leave the salmon to stand for 1 hour, then remove the skin.

3 Meanwhile, halve the cucumber lengthwise, scoop out the seeds, and dice the flesh.

4 Place the cucumber in a colander, sprinkle it with salt and toss lightly. Leave for about 30 minutes to drain, then rinse well and pat dry.

5 Place the butter in a small microwaveproof bowl, add the cucumber and microwave on HIGH for 1 minute until translucent but not soft. Add the wine and microwave on HIGH for 1 to 2 minutes longer.

6 Stir the chopped dill and sour cream into the cooked cucumber. Season the cucumber sauce to taste and serve at once with the salmon.

Herby Fish Cakes with Lemon-Chive Sauce

The wonderful flavor of fresh herbs makes these fish cakes the catch of the day.

INGREDIENTS

Serves 4

12 ounces potatoes, peeled

4 tablespoons water

5 tablespoons skim milk

12 ounces haddock or hoki fillets, skinned

1 tablespoon lemon juice

1 tablespoon creamed horseradish sauce

2 tablespoons chopped fresh parsley

flour, for dusting

2 cups fresh whole wheat bread crumbs

salt and ground black pepper

sprig of flat-leaf parsley, to garnish

sugar-snap peas and a sliced tomato and
  onion salad, to serve

For the lemon-chive sauce

thinly pared peel and juice of $\frac{1}{2}$ small
  lemon

$\frac{1}{2}$ cup dry white wine

2 thin slices fresh ginger root

2 teaspoons cornstarch

2 tablespoons snipped fresh chives

1 Cut the potatoes into small cubes and place in a microwaveproof bowl with 3 tablespoons of the water. Cover and microwave on HIGH for 6 to 8 minutes until tender, stirring halfway through cooking. Drain and mash with the milk and season to taste.

2 Purée the fish with the lemon juice and horseradish sauce in a blender or food processor. Mix the purée with the potatoes and parsley.

3 With floured hands, shape the mixture into eight cakes and coat them with the bread crumbs. Chill the fish cakes for 30 minutes.

4 To make the sauce, cut the lemon peel into julienne strips and place it in a large microwave-proof bowl. Add the lemon juice, wine, ginger, and seasoning to taste. Microwave on HIGH for 3 to 4 minutes, stirring twice.

5 Blend the cornstarch with the remaining 1 tablespoon cold water. Add to the sauce and stir until clear. If necessary, microwave on HIGH for 1 minute, stirring once, until clear and thick.

6 To cook the fish cakes, place them in a shallow microwave-proof dish. Cover and microwave on HIGH for 7 to 8 minutes, turning the cakes over halfway through cooking. Brown lightly under a heated hot broiler, if liked.

7 Stir the chives into the hot sauce and serve immediately with the fish cakes, garnished with sprigs of flat leaf parsley. Sugar-snap peas and a sliced tomato and onion salad are suitable accompaniments.

Mackerel Kabobs with Parsley Dressing

Fish kabobs cook quickly and evenly in the microwave.

Serves 4

1 pound mackerel fillets

finely grated peel and juice of 1 lemon

3 tablespoons chopped fresh parsley

12 cherry tomatoes

8 ripe olives, pitted

salt and ground black pepper

1 Cut the fish into $1\frac{1}{2}$-inch chunks and place in a bowl with half the lemon peel and juice, half the parsley, and the seasoning. Cover and leave to marinate for 30 minutes.

2 Thread the fish onto eight long wooden skewers, alternating the chunks with tomatoes and olives. Place the kabobs on a microwave-proof roasting rack or rest them across a shallow microwaveproof dish. Cover with waxed paper and microwave on HIGH for 4 to 6 minutes, rearranging halfway through cooking, until the fish is cooked.

3 Mix the remaining lemon peel and juice with the remaining parsley in a small bowl, adding seasoning to taste. Spoon the dressing over the kabobs and serve hot, with plain boiled rice or noodles and a leafy green salad.

COOK'S TIP

When using wooden or bamboo kabob skewers, soak them first in a bowl of cold water for a few minutes to help prevent them from drying out and cracking.

VARIATIONS

Other firm-fleshed fish may be used in place of the mackerel—for a special occasion opt for salmon fillet or monkfish tail; or try a mixture of the two, threading the fish chunks alternately onto the skewers with the tomatoes and olives.

Tuna and Mixed Vegetable Pasta

Cook this simple and very speedy sauce in the microwave while the pasta cooks conventionally.

INGREDIENTS

Serves 4

2 tablespoons olive oil

2½ cups sliced button mushrooms

1 garlic clove, crushed

½ red bell pepper, seeded and chopped

1 tablespoon tomato paste

1¼ cups tomato juice

1 cup frozen peas

1 to 2 tablespoons drained pickled green peppercorns, crushed

2½ cups whole wheat pasta shapes

7-ounce can tuna chunks in brine, drained

6 scallions, diagonally sliced

1 Place the oil in a microwave-proof bowl with the mushrooms, garlic, and bell pepper. Cover and microwave on HIGH for 4 minutes, stirring halfway through cooking. Stir in the tomato paste, then add the tomato juice, peas, and some or all of the crushed peppercorns, depending on how spicy you like the sauce.

2 Cover the bowl and microwave on HIGH for 4 minutes longer, stirring halfway through cooking.

3 Bring a large saucepan of lightly salted water to a boil on the stovetop. Add the pasta and cook for about 12 minutes, or according to the package directions, until just tender. When the pasta is almost ready, add the tuna to the sauce and microwave on HIGH for 1 minute to heat though. Stir in the scallions.

4 Drain the pasta and tip it into a warm bowl. Pour the sauce over the pasta and toss to mix. Serve at once.

Sweet-and-Sour Fish

Serve this tasty, nutritious dish with brown rice and stir-fried cabbage or spinach for a delicious, light lunch-time meal.

INGREDIENTS

Serves 4

4 tablespoons apple vinegar

3 tablespoons light soy sauce

¼ cup sugar

1 tablespoon tomato paste

1½ tablespoons cornstarch

1 cup water

1 green bell pepper, seeded and sliced

8-ounce can pineapple pieces in natural juice

1½ cups peeled and chopped tomatoes

3 cups sliced button mushrooms

1½ pounds chunky haddock fillets, skinned

salt and ground black pepper

1 Mix the vinegar, soy sauce, sugar, and tomato paste in a microwaveproof bowl. Gradually blend the cornstarch to a smooth paste with the water, then add to the bowl, stirring well. Microwave on HIGH for 2 to 2½ minutes, stirring three times during cooking, until smooth, boiling, and thick.

2 Add the green bell pepper, canned pineapple pieces with juice, tomatoes, and mushrooms to the sauce and microwave on HIGH for 2 minutes, stirring halfway through cooking. Season to taste with salt and pepper.

3 Place the fish in a single layer in a shallow microwaveproof dish and pour the sauce over. Cover and microwave on HIGH for 8 to 10 minutes, rotating the dish twice during cooking. Leave to stand for 5 minutes before serving.

Spiced Fish with Okra

INGREDIENTS

Serves 4

1 pound monkfish

1 teaspoon ground turmeric

$\frac{1}{2}$ teaspoon ground red pepper

$\frac{1}{2}$ teaspoon salt

1 teaspoon cumin seeds

$\frac{1}{2}$ teaspoon fennel seeds

2 dried red chilies

3 tablespoons oil

1 onion, finely chopped

2 garlic cloves, crushed

4 tomatoes, skinned and finely chopped

$\frac{2}{3}$ cup water

2 cups okra, trimmed and cut into
   1-inch pieces

1 teaspoon garam masala

tomato rice, to serve

1 Remove the membrane and bones from the monkfish. Cut the fillet into 1-inch cubes and place them in a dish. Mix the turmeric, ground red pepper, and $\frac{1}{4}$ teaspoon of the salt. Rub this mixture all over the fish. Marinate the fish for 15 minutes.

2 Mix the cumin seeds, fennel seeds, and chilies in a large microwaveproof bowl, cover, and microwave on HIGH for 1 to 2 minutes. Transfer the spices to a blender or mortar and process or grind them into a coarse powder.

COOK'S TIP

Yellow (flavored with turmeric or saffron) and plain rice also go well with this spiced dish, and the two colors make an attractive presentation.

3 Place 2 tablespoons of the oil in a large microwaveproof bowl and microwave on HIGH for 30 seconds until hot. Add the fish, turning the pieces in the oil. Cover and microwave on HIGH for 4 to 5 minutes, stirring halfway through cooking. Use a perforated spoon to remove the fish from the bowl.

4 Add the remaining oil to the bowl with the onion, garlic, ground spice mixture and the remaining salt. Cover and microwave on HIGH for 2 minutes, stirring once. Stir in the tomatoes and water, cover and microwave on HIGH for 2 to 3 minutes, stirring once.

5 Add the okra, cover, and microwave on HIGH for 4 to 6 minutes, stirring halfway through cooking.

6 Replace the fish. Add the garam masala and lightly mix both with the sauce. Cover and microwave on HIGH for 2 to 3 minutes until the fish is hot and the okra is tender. Serve with rice flavored with a little tomato paste during cooking.

Coconut Salmon

This is an ideal dish to serve at dinner parties

INGREDIENTS

Serves 4

2 teaspoons ground cumin

2 teaspoons chili powder

$\frac{1}{2}$ teaspoon ground turmeric

2 tablespoons white wine vinegar

$\frac{1}{4}$ teaspoon salt

4 salmon steaks, about 6 ounces each

3 tablespoons oil

1 onion, chopped

2 green chilies, seeded and chopped

2 garlic cloves, crushed

1-inch piece fresh ginger root, grated

1 teaspoon ground coriander

$\frac{3}{4}$ cup coconut milk

fresh cilantro sprigs, to garnish

scallion rice, to serve

1 Mix 1 teaspoon of the ground cumin with the chili powder, turmeric, vinegar, and salt. Rub this spice paste over the salmon steaks and leave to marinate for about 15 minutes.

2 Place the oil in a large, deep microwaveproof dish. Add the onion, chilies, garlic, and ginger. Cover and microwave on HIGH for 3 minutes, stirring halfway though cooking. Process this cooked mixture to a paste in a food processor or blender.

3 Return the paste to the dish. Stir in the remaining cumin, the ground coriander, and coconut milk. Microwave on HIGH for 2 to 2$\frac{1}{2}$ minutes, stirring twice during cooking.

4 Add the salmon steaks, cover, and microwave on MEDIUM for 9 to 10 minutes, rearranging halfway through cooking, until the fish is cooked. Leave to stand for 5 minutes before serving, garnished with cilantro. Serve rice flavored with chopped scallions with the salmon.

COOK'S TIP

To make coconut milk, dissolve grated creamed coconut in boiling water and strain it into a pitcher, if necessary.

Green Fish Curry

Serves 4

$\frac{1}{4}$ teaspoon ground turmeric

2 tablespoons lime juice

pinch of salt

4 portions cod fillets, skinned and cut into 2-inch chunks

1 onion, chopped

1 green chili, roughly chopped

1 garlic clove, crushed

$\frac{1}{4}$ cup cashew nuts

$\frac{1}{2}$ teaspoon fennel seeds

2 tablespoons shredded coconut

2 tablespoons oil

$\frac{1}{4}$ teaspoon cumin seeds

$\frac{1}{4}$ teaspoon ground coriander

$\frac{1}{4}$ teaspoon ground cumin

$\frac{1}{4}$ teaspoon salt

$\frac{2}{3}$ cup water

$\frac{3}{4}$ cup light cream

3 tablespoons finely chopped fresh cilantro

fresh cilantro sprig, to garnish

rice with vegetables, to serve

1 Combine the turmeric, lime juice, and pinch of salt, then rub the mixture over the fish. Cover and leave to marinate for 15 minutes.

2 Meanwhile, process the onion, chili, garlic, cashew nuts, fennel seeds, and coconut to a paste in a blender or food processor. Spoon the paste into a bowl; set it aside.

3 Place the oil in a large microwaveproof bowl. Add the cumin seeds and microwave on HIGH for 1 to 1$\frac{1}{2}$ minutes until the seeds begin to splutter. Add the paste, ground coriander, cumin, salt, and water and mix well. Cover and microwave on HIGH for 3 to 5 minutes, stirring twice during cooking.

4 Stir in the cream and fresh cilantro. Microwave on HIGH for 2 to 3 minutes longer, stirring halfway through cooking.

5 Gently stir in the fish. Cover and microwave on HIGH for 7 to 10 minutes, stirring twice, until cooked. Serve, garnished with cilantro, with rice and vegetables or pilaf.

COOK'S TIP

Whole and ground spices, lime, garlic, chilli and coconut make a superb sauce. Fresh cilantro and light cream balance and enliven the flavors.

Shrimp Curry

This rich shrimp curry is flavored with coconut and a delicious blend of aromatic spices.

INGREDIENTS

Serves 4

$1\frac{1}{2}$ pounds uncooked tiger shrimp

4 dried red chilies

1 cup shredded coconut

1 teaspoon black mustard seeds

1 large onion, chopped

3 tablespoons oil

4 bay leaves

1-inch piece fresh ginger root, finely chopped

2 garlic cloves, crushed

1 tablespoon ground coriander

1 teaspoon chili powder

1 teaspoon salt

4 tomatoes, finely chopped

$\frac{3}{4}$ cup water

plain rice, to serve

1 Shell the shrimp. Run a sharp knife along the back of each shrimp to make a shallow cut and carefully remove the thin black intestinal vein.

2 Put the dried red chilies, coconut, mustard seeds, and onion in a large microwaveproof bowl. Microwave on HIGH for 8 minutes, stirring twice. Process the mixture to a coarse paste in a blender or food processor.

3 Place the oil in a microwave-proof bowl with the bay leaves. Add the ginger and garlic, cover, and microwave on HIGH for 2 minutes, stirring twice during cooking.

4 Stir in the coriander, chili powder, salt, and the paste. Cover and microwave on HIGH for 2 to 3 minutes, stirring halfway through cooking.

5 Stir in the tomatoes and water, cover and microwave on HIGH for 4 to 6 minutes, stirring halfway through cooking, until thickened slightly.

6 Stir in the shrimp, cover, and microwave on HIGH for 4 minutes, or until they turn pink and their edges curl slightly. Serve with plain boiled rice.

Seafood Pilaf

This all-in-one main course makes a satisfying meal for any day of the week. For a special meal, substitute dry white wine for the orange juice.

INGREDIENTS

Serves 4

2 teaspoons olive oil

$1\frac{1}{4}$ cups long-grain rice

1 teaspoon ground turmeric

1 red bell pepper, seeded and diced

1 small onion, finely chopped

2 zucchini, sliced

2 cups halved button mushrooms

$1\frac{1}{2}$ cups fish or chicken stock

$\frac{2}{3}$ cup orange juice

12 ounces white fish fillets, skinned

12 cooked mussels, shelled

salt and ground black pepper

grated peel of 1 orange, to garnish

1 Mix the oil with the rice and turmeric in a large microwaveproof bowl. Microwave on HIGH for 1 minute.

2 Add the bell pepper, onion, zucchini and mushrooms. Stir in the stock and orange juice. Cover and microwave on HIGH for 13 minutes, stirring halfway through cooking. Leave to stand, covered.

3 Place the fish on a microwave-proof plate. Cover and microwave on HIGH for 4 to 5 minutes until cooked. Flake the fish and stir it into the rice mixture. Stir in the mussels and microwave on HIGH for 1 minute longer. Adjust the seasoning, sprinkle with orange peel and serve hot.

Salmon Pasta with Parsley Sauce

INGREDIENTS

Serves 4

1 pound salmon fillet, skinned

3 cups pasta shapes, such as penne or twists

6 ounces cherry tomatoes, halved

$\frac{2}{3}$ cup low-fat crème fraîche or sour cream

3 tablespoons chopped fresh parsley

finely grated peel of $\frac{1}{2}$ orange

salt and ground black pepper

COOK'S TIP

If low-fat crème fraîche is not available, use ordinary crème fraîche or sour cream instead.

1 Cut the salmon into bite-size pieces, arrange them on a microwaveproof plate, and cover with greaseproof paper. Microwave on HIGH for 2 to $2\frac{1}{2}$ minutes, rearranging halfway through cooking. Leave to stand for 5 minutes.

2 Cook the pasta in a saucepan of boiling water on the stovetop, following the package directions.

3 Alternatively, cook the pasta in 5 cups boiling water with 1 teaspoon oil in a large microwaveproof bowl. Microwave on HIGH for 10 to 12 minutes.

4 Drain the pasta and toss it with the tomatoes and salmon. Stir together the crème fraîche, parsley, orange peel, and pepper to taste. Toss this sauce into the salmon and pasta and serve hot.

Ginger and Lime Shrimp

Serves 4

8 ounces raw tiger shrimp, peeled

$\frac{1}{3}$ cucumber

1 tablespoon sunflower oil

1 tablespoon sesame seed oil

1 cup snow peas, trimmed

4 scallions, diagonally sliced

2 tablespoons chopped fresh cilantro,
   to garnish

For the marinade

1 tablespoon honey

1 tablespoon light soy sauce

1 tablespoon dry sherry

2 garlic cloves, crushed

small piece of fresh ginger root, peeled
   and finely chopped

juice of 1 lime

1 Mix the marinade ingredients together, stir in the shrimp, and leave to marinate for 1 to 2 hours.

2 Prepare the cucumber: Slice it in half lengthwise, scoop out the seeds, and slice each half neatly into crescents; set aside.

3 Place both types of oil in a large microwaveproof bowl. Microwave on HIGH for 30 seconds. Drain the shrimp (reserving the marinade) and add them to the oils. Cover and microwave on HIGH for $1\frac{1}{2}$ to $2\frac{1}{2}$ minutes, stirring halfway through cooking, until they begin to turn pink.

4 Add the snow peas and the cucumber, cover and microwave on HIGH for 1 to 2 minutes longer, stirring once.

5 Stir in the reserved marinade and microwave on HIGH for 30 seconds longer. Stir in the scallions and serve, sprinkled with fresh cilantro.

Mediterranean Fish Cutlets

Serves 4

4 white fish cutlets, about 5 ounces each

3 tablespoons fish stock

3 tablespoons dry white wine

1 bay leaf, a few black peppercorns,
   and a strip of pared lemon peel,
   for flavoring

chopped fresh parsley, to garnish

For the tomato sauce

14-ounce can crushed tomatoes

1 garlic clove, crushed

1 tablespoon sun-dried tomato paste

1 tablespoon pastis or other anise-
   flavored liqueur

1 tablespoon drained capers

12 to 16 ripe olives, pitted

salt and ground black pepper

1 To make the tomato sauce, place the tomatoes, garlic, tomato paste, pastis or liqueur, capers, olives, and salt and pepper in a microwaveproof bowl. Cover and microwave on HIGH for 4 to 6 minutes, stirring twice.

2 Place the fish cutlets in a microwaveproof dish, pour the stock and wine over, and add the flavorings. Cover and microwave on HIGH for 5 minutes, rotating the dish twice. Leave to stand for 2 minutes.

3 Using a perforated spoon, transfer the fish to a heated dish. Strain the stock into the tomato sauce and stir well. Season the sauce, pour it over the fish, and serve at once, garnished with chopped parsley.

Whole Cooked Salmon

Farmed salmon has made this fish more affordable and less of a treat, but a whole salmon still features as a centerpiece at parties. As with all fish, the taste depends first on freshness and second on not overcooking it. Although you need to start early, the cooking time is short. Cooked salmon is, of course, also delicious served hot with a buttery hollandaise sauce. New potatoes and fine green beans are perfect accompaniments.

INGREDIENTS

Serves 6 to 8 as part of a buffet

4 pounds whole salmon

1 lemon, sliced

salt and ground black pepper

lemon wedges, cucumber ribbons, and
   fresh dill sprigs, to garnish

1 Wash the salmon and dry it well, inside and out. Prick the skin in several places to prevent it bursting and place the salmon in a shallow microwaveproof dish.

2 Put a few slices of lemon inside the salmon and arrange more on the top. Season well and sprinkle a little boiling water over to moisten the fish.

3 Cover with waxed paper or vented plastic wrap and microwave on HIGH for 20 to 22 minutes, rotating the dish three times during cooking. Leave to stand, covered, for 5 minutes, before serving hot. If serving cold, leave to cool completely before uncovering.

4 To serve hot with hollandaise sauce, peel off the skin, and transfer the salmon to a heated serving dish. Keep warm while preparing the sauce.

5 To serve cold and on the same day, remove the skin from the cooked fish and arrange it on a large platter. Garnish with lemon wedges, cucumber cut into thin ribbons, and sprigs of dill. If you intend serving the salmon the following day, leave the skin on and chill the fish overnight before adding the garnish.

HOLLANDAISE SAUCE

Place $1/2$ cup butter in a large microwaveproof pitcher and microwave on HIGH for $1 1/2$ minutes. Whisk in 3 tablespoons lemon juice, 2 egg yolks, a pinch of mustard powder, and salt and pepper to taste. Microwave on MEDIUM for 1 minute. Whisk and serve.

COOK'S TIP

To prevent the head and tail ends of fish from overcooking in the microwave, they can be shielded with small pieces of smooth foil. This may be done at the beginning of the cooking time or after a few minutes if cooking progress is being carefully watched.

MEAT AND POULTRY

Stilton Burgers

Slightly more up-scale than the traditional burger, this recipe contains a delicious surprise. The lightly melted blue Stilton cheese encased in a burger is absolutely delicious.

INGREDIENTS

Serves 4

1 pound ground beef
1 onion, finely chopped
1 celery stalk, chopped
1 teaspoon Italian seasoning
1 teaspoon prepared mustard
$\frac{1}{2}$ cup crumbled Stilton cheese
4 hamburger buns
salt and ground black pepper

1 Place the ground beef in a bowl together with the onion and celery; season well.

2 Stir in the Italian seasoning and mustard, bringing all the ingredients together to form a firm mixture.

3 Divide the mixture into eight equal portions. Place four on a chopping board and flatten each one slightly.

4 Share the crumbled cheese between the burgers, placing a little in the middle of each.

5 Flatten the remaining mixture and place on top. Mold the mixture around the crumbled cheese and shape into four burgers.

6 To cook, place the burgers on a microwaveproof roasting rack and microwave on HIGH, uncovered, for 6 to 7 minutes, turning over once. Leave to stand for 2 to 3 minutes.

7 Alternatively, for a browner and crisper result, heat a microwave browning dish or special microwave hamburger cooker according to the manufacturer's directions. Add the burgers, pressing them down well onto the base, and microwave on HIGH for 5 to $5\frac{1}{2}$ minutes, turning over once. If using a microwave burger cooker to cook the burgers individually, read and follow the manufacturer's directions, particularly for timing. Leave to stand for 2 to 3 minutes.

8 Serve in hamburger buns or pita bread with salad leaves and a relish of your choice.

COMBINATION MICROWAVE

This recipe is suitable for cooking in a combination microwave. Follow the oven manufacturer's timing guide for the best results.

Beef and Mushroom Burgers

It's worth making your own burgers to cut down on fat—in these, the meat is extended with mushrooms for extra fiber.

INGREDIENTS

Serves 4

2 cups small button mushrooms

1 small onion, chopped

1 pound ground beef

1 cup fresh whole wheat
   bread crumbs

1 teaspoon Italian seasoning

1 tablespoon tomato paste

all-purpose flour, for shaping

salt and ground black pepper

relish, lettuce, hamburger buns or pita
   bread, to serve

1 Place the mushrooms and onion in a food processor, and process until finely chopped. Add the beef, bread crumbs, Italian seasoning, tomato paste, salt and pepper. Process for a few seconds until the mixture binds together but still has some texture.

2 Divide the mixture into four, then press into hamburger shapes using lightly floured hands.

3 To cook, place the burgers on a microwaveproof roasting rack and microwave on HIGH, uncovered, for 6 to 7 minutes, turning over once. Leave to stand for 2 to 3 minutes.

4 Alternatively, for a browner and crisper result, heat a microwave browning dish according to the manufacturer's directions. Add the burgers, pressing down well onto the base and microwave on HIGH for 5 to $5\frac{1}{2}$ minutes, turning over once. Leave to stand for 2 to 3 minutes. Serve with relish and lettuce, in hamburger buns or pita bread.

VARIATION

To make Lamb and Mushroom Burgers, substitute lean ground lamb for the ground beef.

COMBINATION MICROWAVE

This recipe is suitable for cooking in a combination microwave. Follow the oven manufacturer's timing guide for the best results.

Stuffed Tomatoes

Ever popular, this simple recipe demonstrates the versatility of ground beef as a stuffing.

INGREDIENTS

Serves 4

4 large beefsteak tomatoes

$1\frac{1}{2}$ teaspoons oil

3 ounces ground beef

1 small red onion, thinly sliced

$\frac{1}{4}$ cup bulgar wheat

2 tablespoons freshly grated
    Parmesan cheese

1 tablespoon cashew nuts, chopped

1 small celery stalk, chopped

salt and ground black pepper

crisp green salad, to serve

1 Trim the tops from the tomatoes and scoop out the flesh with a teaspoon, reserve.

2 Place the oil in a large microwaveproof bowl. Add the ground beef and onion, cover, and microwave on HIGH for 5 to 6 minutes until the beef is cooked, stirring twice to break up the meat. Stir in the tomato flesh.

3 Place the bulgar wheat in a bowl, cover with boiling water, and leave to soak for 10 minutes; drain if necessary.

4 Mix the ground beef and bulgar wheat, Parmesan cheese, nuts, and celery together; season well.

5 Spoon the filling into the tomatoes and place in a shallow microwaveproof dish. Microwave on HIGH for 3 to 5 minutes until the tomatoes and their filling are tender. Serve with a crisp green salad.

Beef Casserole and Dumplings

This delicious casserole is topped with light herby dumplings for a filling and nutritious meal. Accompany with broccoli.

INGREDIENTS

Serves 4

1 tablespoon oil

16 pearl onions

2 carrots, sliced

2 celery stalks, sliced

2 tablespoons all-purpose flour

1 pound ground beef

$2\frac{1}{2}$ cups hot beef stock

salt and ground black pepper

For the dumplings

$\frac{3}{4}$ cup all-purpose flour

$1\frac{1}{2}$ teaspoons baking powder

$\frac{1}{2}$ teaspoon salt

4 tablespoons margarine

1 tablespoon chopped fresh parsley

4 to 5 tablespoons water

1 Place the oil, onions, carrots, and celery in a large microwaveproof casserole. Cover and microwave on HIGH for 6 to 8 minutes, stirring twice, until softened.

2 Stir in the flour, mixing well. Microwave for 1 minute, stirring halfway through cooking.

3 Stir in the ground beef, stock, and salt and pepper to taste.

4 Three-quarters cover with plastic wrap or the casserole lid. Microwave on HIGH for 20 to 25 minutes, stirring three times. Leave to stand while cooking the dumplings.

5 To make the dumplings, stir the flour, baking powder, and salt together. Cut in the margarine, then stir in the parsley and water to form a smooth dough.

6 Roll into eight equal-size balls and place in a shallow microwaveproof dish in a circle. Pour in $2\frac{1}{2}$ cups boiling water. Microwave on HIGH for 2 minutes. Rearrange and cover, then microwave on HIGH for 2 minutes longer. Remove the dumplings with a perforated spoon and serve with the beef casserole.

Beef and Lentil Pie

In this variation of British cottage pie, lentils are substituted for some of the meat to produce a dish that is lower in fat and higher in fiber.

INGREDIENTS

Serves 4

1 cup green lentils

1 onion, chopped

2 celery stalks, chopped

1 large carrot, chopped

1 garlic clove, crushed

$\frac{1}{2}$ pound lean ground beef

15-ounce can crushed tomatoes

2 teaspoons yeast extract

1 bay leaf

For the topping

3 cups potatoes peeled and cut into large chunks

3 cups parsnips peeled and cut into large chunks

4 tablespoons low-fat plain yogurt

3 tablespoons snipped chives

4 teaspoons freshly grated Parmesan cheese

2 tomatoes, sliced

$\frac{1}{4}$ cup pine nuts (optional)

1 Place the lentils in a microwave-proof bowl and pour in boiling water to cover. Cover and microwave on HIGH for 6 minutes.

2 Place onion, celery, carrot, and garlic in a microwaveproof bowl. Cover, microwave on HIGH for 4 minutes and stir once. Add the beef, stir, and microwave on HIGH for 2 minutes. Mix in the tomatoes.

3 Drain the lentils, reserving 1 cup of the cooking water in a measuring jug. Add the lentils to the meat mixture. Dissolve the yeast extract in the cooking water and stir it into the meat with the bay leaf. Cover loosely, then microwave on HIGH for 12 to 15 minutes, stirring twice.

4 Make the topping. Place the potatoes and parsnips in a microwaveproof bowl with 5 tablespoons water. Cover and microwave on HIGH for 11 to 13 minutes, stirring once, until tender. Mash the potatoes and parsnips together and stir in the yogurt and chives.

5 Remove the bay leaf and divide the meat mixture between four small dishes or one large dish suitable for broiling. Spoon the potato mixture over. Sprinkle with Parmesan and garnish with tomato slices. Scatter pine nuts over the top, if using, and broil the pies for a few minutes until the topping is crisp and golden brown.

Spicy Spaghetti Sauce

A spicy version of a popular dish. Worcestershire sauce and chorizo sausages add an extra element to this perfect family standby.

INGREDIENTS

Serves 4

1 tablespoon oil

1 onion, chopped

$\frac{1}{2}$ pound ground beef

1 teaspoon chili powder

1 tablespoon Worcestershire sauce

2 tablespoons all-purpose flour

$\frac{2}{3}$ cup beef stock

4 chorizo sausages

7-ounce can crushed tomatoes

2 ounces baby corn

1 tablespoon chopped fresh basil

salt and ground black pepper

1 Place the oil and onion in a large microwaveproof bowl. Microwave on HIGH for 2 minutes. Add the ground beef and chili powder, stirring well. Microwave on HIGH for 4 to 5 minutes, breaking up the beef twice during cooking.

2 Stir in the Worcestershire sauce and flour. Microwave on HIGH for 30 seconds, stirring once, before pouring in the stock.

3 Slice the chorizo sausages and halve the corn lengthwise.

4 Stir in the sausages, tomatoes, corn, and chopped basil. Season well, cover loosely, and microwave on HIGH for 15 to 20 minutes, stirring twice. Serve with spaghetti, garnished with fresh basil.

COOK'S TIP

If you like, cool the spaghetti sauce and freeze it in conveniently sized portions for up to two months.

Chili Con Carne

An old-fashioned recipe that has become a regular feature in many homes. Simple and economical, it is one of the most popular ground beef recipes developed. This recipe isn't highly spiced, so it is suitable for young children, too.

INGREDIENTS

Serves 4

1 tablespoon oil

$\frac{1}{2}$ pound ground beef

1 onion, quartered

1 teaspoon chili powder

2 tablespoons all-purpose flour

2 tablespoons tomato paste

$\frac{2}{3}$ cup beef stock

7-ounce can chopped tomatoes

7-ounce can kidney beans, drained

1 green bell pepper, seeded and chopped

1 tablespoon Worcestershire sauce

$\frac{1}{2}$ cup long-grain rice

salt and ground black pepper

sour cream, to serve

chopped fresh parsley, to garnish

1 Place the oil, ground beef, onion, and chili powder in a microwaveproof bowl and microwave on HIGH for 6 to 8 minutes, stirring twice.

2 Add the flour and tomato paste and microwave on HIGH for 30 seconds, stirring once. Stir in the stock and tomatoes, cover, and microwave on HIGH for 12 to 15 minutes, stirring once.

3 Stir in the kidney beans, chopped green bell pepper, and Worcestershire sauce. Cover and microwave on HIGH for 5 to 7 minutes, stirring once.

4 Place the rice in a large microwaveproof bowl. Add 1 cup boiling water and a pinch of salt. Cover loosely and microwave on HIGH for 3 minutes. Stir, re-cover, and microwave on MEDIUM for 12 minutes. Leave to stand, covered, for 5 minutes.

5 Fluff up the rice and spoon it onto serving plates. Serve the chili con carne on the rice. To complete the dish, add a spoonful of sour cream and garnish with fresh parsley.

Butterflied Lamb with Cumin and Garlic

Ground cumin and garlic give the lamb a wonderful Middle-Eastern flavor. Vary the recipe by making a simple oil, lemon, and herb marinade instead.

INGREDIENTS

Serves 6

4 pounds leg of lamb

4 tablespoons olive oil

2 tablespoons ground cumin

4 to 6 garlic cloves, crushed

salt and ground black pepper

pilaf with raisins and toasted almonds, to serve

cilantro sprigs and lemon wedges, to garnish

1 To butterfly the lamb, cut away the meat from the bone using a small sharp knife. Remove any excess fat and the thin, parchment-like membrane. Bat out the meat to an even thickness, then prick the fleshy side with a knife tip.

2 In a bowl, mix together the oil, cumin, and garlic; season with pepper. Spoon the mixture all over the lamb, then rub it well into the crevices. Cover and leave to marinate overnight.

3 Spread the lamb, skin-side down, on a microwave roasting rack or upturned saucer in a microwaveproof shallow dish. Season with salt and microwave on HIGH for 5 minutes. Reduce the power setting to MEDIUM and microwave for 30 to 35 minutes longer, or until the meat is cooked but still pink inside, turning it over once.

4 Brown the lamb under a heated hot broiler to crisp the outside, if liked. Leave to stand, covered with foil, for 10 to 15 minutes before carving.

5 Cut the lamb into diagonal slices and serve it with a rice pilaf with toasted almonds and raisins. Garnish with cilantro sprigs and lemon wedges.

COMBINATION MICROWAVE

This recipe is suitable for cooking in a combination microwave. Follow the oven manufacturer's timing guide for the best results.

Rack of Lamb with Red Currant Bunches

Bunches of red currants tied with chives provide a strong color contrast to glazed rack of lamb.

INGREDIENTS

Serves 4 to 6

3 tablespoons red currant jelly

1 teaspoon wholegrain mustard

2 best ends of lamb, each with 6 chops, trimmed of all fat

$\frac{1}{2}$ cup red wine

$\frac{1}{2}$ cup stock or water

salt and ground black pepper

For the garnish

4 to 6 chives, wilted

8 to 12 small bunches of red currants

1 Place the red currant jelly with the mustard in a small microwaveproof bowl and microwave on HIGH for 1 to 2 minutes, stirring once, until the jelly melts. Brush the mixture over the lamb.

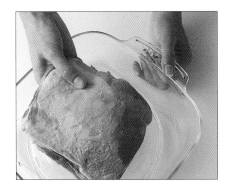

2 Place the racks of lamb on a microwave roasting rack or upturned saucer in a microwave-proof shallow dish. Microwave on HIGH for 18 to 22 minutes, or until cooked to your taste, rotating the dish and basting the lamb four times during cooking. Transfer the lamb to a warm platter, loosely cover with foil, and leave to rest for 10 minutes.

3 Drain the fat from the roasting dish, leaving the sediment behind. Stir in the red wine and microwave on HIGH for 2 to 3 minutes until most of the liquid evaporates.

4 Add the stock or water. Microwave on HIGH for 3 to 4 minutes until reduced and very slightly syrupy. Season, strain into a gravyboat; keep hot.

5 Wrap the chives around the red currant stems, tie them in a neat knot, and then trim the ends. Make four bunches of red currants in this way. Carve the lamb into chops, arrange them on four or six dinner plates and spoon a little of the sauce over. To complete the dish, garnish with the red currant bunches.

COMBINATION MICROWAVE

This recipe is suitable for cooking in a combination microwave. Follow the oven manufacturer's timing guide for the best results.

Turkish Lamb and Apricot Stew

Cooking this stew on medium power makes sure that the lamb is deliciously moist and tender.

INGREDIENTS

Serves 4

1 large eggplant, cubed

2 tablespoons sunflower oil

1 onion, chopped

1 garlic clove, crushed

1 teaspoon ground cinnamon

3 whole cloves

1 pound boned leg of lamb, cubed

14-ounce can crushed tomatoes

$1\frac{1}{4}$ cups boiling water

$\frac{2}{3}$ cup ready-to-eat dried apricots

$\frac{2}{3}$ cup canned garbanzo beans, drained

1 teaspoon honey

salt and ground black pepper

couscous, to serve

2 tablespoons olive oil

2 tablespoons chopped almonds, fried in a little oil

chopped fresh parsley

1 Place the eggplant in a colander, sprinkle with salt, and leave for 30 minutes. Place the oil in a microwaveproof casserole, add the onion and garlic, cover, and microwave on HIGH for 2 minute, until soft.

2 Stir in the ground cinnamon and cloves and microwave on HIGH for 30 seconds. Add the lamb and microwave on HIGH for 5 minutes, stirring once.

3 Rinse, drain, and pat the eggplant dry. Add it to the casserole with the tomatoes, boiling water, apricots, and seasoning. Cover and microwave on MEDIUM for 30 minutes, or until the meat is almost tender.

4 Stir in the garbanzo beans and honey. Cover and microwave on HIGH for 3 to 5 minutes until the lamb is tender. Serve the stew accompanied by couscous with the olive oil, fried almonds, and chopped parsley stirred in.

Lamb Pie with a Potato Crust

INGREDIENTS

Serves 4

$4\frac{1}{2}$ cups diced potatoes

3 tablespoons water

2 tablespoons skim milk

1 tablespoon wholegrain or
  French mustard

1 onion, chopped

2 celery stalks, sliced

2 carrots, diced

1 pound lean ground lamb

$\frac{2}{3}$ cup beef or lamb stock

4 tablespoons rolled oats

1 tablespoon Worcestershire sauce

2 tablespoons chopped fresh rosemary

salt and ground black pepper

1 Place the potatoes in a microwaveproof bowl with the water. Cover and microwave on HIGH for 8 to 10 minutes until tender, stirring once. Drain and mash until smooth, then stir in the milk and mustard.

2 Place the onion, celery, and carrots in a large microwave-proof bowl. Cover and microwave on HIGH for 5 minutes, stirring once. Add the ground lamb, stirring well. Microwave on HIGH for 2 minutes, stirring once.

3 Stir in the stock, rolled oats, Worcestershire sauce, rosemary, and seasoning to taste. Cover loosely and microwave on HIGH for 20 to 25 minutes until cooked, stirring twice.

4 Spoon the meat mixture into a 2-quart microwaveproof dish that is suitable for broiling. Swirl the potato evenly over the top. Microwave, uncovered, on HIGH for 4 to 5 minutes until hot. Brown under a broiler, if liked. Serve with freshly cooked vegetables.

COMBINATION MICROWAVE

This recipe is suitable for cooking in a combination microwave. Follow the oven manufacturer's timing guide for the best results.

Rogan Josh

For this popular Indian dish, the lamb is traditionally marinated in yogurt, then cooked with spices and tomatoes to give the dish its rich, red appearance.

INGREDIENTS

Serves 4

2 pounds lamb tenderloin

3 tablespoons lemon juice

1 cup plain yogurt

1 teaspoon salt

2 garlic cloves, crushed

1-inch piece fresh gingerroot, grated

2 tablespoons oil

$\frac{1}{2}$ teaspoon cumin seeds

2 bay leaves

4 green cardamom pods

1 onion, finely chopped

2 teaspoons ground coriander

2 teaspoons ground cumin

1 teaspoon chili powder

14-ounce can crushed tomatoes

2 tablespoons tomato paste

$\frac{2}{3}$ cup water

toasted cumin seeds and bay leaves, to garnish

plain rice, to serve

1 Discard any excess fat from the meat and cut it into 1-inch cubes.

2 In a bowl, combine the lemon juice, yogurt, salt, 1 garlic clove, and the ginger. Add the lamb and leave to marinate overnight.

3 Place the oil in a large microwaveproof bowl and microwave on HIGH for 1 minute. Add the cumin seeds, bay leaves, and cardamom pods and microwave on HIGH for 2 minutes.

4 Add the onion and remaining garlic, cover, and microwave on HIGH for 3 minutes, stirring once. Stir in the ground coriander, cumin and chili powder. Microwave on HIGH for 1 minute, stirring once.

5 Stir in the marinated lamb, cover, and microwave on HIGH for 10 minutes, stirring once.

6 Mix in the tomatoes, tomato paste, and water. Cover and microwave on HIGH for 5 to 8 minutes until hot and bubbling. Reduce the power setting to MEDIUM and microwave for 30 to 40 minutes until tender. Leave to stand, covered, for 10 minutes before serving, garnished with cumin seeds and bay leaves, with plain rice.

Spicy Lamb Curry

One of the simplest Indian dishes to make, this spicy mixture can be used as a filling for stuffed vegetables, such as peppers and large beefsteak tomatoes.

INGREDIENTS

Serves 4

3 tablespoons oil

1 onion, finely chopped

2 garlic cloves, crushed

1-inch piece fresh gingerroot, grated

2 green chilies, finely chopped

$1\frac{1}{2}$ pounds ground lamb

1 teaspoon ground cumin

1 teaspoon ground coriander

1 teaspoon chili powder

1 teaspoon salt

1 cup water

1 cup frozen peas, thawed

2 tablespoons lemon juice

naan bread and plain yogurt, to serve

1 Place the oil, onion, garlic, ginger, and chilies in a large microwaveproof bowl. Cover and microwave on HIGH for 5 minutes, stirring once.

2 Add the ground lamb and stir well to break up the meat. Microwave on HIGH for 5 minutes, stirring once.

3 Stir in the cumin, coriander, chili powder, salt, and water. Cover and microwave on HIGH for 10 minutes, stirring once.

4 Finally, stir in the peas and lemon juice. Microwave on HIGH, uncovered, for 6 to 8 minutes until the meat is tender. Serve with naan bread and plain yogurt.

Curried Lamb and Lentils

This colorful curry is packed with protein and is low in fat, too.

INGREDIENTS

Serves 4

8 lean, boneless lamb leg steaks, about
$1\frac{1}{4}$ pounds total weight

1 onion, chopped

2 carrots, diced

1 celery stalk, chopped

1 tablespoon hot curry paste

2 tablespoons tomato paste

2 cups stock

1 cup green lentils

salt and ground black pepper

fresh cilantro leaves, to garnish

boiled rice, to serve

1 Heat a large browning dish according to the manufacturer's directions. Add the lamb steaks, pressing them down well on the dish, and microwave on HIGH for 7 to 8 minutes, turning over halfway through cooking. Alternatively, cook the lamb steaks on a microwave-proof plate, but they will not brown in the same way.

2 Place the onion, carrots, and celery in a microwaveproof casserole. Cover and microwave on HIGH for 4 minutes, stirring once. Stir in the curry paste, tomato paste, stock and lentils. Cover and microwave on HIGH for 10 to 15 minutes until the lentils are almost cooked.

3 Add the lamb steaks, cover, and microwave on HIGH for 5 to 10 minutes, until tender. Season the lamb to taste, sprinkle with cilantro, and serve with rice.

Golden Pork and Apricot Casserole

The rich golden color and warm spicy flavor of this simple casserole make it ideal for chilly winter days.

INGREDIENTS

Serves 4

4 lean pork loin chops

1 onion, thinly sliced

2 yellow bell peppers, seeded and sliced

2 teaspoons medium-hot curry powder

1 tablespoon all-purpose flour

1 cup chicken stock

$\frac{2}{3}$ cup ready-to-eat dried apricots

2 tablespoons wholegrain mustard

salt and ground black pepper

rice or new potatoes, to serve

1 Heat a large browning dish according to the manufacturer's directions.

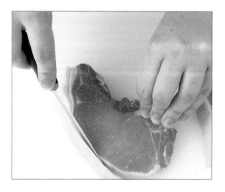

2 Meanwhile, trim the rind and fat off the pork chops. Place them in the browning dish, pressing them down well, and microwave on HIGH for 5 to 6 minutes, turning halfway through cooking. Alternatively, cook the chops on a microwaveproof plate, but they will not brown in the same way.

3 Place the onion and bell peppers in a microwaveproof casserole. Cover and microwave on HIGH for 4 minutes, stirring once. Stir in the curry powder and flour.

4 Pour in the stock, stirring, then add the apricots, mustard, and pork chops. Cover and microwave on HIGH for 8 to 10 minutes, stirring once. Leave to stand, covered, for 10 minutes. Adjust the seasoning and serve hot, with rice or new potatoes.

Hot-and-Sour Pork

Chinese five-spice powder, made from a mixture of ground star anise, Szechuan pepper, cassia, cloves, and fennel seed, has a flavor similar to licorice. If you can't find any, use apple-pie spice instead.

INGREDIENTS

Serves 4

12 ounces pork tenderloin

1 teaspoon sunflower oil

1-inch piece fresh ginger root, grated

1 red chili, seeded and finely chopped

1 teaspoon Chinese five-spice powder

1 tablespoon sherry vinegar

1 tablespoon soy sauce

8-ounce can pineapple chunks in
   natural juice

¾ cup chicken stock

4 teaspoons cornstarch

1 tablespoon water

1 small green bell pepper, seeded and sliced

1 cup baby corn, halved

salt and ground black pepper

sprig of flat-leaf parsley, to garnish

boiled rice, to serve

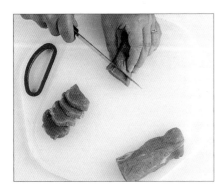

1 Trim away any visible fat from the pork and cut it into ½ inch thick slices.

2 Brush the sunflower oil over the bottom of a microwaveproof casserole. Microwave on HIGH for 3 minutes, stirring once.

3 Blend the ginger, chili, five-spice powder, sherry vinegar and soy sauce. Drain the pineapple, reserving the juice. Make the stock up to 1¼ cups with the juice and mix it with the spices, then pour over the pork.

4 Blend the cornstarch with the water and gradually stir it into the pork. Add the vegetables and season to taste.

5 Cover loosely and microwave on HIGH for 14 to 16 minutes, stirring twice, until the pork and vegetables are almost tender. Stir in the pineapple, cover, and microwave on HIGH for 3 minutes, stirring once, until the pineapple is hot and the pork tender. Garnish with flat-leaf parsley and serve with rice.

Chow Mein

One of the best known of Chinese dishes, this recipe is easy to prepare and a healthy choice for everyday meals.

INGREDIENTS

Serves 4

8 ounces dried egg noodles

2 tablespoons vegetable oil

1 onion, chopped

$\frac{1}{2}$-inch piece fresh gingerroot, chopped

2 garlic cloves, crushed

2 tablespoons soy sauce

$\frac{1}{4}$ cup dry white wine

2 teaspoons Chinese five-spice powder

1 pound ground pork

4 scallions, sliced

2 ounces oyster mushrooms

3 ounces canned bamboo shoots, sliced
   if necessary

1 tablespoon sesame oil

shrimp crackers, to serve

1 Place the noodles in a microwaveproof bowl, cover with boiling water, and microwave on HIGH for 4 minutes, stirring once; drain thoroughly.

2 Place the oil in a large microwaveproof bowl and add the onion, ginger, garlic, soy sauce, and wine. Cover and microwave on HIGH for 2 to 3 minutes, stirring once. Stir in the Chinese five-spice powder.

3 Add the ground pork, cover, and microwave on HIGH for 6 minutes, stirring three times to break up the meat during cooking. Stir in the scallions, mushrooms, and bamboo shoots. Cover and microwave on HIGH for 3 minutes, stirring once.

4 Stir in the noodles and sesame oil. Stir all the ingredients together well and serve with shrimp crackers.

COOK'S TIP

Lean ground lamb also makes delicious chow mein. Canned bamboo shoots can be replaced by canned water chestnuts for a crunchy texture.

Pork Crumble

Ground pork combines well with the sweetness of apple and the texture of crunchy vegetables. Served with the satisfying oat topping, this is a meal to tempt all the family.

INGREDIENTS

Serves 4

1 tablespoon oil
1 onion, sliced
1 pound ground pork
2 tablespoons all-purpose flour
$2/3$ cup hot milk
$2/3$ cup hot vegetable stock
$1/2$ cup broccoli flowerets
$1/2$ cup canned corn kernels, drained
1 green eating apple, cored and diced
salt and ground black pepper

For the topping
$1/2$ cup instant oatmeal
$1/2$ cup all-purpose flour
1 tablespoon butter
$1/4$ cup grated Red Leicester or cheddar cheese

1 Place the oil in a large microwaveproof bowl with the onion. Cover and microwave on HIGH for 2 minutes. Stir in the pork, cover, and microwave on HIGH for 4 to 6 minutes, stirring twice to break up the meat.

2 Stir in the flour, then stir in the milk and stock. Cover and microwave on HIGH for 3 minutes, stirring twice.

3 Mix the broccoli, corn, and apple into the pork mixture; season.

4 Spoon the mixture into four individual microwaveproof dishes that are suitable for broiling.

5 To make the crumble topping, mix the oatmeal and flour, then cut in the butter.

6 Spoon the topping onto the pork mixture and press down with the back of a spoon. Scatter the cheese over the top and microwave on HIGH for 6 to 8 minutes, repositioning the dishes halfway through cooking. Brown under a heated hot broiler, if liked.

VARIATION

For a rich cheesy topping, mix together crushed potato chips and grated cheese. Cook as above.

COOK'S TIP

Vary the choice of vegetables according to personal preference. For example, use finely shredded white cabbage instead of the broccoli and/or frozen peas instead of the corn.

Chicken Roll

The roll can be prepared and cooked the day before and it will also freeze well. Remove from the refrigerator about an hour before serving.

INGREDIENTS

Serves 8

4 pound chicken

For the stuffing

1 onion, finely chopped

4 tablespoons butter, melted

12 ounces lean ground pork

4 ounces bacon, chopped

1 tablespoon chopped fresh parsley

2 teaspoons chopped fresh thyme

2 cups fresh white bread crumbs

2 tablespoons sherry

1 large egg, beaten

$\frac{1}{4}$ cup shelled pistachio nuts

$\frac{1}{4}$ cup ripe olives,
   about 12, pitted

salt and ground black pepper

1 To make the stuffing, place the onion and 2 tablespoons of the butter in a microwaveproof bowl. Cover and microwave on HIGH for 2 minutes until soft.

2 Turn into a bowl and cool slightly before adding the remaining ingredients. Stir thoroughly and season with salt and ground black pepper.

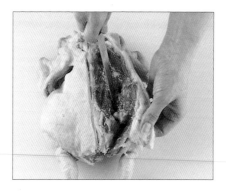

3 To bone the chicken, use a small, sharp knife to remove the wingtips. Turn the chicken on to its breast and cut a line down the backbone.

4 Cut the flesh away from the carcass, scraping the bones clean. Carefully cut through the sinews around the leg and wing joints and scrape down the bones to free them. Remove the carcass, taking care not to cut through the skin along the breastbone.

5 To stuff the chicken, lay it flat, skin side down and smooth the flesh out as much as possible. Shape the stuffing down the center of the chicken and fold the sides over the stuffing.

6 Sew the flesh neatly together, using a needle and dark thread. Tie with fine string into a roll. Weigh the stuffed chicken roll. Brush with the remaining butter.

7 Place the roll, with the seam underneath, in a roasting bag. Secure with string or an elastic band, making sure there is room for steam to escape. Place in a shallow microwaveproof dish. Microwave on MEDIUM for 9 minutes per 1 pound, turning over twice during cooking.

8 Remove the chicken from the bag and brown it under a heated hot broiler, if liked. Leave to cool completely before removing the string and thread. Wrap in foil and chill until ready for serving or freezing.

COMBINATION MICROWAVE

This recipe is suitable for cooking in a combination microwave. Follow the oven manufacturer's timing guide for the best results.

COOK'S TIP

Use dark thread for sewing, because it is easier to see than white so you can remove it after the roll is cooked.

Spiced Chicken with Spinach

A mildly spiced dish using a popular combination of spinach and chicken. This recipe is best made using fresh spinach, but if this is unavailable use frozen instead.

INGREDIENTS

Serves 4

8 ounces fresh spinach leaves, washed but not dried

1-inch piece fresh ginger root, grated

2 garlic cloves, crushed

1 green chili, roughly chopped

scant 1 cup water

2 tablespoons oil

2 bay leaves

$\frac{1}{4}$ teaspoon black peppercorns

1 onion, finely chopped

4 tomatoes, skinned and finely chopped

2 teaspoons curry powder

1 teaspoon salt

1 teaspoon chili powder

3 tablespoons plain yogurt

8 chicken thighs, skinned

plain yogurt and chili powder, to garnish

store-bought masala naan, to serve

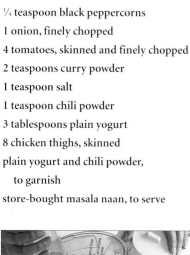

1 Place the spinach, without water, in a microwaveproof bowl. Cover and microwave on HIGH for 4 minutes, stirring once. Puree the spinach, ginger, garlic and chilli with $\frac{1}{4}$ cup of the water in a food processor or blender.

2 Place the oil in a large microwaveproof dish. Add the bay leaves, black peppercorns, and onion. Cover and microwave on HIGH for 4 minutes, stirring once.

3 Stir in the tomatoes, curry powder, salt, and chili powder. Cover and microwave on HIGH for 3 minutes, stirring once.

4 Stir in the puree and remaining water. Cover and microwave on HIGH for 2 minutes.

5 Stir in half the yogurt and add the chicken, arranging the pieces in the sauce. Cover and microwave on HIGH for 10 minutes, stirring once.

6 Add the remaining yogurt. Cover and microwave on HIGH for 7 to 8 minutes longer until the chicken is tender. Serve on masala naan, drizzle plain yogurt over and dust with chili powder.

Hot Chili Chicken

Not for the faint-hearted, this fiery, hot curry is made with a spicy chili masala paste.

INGREDIENTS

Serves 4

2 tablespoons tomato paste

2 garlic cloves, roughly chopped

2 green chilies, roughly chopped

5 dried red chilies

$\frac{1}{2}$ teaspoon salt

$\frac{1}{4}$ teaspoon sugar

1 teaspoon chili powder

$\frac{1}{2}$ teaspoon paprika

1 tablespoon curry paste

2 tablespoons oil

$\frac{1}{2}$ teaspoon cumin seeds

1 onion, finely chopped

2 bay leaves

1 teaspoon ground coriander

1 teaspoon ground cumin

$\frac{1}{4}$ teaspoon ground turmeric

14-ounce can crushed tomatoes

$\frac{2}{3}$ cup water

8 chicken thighs, skinned

1 teaspoon garam masala

sliced green chilies, to garnish

chappatis and plain yogurt, to serve

1 Process the tomato paste, garlic, green and dried red chilies, salt, sugar, chili powder, paprika, and curry paste to a smooth paste in a food processor or blender.

2 Place the oil in a large microwaveproof bowl and add the cumin seeds. Microwave on HIGH for $1\frac{1}{2}$ minutes. Add the onion and bay leaves, cover, and microwave on HIGH for 3 minutes.

3 Stir in the chili paste. Cover and microwave on HIGH for $1\frac{1}{2}$ minutes, then stir in the remaining ground spices, crushed tomatoes, and water. Cover and microwave on HIGH for 3 minutes.

4 Add the chicken and garam masala. Cover and microwave on HIGH for 18 to 22 minutes, stirring twice, until the chicken is tender. Garnish with sliced green chilies and serve with chappatis and plain yogurt.

Dijon Chicken Salad

An attractive and elegant dish to serve for lunch with herb and garlic bread.

INGREDIENTS

Serves 4

4 boned and skinned chicken
   breast halves
mixed salad leaves, to serve

For the marinade
2 tablespoons Dijon mustard
3 garlic cloves, crushed
1 tablespoon grated onion
4 tablespoons white wine

For the mustard dressing
2 tablespoons tarragon wine vinegar
1 teaspoon Dijon mustard
1 teaspoon honey
6 tablespoons olive oil
salt and ground black pepper

1 Stir all the marinade ingredients together in a shallow glass or earthenware dish that is large enough to hold the chicken in a single layer.

2 Turn the chicken over in the marinade to coat it completely and cover with plastic wrap; chill overnight.

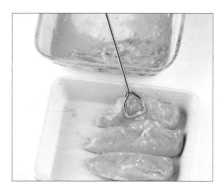

3 Transfer the chicken and the marinade to a microwave-proof dish. Cover and microwave on HIGH for 4 to 5 minutes, turning over and rearranging twice during cooking.

4 Put all the mustard dressing ingredients into a screw-top jar and shake it vigorously to emulsify the mixture. Adjust the seasoning. This dressing can be stored in the refrigerator for several days.

5 Cut the cooked chicken meat into thin, even slices.

6 Fan out the chicken slices and arrange them on a serving dish with the salad leaves. Spoon some of the mustard dressing over and serve.

COMBINATION MICROWAVE

This recipe is suitable for cooking in a combination microwave. Follow the oven manufacturer's timing guide for the best results.

COOK'S TIP

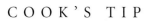

Dijon mustard is smooth and fairly mild. A hot variety is not suitable for this dish.

Chicken and Fruit Salad

The chicken may be cooked a day before serving and the salad assembled at the last minute. Serve with warm garlic bread.

INGREDIENTS

Serves 8

4 tarragon or rosemary sprigs

2 x 3- to $3\frac{1}{2}$-pound chickens

5 tablespoons butter, soft

$\frac{2}{3}$ cup chicken stock

$\frac{2}{3}$ cup white wine

1 small cantaloupe melon

1 cup walnut pieces

lettuce leaves

1 pound seedless grapes or cherries, pitted

salt and ground black pepper

For the dressing

2 tablespoons tarragon vinegar

$\frac{1}{2}$ cup olive oil

2 tablespoons chopped mixed fresh herbs, such as parsley, mint, and tarragon

1 Put the sprigs of tarragon or rosemary inside the chickens and season with salt and pepper. Tie the chickens in a neat shape with string and spread with 4 tablespoons of the butter. Place breast-side down in a microwave-proof shallow dish and pour in the stock. Cover loosely and microwave on HIGH for 30 to 35 minutes, turning breast-side up halfway through cooking. Cover with foil and leave to stand for 10 to 15 minutes. Prick to release excess juices and leave to cool.

2 Add the wine to the cooking juices. Transfer to a microwaveproof pitcher or bowl and microwave on HIGH for about 5 minutes, or until syrupy. Strain and leave the juices to cool. Scoop the melon into balls or cut into cubes. Joint the chickens.

3 Place the remaining butter in a microwaveproof bowl with the walnuts. Microwave on HIGH for 2 to 3 minutes to brown, stirring once; drain and cool.

4 To make the dressing, whisk the vinegar and oil together with some seasoning. Remove the fat from the chicken juices and add the juices to the dressing with the herbs. Adjust the seasoning.

5 Arrange the chicken pieces on a bed of lettuce, scatter the grapes or pitted cherries over, melon balls or cubes, and coat with the herb dressing. Sprinkle with toasted walnuts and serve.

COMBINATION MICROWAVE

This recipe is suitable for cooking in a combination microwave. Follow the oven manufacturer's timing guide for the best results.

COOK'S TIP

The chickens can be cooked in roasting bags, but do not use metal ties for securing the bags; replace them with elastic bands or string.

Chicken Liver Salad

This salad may be served as a first course on individual plates.

INGREDIENTS

Serves 4

mixed salad leaves

1 avocado, diced

2 pink grapefruits, segmented

12 ounces chicken livers

2 tablespoons olive oil

1 garlic clove, crushed

salt and ground black pepper

crusty bread, to serve

For the dressing

2 tablespoons lemon juice

4 tablespoons olive oil

$1/2$ teaspoon wholegrain mustard

$1/2$ teaspoon honey

1 tablespoon snipped fresh chives

1 First prepare the dressing. Put all the ingredients into a screw-top jar and shake vigorously to emulsify the mixture. Taste and adjust the seasoning.

2 Wash and dry the salad. Arrange attractively on a serving plate with the avocado and grapefruit.

3 Dry the chicken livers on paper towels and remove any sinew or membrane. Cut the larger livers in half and leave the smaller ones whole. Prick thoroughly with a fork.

4 Place the oil in a large microwaveproof bowl. Add the livers and garlic, mixing well. Cover loosely and microwave on HIGH for 3 to 4 minutes, stirring twice until cooked, but still slightly pink inside.

5 Season with salt and ground black pepper and drain on paper towels.

6 Place the liver on the salad and spoon the dressing over the top. Serve immediately, with warm crusty bread.

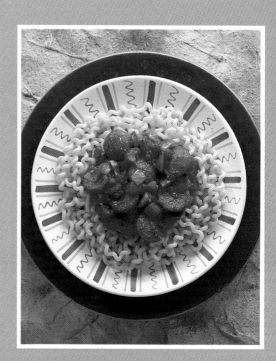

LEGUMES, PASTA, AND GRAINS

Lemon and Ginger Spicy Beans

A quick meal, made with canned beans. You won't need extra salt because most canned beans are salted.

INGREDIENTS

Serves 4

2-inch piece fresh gingerroot, peeled and roughly chopped

3 garlic cloves, roughly chopped

1 cup cold water

1 tablespoon sunflower oil

1 large onion, thinly sliced

1 fresh red chili, seeded and finely chopped

$\frac{1}{4}$ teaspoon cayenne pepper

2 teaspoons ground cumin

1 teaspoon ground coriander

$\frac{1}{2}$ teaspoon ground turmeric

2 tablespoons lemon juice

$\frac{1}{3}$ cup chopped fresh cilantro leaves

14-ounce can black-eye peas, drained and rinsed

14-ounce can aduzki beans, drained and rinsed

14-can can haricot beans, drained and rinsed

ground black pepper

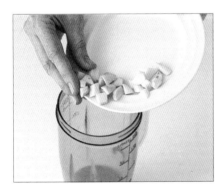

1 Place the ginger, garlic, and 4 tablespoons of the cold water in a blender or food processor and process until smooth.

2 Place the oil in a large microwaveproof bowl with the onion and chili. Microwave on HIGH for 3 minutes, stirring halfway through cooking.

3 Add the cayenne pepper, cumin, ground coriander, and turmeric. Microwave on HIGH for 1 minute.

4 Stir in the ginger and garlic paste and microwave on HIGH for 1 minute longer.

5 Stir in the remaining water, lemon juice, and fresh cilantro. Cover and microwave on HIGH for 4 minutes.

6 Add all the beans to the mixture in the bowl and stir well. Cover and microwave on HIGH for 4 to 6 minutes, stirring halfway through cooking. Season with pepper and serve.

Borlotti Beans with Mushrooms

A mixture of wild and cultivated mushrooms helps to give this dish a rich and nutty flavor.

INGREDIENTS

Serves 4

2 tablespoons olive oil

4 tablespoons butter

2 shallots, chopped

2 or 3 garlic cloves, crushed

$1\frac{1}{2}$ pounds mixed mushrooms, thickly sliced

4 sun-dried tomatoes in oil, drained and chopped

3 tablespoons dry white wine

14-ounce can borlotti beans

3 tablespoons grated Parmesan cheese

2 tablespoons chopped fresh parsley

salt and ground black pepper

freshly cooked pappardelle pasta, to serve

1 Place the oil and butter in a microwaveproof bowl with the shallots. Microwave on HIGH for 1 minute.

2 Add the garlic and mushrooms and microwave on HIGH for 3 to 4 minutes, stirring halfway through cooking. Stir in the sun-dried tomatoes, wine, and seasoning to taste.

3 Stir in the borlotti beans and microwave on HIGH for 2 to 3 minutes until the beans are heated through.

4 Stir in the grated Parmesan and sprinkle with parsley. Serve immediately with hot pappardelle pasta.

COOK'S TIP

When buying wild mushrooms, examine them carefully and reject any mushrooms that have tiny holes or show signs of being eaten because they may contain tiny maggots.

Mung Beans with Potatoes

Mung beans are one of the quicker-cooking legumes that do not require soaking and are therefore very easy to use. In this recipe, they are cooked with potatoes and traditional Indian spices to make a tasty, nutritious dish.

INGREDIENTS

Serves 4

1 cup mung beans

3 cups boiling water

$1\frac{1}{2}$ cups potatoes cut into
    $\frac{3}{4}$-inch chunks

2 tablespoons oil

$\frac{1}{2}$ teaspoon cumin seeds

1 green chili, seeded and finely chopped

1 garlic clove, crushed

1-inch piece fresh gingerroot,
    finely chopped

$\frac{1}{4}$ teaspoon ground turmeric

$\frac{1}{2}$ teaspoon chili powder

1 teaspoon salt

1 teaspoon sugar

4 curry leaves

5 tomatoes, peeled and finely chopped

1 tablespoon tomato paste

plain rice, to serve

curry leaves, to garnish

1 Wash the beans and place them in a large microwave-proof bowl with the boiling water and potatoes. Cover and microwave on HIGH for 4 minutes, stirring once. Reduce the power setting to MEDIUM and microwave for 12 to 15 minutes longer until the beans are almost tender. Set aside to stand, covered, for 10 minutes.

2 Meanwhile, place the oil and cumin seeds in another large microwaveproof bowl and microwave on HIGH for $1\frac{1}{2}$ minutes. Add the chili, garlic and ginger. Microwave on HIGH for 2 minutes, stirring once.

3 Add the turmeric, chili powder, salt, and sugar. Microwave on HIGH for 1 minute, stirring once.

4 Stir in the curry leaves, tomatoes, and tomato paste. Cover and microwave on HIGH for 3 to 4 minutes, stirring once, until the sauce thickens slightly. Drain the beans and potatoes, then mix them into the tomato sauce. Serve with plain boiled rice and garnish with curry leaves.

Garbanzo Bean Curry

Garbanzo are used and cooked in a variety of ways all over India.

Serves 4

$1\frac{1}{4}$ cups dried garbanzo beans

2 ounces tamarind pulp

$\frac{1}{2}$ cup boiling water, plus extra for cooking garbanzo beans

3 tablespoons oil

$\frac{1}{2}$ teaspoon cumin seeds

1 onion, finely chopped

2 garlic cloves, crushed

1-inch piece fresh gingerroot, grated

1 green chili, seeded and finely chopped

1 teaspoon ground cumin

1 teaspoon ground coriander

$\frac{1}{4}$ teaspoon ground turmeric

$\frac{1}{2}$ teaspoon salt

$1\frac{1}{2}$ cups peeled and finely chopped tomatoes

$\frac{1}{2}$ teaspoon garam masala

chopped chilies and onion, to garnish

1 Put the garbanzo beans in a large bowl and cover with plenty of cold water. Leave to soak overnight.

2 Drain the garbanzos. Place in a large microwaveproof bowl and pour in boiling water to cover them. Cover and microwave on HIGH for 10 minutes. Reduce the power setting to MEDIUM and microwave for 20 to 25 minutes longer, stirring twice and adding extra boiling water to cover the beans, if necessary; drain thoroughly.

3 Meanwhile, break up the tamarind and soak it in the measured boiling water for about 15 minutes. Rub the resulting tamarind pulp through a strainer into a bowl, discarding any stones and fiber. The tamarind gives the dish a delicious, sharp flavor.

4 Place the oil in a large microwaveproof bowl with the cumin seeds and microwave on HIGH for $1\frac{1}{2}$ minutes. Add the onion, garlic, ginger, and chili, cover, and microwave on HIGH for 3 minutes, stirring once.

5 Add the cumin, coriander, turmeric, and salt and microwave on HIGH for 1 minute. Stir in the tomatoes and tamarind pulp. Cover and microwave on HIGH for 3 minutes, stirring once.

6 Stir in the beans and garam masala. Cover, microwave on HIGH for 6 to 8 minutes, stir once. Garnish with chilies and onion.

Cannelloni al Forno

Filled with chicken, this is a lighter alternative to the usual beef-filled, béchamel-coated version. For a vegetarian recipe, fill with ricotta cheese, onion, and mushroom, then top with tomato sauce.

INGREDIENTS

Serves 4 to 6

1 pound skinned and boned chicken
   breast meat, cooked

3 cups mushrooms

2 garlic cloves, crushed

2 tablespoons chopped fresh parsley

1 tablespoon chopped fresh tarragon

1 egg, beaten

fresh lemon juice

12 to 18 cannelloni tubes

1¼ cups tomato sauce

½ cup freshly grated Parmesan
   cheese

salt and ground black pepper

fresh parsley sprig, to garnish

1 Process the chicken in a blender or food processor until finely ground. Transfer to a bowl.

2 Process the mushrooms, garlic, parsley, and tarragon until finely ground.

3 Beat the mushroom mixture into the chicken with the egg, salt and pepper, adding lemon juice to taste.

4 Place the cannelloni in a microwaveproof dish and cover with boiling water. Cover and microwave on HIGH for 1 minute. Drain well and dry on a clean dishcloth.

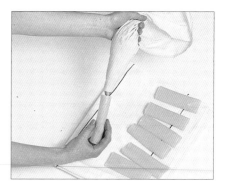

5 Place the filling in a pastry bag fitted with a large plain tip. Use this to fill each of the tubes of cannelloni.

6 Lay the filled cannelloni tightly together in a single layer in a buttered, shallow microwaveproof dish that is suitable for broiling. Spoon the tomato sauce over and sprinkle with Parmesan cheese. Microwave on HIGH for 5 to 8 minutes. Reduce the power setting to MEDIUM and microwave for 5 minutes longer. Brown under a heated hot broiler, if liked. Garnish with a sprig of fresh parsley

COMBINATION MICROWAVE

This recipe is suitable for cooking in a combination microwave. Follow the oven manufacturer's timing guide for the best results.

Ravioli with Four Cheese Sauce

This is a smooth cheese sauce that coats the pasta very evenly.

INGREDIENTS

Serves 4

12 ounces ravioli

2 quarts boiling water

$\frac{1}{4}$ cup butter

$\frac{1}{3}$ cup all-purpose flour

2 cups milk

2 ounces Parmesan cheese

2 ounces Edam cheese

2 ounces Gruyère cheese

2 ounces fontina cheese

salt and ground black pepper

chopped fresh parsley, to garnish

1 Place the ravioli in a large microwaveproof bowl and pour in the boiling water. Microwave on HIGH for 10 minutes, stirring halfway through cooking. Leave to stand for 3 minutes.

2 Whisk the butter, flour, and milk together in a microwave-proof pitcher. Microwave on HIGH for 5 to 7 minutes, whisking every minute, until smooth, boiling, and thick.

3 Grate the cheeses and stir them into the sauce until they are just beginning to melt. Add seasoning to taste.

4 Drain the pasta thoroughly and turn it into a large serving bowl. Pour the sauce over and toss to coat. Serve immediately, garnished with chopped parsley.

COOK'S TIP

If you cannot find all of the recommended cheeses, simply substitute your favorite types. Strong-flavored hard cheeses are best for this type of sauce.

Turkey Lasagne

This delicious low-fat version of a classic lasagne is very easy to cook in the microwave.

INGREDIENTS

Serves 6 to 8

1 large onion, chopped

2 garlic cloves, crushed

$1\frac{1}{4}$ pounds ground turkey meat

2 cups smooth, thick, strained tomatoes

1 teaspoon Italian seasoning

7 ounces dried lasagne verdi

$3\frac{3}{4}$ cups boiling water

8 ounces frozen leaf spinach, thawed

7 ounces low-fat cottage cheese

For the sauce

2 tablespoons low-fat margarine spread

2 tablespoons all-purpose flour

$1\frac{1}{4}$ cups skim milk

$\frac{1}{4}$ teaspoon ground nutmeg

$\frac{1}{4}$ cup grated Parmesan cheese

salt and ground black pepper

mixed salad, to serve

1 Mix the onion, garlic, and ground turkey in a microwaveproof bowl. Cover and microwave on HIGH for 4 minutes, stirring twice to separate the pieces.

2 Add the strained tomatoes, Italian seasoning, and salt and pepper to taste. Cover and microwave on HIGH for 8 minutes, stirring once.

3 Whisk all the sauce ingredients, except the Parmesan cheese, together in a microwaveproof pitcher. Microwave on HIGH for 4 to 6 minutes, whisking every minute, until smooth, boiling, and thick. Adjust the seasoning and stir in the cheese.

4 Place the lasagne in a deep, rectangular microwaveproof dish. Add the boiling water. Cover and microwave on HIGH for 9 minutes. Leave to stand for 15 minutes; drain well and rinse under cold water. Lay the spinach leaves on paper towels and pat dry.

5 Layer the turkey mixture, prepared lasagne, cottage cheese, and spinach in a 2-quart microwaveproof dish which is suitable for broiling, starting and ending with a layer of turkey.

6 Spoon the sauce over the top to coat the turkey and microwave on HIGH for 2 to 3 minutes until heated through. Brown under a heated hot broiler, if liked. Serve with a mixed salad.

COMBINATION MICROWAVE

This recipe is suitable for cooking in a combination microwave. Follow the oven manufacturer's timing guide for the best results.

Pasta Shells with Smoked Haddock

INGREDIENTS

Serves 4

1 pound smoked haddock fillet

1 small leek or onion, thickly sliced

$1\frac{1}{4}$ cups hot skim milk

1 bouquet garni (bay leaf, thyme, and parsley stems)

2 tablespoons low-fat margarine spread

2 tablespoons all-purpose flour

2 tablespoons chopped fresh parsley

8 ounces dried pasta shells

salt and ground black pepper

1 tablespoon slivered almonds, toasted, to serve

1 While preparing the sauce in the microwave, cook the pasta conventionally in a large saucepan of boiling salted water on the stovetop according to the package directions.

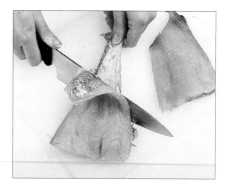

2 Remove all the skin and any bones from the haddock. Arrange the fish fillets in a large microwaveproof dish with the thicker portions to the outside of the dish. Sprinkle with the leek or onion. Add half the milk and the bouquet garni. Cover and microwave on HIGH for 5 to 6 minutes, rearranging once. Leave to stand for 3 minutes.

3 Strain, reserving the milk for making the sauce; discard the bouquet garni.

4 Whisk the margarine, flour, and remaining milk together in a microwave pitcher. Microwave on HIGH for 4 to 6 minutes, whisking every minute, until smooth, boiling, and thick. Season and add the fish and leek or onion.

5 Drain the pasta thoroughly and stir it into the sauce with the chopped parsley. Serve immediately, scattered with toasted slivered almonds.

Pasta Bows with Smoked Salmon and Dill

In Italy, pasta cooked with smoked salmon has become very fashionable. This is a quick and very luxurious sauce.

INGREDIENTS

Serves 4

4 tablespoons butter

6 scallions, sliced

6 tablespoons dry white wine or vermouth

2 cups heavy cream

freshly grated nutmeg

8 ounces smoked salmon

2 tablespoons chopped fresh dill, or
   1 tablespoon dried dill

freshly squeezed lemon juice

4 cups dried pasta bows (farfalle)

salt and ground black pepper

1 While preparing the sauce in the microwave, cook the pasta conventionally in a large saucepan of boiling salted water on the stovetop according to the package directions.

2 Place the butter and scallions in a microwaveproof bowl. Cover and microwave on HIGH for 1 minute.

3 Add the wine and microwave on HIGH for 2 to 3 minutes to reduce the liquid to about 2 tablespoons. Stir in the cream and add salt, pepper, and nutmeg to taste. Microwave on HIGH for 1 to 2 minutes, stirring twice, until slightly thick.

4 Cut the smoked salmon into 1-inch pieces and stir into the sauce with the dill. Taste and add a little lemon juice.

5 Drain the pasta well. Toss the pasta with the sauce and serve immediately.

Pasta with Tuna, Capers, and Anchovies

This piquant sauce can be made without the tomatoes—just heat the oil, add the other ingredients, and microwave on HIGH for 2 to 3 minutes, stirring once, before tossing with the pasta.

INGREDIENTS

Serves 4

2 x 7-ounce cans tuna fish in oil

2 tablespoons olive oil

2 garlic cloves, crushed

20 ounces canned crushed tomatoes

6 canned anchovy fillets, drained

2 tablespoons capers in vinegar, drained

2 tablespoons chopped fresh basil

1 pound rigatoni, penne, or garganelle

salt and ground black pepper

fresh basil sprigs, to garnish

1 While preparing the sauce in the microwave, cook the pasta conventionally in a large saucepan of boiling salted water on the stovetop according to the package directions.

2 Drain the oil from the tuna into a microwaveproof bowl. Add the olive oil and microwave on HIGH for 1 minute.

3 Add the garlic and microwave on HIGH for 30 seconds. Stir in the tomatoes, cover, and microwave on HIGH for 4 to 6 minutes, stirring twice, until thick.

4 Flake the tuna and cut the anchovies in half. Stir into the sauce with the capers and chopped basil. Season well.

5 Drain the pasta well and toss it with the sauce. Garnish with fresh basil sprigs and serve at once.

COOK'S TIP

For a slightly lighter version of this recipe, use tuna canned in brine and drain off the brine. Use 1 tablespoon olive oil and heat it with the garlic for 30 seconds; continue as in the main recipe.

Spaghetti with Tomato and Clam Sauce

Small, sweet clams make this a delicately succulent sauce. Mussels would make a good substitute. Don't, however, be tempted to use seafood pickled in vinegar—the result will be inedible!

INGREDIENTS

Serves 4

2 pounds small clams, or 2 x 14-ounce
  cans clams in brine, drained
6 tablespoons olive oil
2 garlic cloves, crushed
21 ounces canned crushed tomatoes
3 tablespoons chopped fresh parsley
1 pound spaghetti
salt and ground black pepper

1 While preparing the sauce in the microwave, cook the pasta conventionally in a large saucepan of boiling salted water on the stovetop according to the package directions.

2 If using fresh (live) clams, rinse them in several changes of cold water to remove any grit or sand; drain.

3 Heat the oil in a large microwaveproof bowl. Add the clams, cover loosely, and microwave on HIGH for 4 to 5 minutes, stirring once, until the clams open. Throw away any that do not open. Transfer the clams to a bowl with a perforated spoon.

4 Microwave the clam juice on HIGH for 2 to 3 minutes to reduce it to about 1 tablespoon. Add the garlic and microwave on HIGH for 30 seconds. Stir in the tomatoes and microwave on HIGH for 3 to 4 minutes.

5 Stir in the cooked or canned clams with half the parsley and microwave on HIGH for 2 minutes until hot. Season to taste with salt and pepper.

6 Drain the pasta well and turn it into a warm serving dish. Pour the sauce over and sprinkle with the remaining parsley. Serve at once.

Rigatoni with Spicy Sausage and Tomato

This is really a cheat's spaghetti sauce using the wonderful fresh spicy sausages sold in every Italian delicatessen.

INGREDIENTS

Serves 4

1 pound fresh spicy Italian sausage

2 tablespoons olive oil

1 onion, chopped

2 cups smooth, thick, strained tomatoes

$2/3$ cup dry red wine

6 sun-dried tomatoes in oil, drained

1 pound rigatoni or similar pasta

salt and ground black pepper

freshly grated Parmesan cheese, to serve

1 Squeeze the sausage meat out of the skins into a bowl and break it up.

2 While preparing the sauce, cook the pasta conventionally in a saucepan of boiling salted water on the stovetop according to the package directions.

3 Place the oil in a microwave-proof bowl and add the onion. Microwave on HIGH for 3 minutes. Stir in the sausage meat and microwave on HIGH for 5 minutes, stirring every minute to break up the meat. Stir in the tomatoes and wine. Cover and microwave on HIGH for 4 minutes, stirring once.

4 Slice the sun-dried tomatoes and add them to the sauce. Microwave, uncovered, for 2 minutes, stirring once, then season to taste.

5 Drain the pasta well and top with the sauce. Serve with grated Parmesan cheese.

COOK'S TIP

If you cannot find fresh Italian sausage, season pork sausage meat with a crushed garlic clove, a little dried oregano, grated nutmeg, and a pinch of paprika; stir well.

Pasta with Tomato and Smoky Bacon Sauce

This is a wonderful sauce to prepare in midsummer when the tomatoes are ripe and sweet.

INGREDIENTS

Serves 4

2 pounds ripe tomatoes

1 pound pasta, any variety

6 slices smoked bacon

4 tablespoons butter

1 onion, chopped

1 tablespoon chopped fresh oregano, or
    1 teaspoon dried oregano

salt and ground black pepper

freshly grated Parmesan cheese, to serve

1 Plunge the tomatoes into boiling water for 1 minute, then into cold water to stop them from becoming mushy. Slip off the skins. Halve the tomatoes, remove the seeds and cores, and roughly chop the flesh.

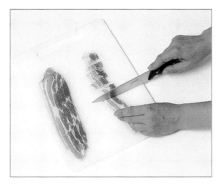

2 Cook the pasta in a saucepan of boiling water according to the package directions. Remove and discard the rind from the bacon, if necessary, and chop the slices.

3 Place the butter in a microwaveproof bowl and add the bacon. Microwave on HIGH for 5 minutes, stirring once, then add the onion.

4 Microwave on HIGH for 1½ minutes longer. Add the tomatoes, seasoning, and oregano. Cover and microwave on HIGH for 5 to 6 minutes, stirring twice.

5 Drain the pasta well and toss it with the sauce. Serve with grated Parmesan cheese.

Pasta Carbonara

Cooking the pasta conventionally on the stovetop and the sauce in the microwave makes this a very speedy dish to prepare.

INGREDIENTS

Serves 4

12 ounces to 1 pound fresh tagliatelle
1 tablespoon olive oil
$1\frac{1}{2}$ cups ham, thick bacon or pancetta cut into 1-inch sticks
$1\frac{1}{2}$ cups sliced button mushrooms
4 eggs, lightly beaten
5 tablespoons light cream
2 tablespoons finely grated Parmesan cheese
salt and ground black pepper
fresh basil sprigs, to garnish

1 While preparing the sauce in the microwave, cook the pasta conventionally in a large saucepan of boiling salted water on the stovetop according to the package directions.

2 Meanwhile, place the oil and ham in a microwaveproof bowl. Microwave on HIGH for 3 minutes, then add the mushrooms. Microwave on HIGH for 3 minutes longer, stirring once during cooking. Meanwhile, lightly beat the eggs and cream together and season well.

3 Drain the cooked pasta well and add to the ham and mushroom mixture, stirring well.

4 Pour in the eggs and cream and add half the Parmesan cheese. Stir well and, as you do this, the eggs will cook in the heat of the pasta. If you like your sauce slightly thicker, microwave on HIGH for 30 seconds, stirring once during cooking. Pile onto warm serving plates. Sprinkle with the remaining Parmesan and garnish with basil.

Baked Macaroni and Cheese

A delicious suppertime dish—replace the cheddar with your family's favorite cheese.

INGREDIENTS

Serves 4

$2\frac{1}{3}$ cups macaroni
5 cups boiling water
1 tablespoon olive oil
2 leeks, chopped
4 tablespoons butter
$\frac{1}{3}$ cup all-purpose flour
$3\frac{3}{4}$ cups milk
2 cups grated strong cheddar cheese
2 tablespoons fromage blanc
1 teaspoon wholegrain mustard
1 cup fresh white bread crumbs
$\frac{1}{4}$ cup grated Double Gloucester cheese, or other semihard cheese
salt and ground black pepper
1 tablespoon chopped fresh parsley, to garnish

1 Place the macaroni in a large microwaveproof bowl with the boiling water and the olive oil. Add the leeks and microwave on HIGH for 10 minutes, stirring once. Leave to stand, covered, while cooking the sauce.

2 Stir the butter with the flour and milk in a large microwaveproof pitcher. Microwave on HIGH for 6 to 8 minutes, whisking every minute, until smooth, boiling, and thickened.

3 Whisk in the cheddar cheese, fromage blanc, and mustard, adding salt and pepper to taste.

4 Drain the macaroni and leeks and rinse under cold water. Stir the drained macaroni and leeks into the cheese sauce and pour into a dish that is suitable for broiling. Level the top with the back of a spoon and sprinkle the bread crumbs and Double Gloucester cheese over.

5 Cook under a heated hot broiler until golden and bubbly. Serve hot, garnished with chopped fresh parsley.

Tagliatelle with Tomatoes and Zucchini

INGREDIENTS

Serves 3 to 4

5 or 6 ripe tomatoes

8 ounces wholewheat tagliatelle

5 cups boiling water

2 tablespoons olive oil

1 onion, chopped

2 celery stalks, chopped

1 garlic clove, crushed

2 zucchini, sliced

2 tablespoons sun-dried tomato paste

$\frac{1}{2}$ cup slivered almonds, toasted,
   to serve

salt and ground black pepper

1 Place the tomatoes in a bowl and pour in boiling water to cover. Leave to stand for 30 seconds to loosen their skins; drain. Peel and chop.

2 Place the tagliatelle in a large microwaveproof bowl with the boiling water. Microwave on HIGH for 6 minutes, stirring once. Leave to stand, covered, while cooking the sauce.

3 Place the oil in another microwaveproof bowl and add the onion, celery, garlic, and zucchini. Cover and microwave on HIGH for 3 to 4 minutes, or until the onions are soft.

4 Stir in the tomatoes and sun-dried tomato paste. Microwave on HIGH for 3 to 4 minutes. Add salt and pepper.

5 Drain the pasta, return it to the bowl and add the sauce. Toss well. Transfer to a serving dish and scatter the toasted almonds over the top to serve.

COOK'S TIP

If using fresh pasta, you'll need double the quantity (1 pound) to satisfy 3 to 4 hearty appetites. Fresh tagliatelle usually only takes 2 to 3 minutes to cook and is ready when it's tender, but still *al dente*, or with a bit of bite.

Arugula, Snow Peas, and Pine Nut Pasta

A light but filling pasta dish flavored with the peppery taste of fresh arugula.

INGREDIENTS

Serves 4

9 ounces capellini or angel-hair pasta

$\frac{1}{4}$ cup pine nuts

8 ounces snow peas

2 tablespoons water

6 ounces arugula

2 tablespoons finely grated Parmesan cheese (optional)

2 tablespoons olive oil (optional)

1 While preparing the sauce in the microwave, cook the pasta conventionally in a large saucepan of boiling salted water on the stovetop according to the package directions.

2 Place the pine nuts in a microwaveproof dish and microwave on HIGH for 3 to 5 minutes, stirring every minute, until golden.

3 Top and tail the snow peas. Place them in a large microwaveproof bowl and add the water. Cover and microwave on HIGH for 2 minutes. Add the arugula and stir lightly.

4 As soon as the pasta is cooked, drain it immediately and toss it with the snow peas and arugula.

5 Toss the pine nuts into the pasta. Add the Parmesan and olive oil, if using. Serve at once.

Thai Fragrant Rice

A delicious soft, fluffy rice dish, perfumed with fresh lemongrass.

INGREDIENTS

Serves 4

1 piece lemongrass

2 limes

1 cup brown basmati rice

1 tablespoon olive oil

1 onion, chopped

1-inch piece fresh gingerroot, finely chopped

$1\frac{1}{2}$ teaspoons coriander seeds

$1\frac{1}{2}$ teaspoons cumin seeds

$2\frac{1}{4}$ cups boiling vegetable stock

4 tablespoons chopped fresh cilantro leaves

lime wedges, to serve

3 Rinse the rice in plenty of cold water until the water runs clear; drain it in a strainer.

4 Place the oil in a large microwaveproof bowl. Add the onion and ginger.

5 Stir in the coriander and cumin seeds, lemongrass, and lime peel and microwave on HIGH for 2 minutes.

6 Add the rice and the stock. Cover loosely with a lid or vented plastic wrap and microwave on HIGH for 3 minutes. Reduce the power setting to MEDIUM and microwave for 25 minutes longer, stirring two or three times during cooking.

7 Stir in the fresh cilantro, fluff up the grains of rice, then cover and leave to stand for 5 minutes before serving. Serve lime wedges with the rice.

1 Finely chop the lemongrass using a sharp knife.

2 Remove the peel from the limes using a zester or fine grater. Avoid the white pith that has a bitter taste.

COOK'S TIP

Other varieties of rice, such as white basmati or long grain, can be used for this dish, but you will need to adjust the cooking times according to type.

Golden Vegetable Paella

Serves 4

pinch of saffron strands or 1 teaspoon
   ground turmeric

3 cups boiling vegetable or spicy stock

6 tablespoons olive oil

2 large onions, sliced

3 garlic cloves, chopped

$1\frac{1}{3}$ cups long grain rice

$\frac{1}{3}$ cup wild rice

$1\frac{1}{4}$ cups chopped pumpkin or
   butternut squash

generous 1 cup carrots cut into
   matchstick strips

1 yellow bell pepper, seeded and sliced

4 tomatoes, peeled and chopped

$1\frac{1}{2}$ cups quartered oyster mushrooms

salt and ground black pepper

strips of red, yellow, and green bell
   pepper, to garnish

1 If using saffron, place it in a small bowl with 3 to 4 tablespoons of the stock. Leave to stand for 5 minutes. Meanwhile, place the oil in a large microwave-proof bowl with the onions and garlic. Microwave on HIGH for 4 to $4\frac{1}{2}$ minutes, stirring once.

2 Stir both types of rice into the onion mixture and toss until coated in oil. Add the remaining stock, with the pumpkin or squash, and the saffron strands and liquid or turmeric.

3 Cover and microwave on HIGH for 3 minutes. Add the carrots, pepper, tomatoes, and salt and black pepper. Cover again and microwave on HIGH for 2 minutes. Reduce the power setting to MEDIUM and microwave for 12 minutes longer, stirring twice, or until the rice is almost tender.

4 Finally, stir in the oyster mushrooms. Check the seasoning, cover, and microwave on HIGH for 1 minute. Leave to stand for 10 minutes. Fluff up the rice with a fork, top with the peppers, and serve.

Spiced Lentils and Rice

Lentils are cooked with whole and ground spices, potatoes, rice, and onions to produce an authentic Indian-style risotto.

INGREDIENTS

Serves 4

$3/4$ cup toovar dhal or split red lentils

generous $1/2$ cup basmati rice

1 large potato

1 large onion

2 tablespoons sunflower oil

4 whole cloves

$1/4$ teaspoon cumin seeds

$1/4$ teaspoon ground turmeric

2 teaspoons salt

$1^1/4$ cups boiling water

1 Rinse the toovar dhal or lentils and rice in several changes of cold water. Then leave to soak in plenty of cold water for 15 minutes. Drain well.

2 Peel the potato and cut it into 1-inch chunks.

3 Thinly slice the onion and set it aside until the whole spices are lightly cooked.

4 Place the sunflower oil in a large microwaveproof bowl with the cloves and cumin seeds. Microwave on HIGH for 2 minutes.

5 Add the onion and potatoes, cover and microwave on HIGH for 4 minutes, stirring once. Stir in the lentils and rice, turmeric, salt, and water.

6 Cover and microwave on HIGH for 3 minutes. Reduce the power setting to MEDIUM and microwave for 12 minutes longer, stirring twice. Leave to stand, covered, for about 10 minutes before serving.

Mushroom, Leek, and Cashew Nut Risotto

Serves 4

$1\frac{1}{3}$ cups brown rice

3 cups boiling vegetable stock or a
  mixture of boiling stock and dry white
  wine in the ratio 5:1

1 tablespoon walnut or hazelnut oil

2 leeks, sliced

3 cups trimmed and sliced mixed wild or
  cultivated mushrooms

$\frac{1}{2}$ cup cashews

grated peel of 1 lemon

2 tablespoons chopped fresh thyme

scant $\frac{1}{4}$ cup pumpkin seeds

salt and ground black pepper

fresh thyme sprigs and lemon wedges,
  to garnish

1 Place the rice in a large
microwaveproof bowl with the
boiling stock (or stock and wine).
Cover loosely and microwave on
HIGH for 3 minutes. Reduce the
power setting to MEDIUM and
microwave for 25 minutes longer,
stirring twice. Leave to stand,
covered, while cooking the
vegetable and nut mixture.

2 Place the oil in a large
microwaveproof bowl with the
leeks and mushrooms. Cover and
microwave on HIGH for 3 to
4 minutes, stirring once.

3 Add the cashews, grated
lemon peel and chopped
fresh thyme to the leeks and
mushrooms and microwave on
HIGH for 1 minute. Season to
taste with salt and freshly ground
black pepper.

4 Drain off any excess stock
from the cooked rice and stir
in the vegetable mixture. Turn the
risotto into a warm serving dish.
Scatter the pumpkin seeds over the
top and garnish with the fresh
thyme sprigs and lemon wedges.
Serve the risotto at once.

Chicken and Vegetable Risotto

An Italian dish classic with short-grain arborio rice, which gives this easy one-pot recipe a creamy consistency.

INGREDIENTS

Serves 4

1 tablespoon oil

1 onion, chopped

8 ounces ground chicken

$1\frac{1}{2}$ cups arborio rice

$2\frac{1}{2}$ cups boiling chicken stock

1 red bell pepper, seeded and chopped

1 yellow bell pepper, seeded and chopped

3 ounces frozen green beans

$1\frac{1}{2}$ cups sliced cremini mushrooms

1 tablespoon chopped fresh parsley

salt and ground black pepper

fresh parsley sprigs, to garnish

1 Place the oil, onion, and chicken in a large microwave-proof bowl. Cover the bowl and microwave on HIGH for 6 to 7 minutes, stirring twice.

3 Add the mushrooms and microwave on HIGH for 1 minute. Leave to stand, covered, for 10 minutes.

4 Stir in the chopped parsley and season well to taste. Serve, garnished with parsley sprigs.

2 Stir in the rice, stock, red and yellow bell peppers, and green beans. Cover the bowl and microwave on HIGH for 13 minutes, stirring twice.

VARIATIONS

Make a country-style risotto by using thinly sliced garlic sausage or spicy sausage instead of the chicken and replacing the peppers with shelled fava or lima beans. The green beans can also be replaced with sliced zucchini. To enrich a risotto, use a proportion of dry white wine instead of all chicken stock. For example, use one-third white wine, making it up to the full quantity with boiling stock. Heat the mixture in the microwave before adding it to the risotto, otherwise the overall cooking time will be longer to compensate for the cool liquid.

COOK'S TIP

A traditional risotto has a moist, creamy consistency. Risotto rice, the best being arborio, is short in length, but it has the capacity for absorbing a large proportion of liquid during cooking while retaining its shape and some texture. The cooked rice is slightly sticky, so it acts as thickening agent for the excess liquid.
In fact, a risotto rice is halfway between familiar long-grain rice and traditional short-grain rice used for making rice puddings in terms of cooking quality.

Creamy Risotto with Asparagus

Fine asparagus spears look great gathered in a bundle and tied with a scallion stem.

Serves 4

2 tablespoons olive oil

1 onion, finely chopped

2 garlic cloves, crushed

generous 1 cup arborio rice

$1\frac{1}{2}$ quarts hot vegetable stock

$\frac{2}{3}$ cup dry white wine

$1\frac{1}{2}$ cups asparagus spears cut into
   1-inch pieces

4 tablespoons butter

3 tablespoons freshly grated
   Parmesan cheese

salt and ground black pepper

For the garnish

12 slender asparagus spears

5 tablespoons water

4 long green scallion stems, wilted

1 Place the oil, onion, and garlic in a large microwaveproof bowl. Cover and microwave on HIGH for 3 minutes, stirring once. Add the rice, stock, and wine. Cover and microwave on HIGH for 7 minutes, stirring once. Stir in the chopped asparagus, cover, and microwave on HIGH for 6 minutes longer, stirring once. Leave to stand, covered, for 10 minutes.

2 Meanwhile, place the whole asparagus in a microwave-proof bowl with the water. Cover and microwave on HIGH for 3 to 5 minutes, stirring once, until the spears are just tender.

3 Place three asparagus spears together, positioning them $\frac{3}{4}$-inch below one another. Tie the spears together with a wilted scallion stem. Make three more asparagus bundles.

4 Trim the base of each bundle of spears across at an angle. Trim the ends of the ties neatly.

5 Stir the butter and Parmesan into the risotto and check the seasoning. Serve at once, garnishing each portion with an asparagus bundle.

Sweet Vegetable Couscous

A wonderful combination of sweet vegetables and spices, this makes a substantial winter dish.

INGREDIENTS

Serves 4 to 6

1 generous pinch of saffron threads

3 tablespoons boiling water

1 tablespoon olive oil

1 red onion, sliced

2 garlic cloves, crushed

1 or 2 fresh red chilies, seeded and finely chopped

$\frac{1}{2}$ teaspoon ground ginger

$\frac{1}{2}$ teaspoon ground cinnamon

14-ounce can crushed tomatoes

$1\frac{1}{4}$ cups hot vegetable stock or water

4 carrots, peeled and cut into $\frac{1}{4}$-inch slices

2 turnips, peeled and cut into $\frac{3}{4}$-inch cubes

3 cups sweet potatoes peeled and cut into $\frac{3}{4}$-inch cubes

$\frac{1}{3}$ cup raisins

2 zucchini, cut into $\frac{1}{4}$-inch slices

14-ounce can garbanzo beans, drained and rinsed

3 tablespoons chopped fresh parsley

3 tablespoons chopped fresh cilantro leaves

1 pound quick-cook couscous

1 Sprinkle the saffron into the boiling water and set this aside to infuse.

2 Place the oil in a large microwaveproof bowl. Add the onion, garlic, and chilies. Microwave on HIGH for 2 minutes, stirring halfway through cooking.

3 Add the ground ginger and cinnamon and microwave on HIGH for 1 minute.

4 Stir in the tomatoes, stock or water, infused saffron and liquid, carrots, turnips, sweet potatoes, and raisins. Cover and microwave on HIGH for 15 minutes, stirring twice during cooking.

5 Add the zucchini, garbanzo beans, parsley, and cilantro, cover and microwave on HIGH for 5 to 8 minutes, stirring once, until the vegetables are tender.

6 Meanwhile, prepare the couscous following the package directions and serve it with the vegetables.

VEGETABLES AND SALADS

Ratatouille

Serves 4

2 large eggplants, roughly chopped

4 zucchini, roughly chopped

$2/3$ cup olive oil

2 onions, sliced

2 garlic cloves, chopped

1 large red bell pepper, seeded and
   roughly chopped

2 large yellow bell peppers, seeded and
   roughly chopped

1 fresh rosemary sprig

1 fresh thyme sprig

1 teaspoon coriander seeds, crushed

3 plum tomatoes, peeled, seeded,
   and chopped

8 basil leaves, torn

salt and ground black pepper

fresh parsley or basil sprigs, to garnish

1 Sprinkle the eggplants and zucchini with salt, then put them in a colander. Cover with a plate and place a weight on top to press out the bitter juices. Leave for about 30 minutes.

2 Place the olive oil in a large microwaveproof bowl. Add the onions, cover, and microwave on HIGH for 5 minutes until just soft. Add the garlic and microwave on HIGH for 1 minute longer.

3 Rinse the eggplants and zucchini and pat dry with paper towels or a dishcloth. Stir into the onions with the red and yellow bell peppers, rosemary, thyme, and coriander seeds.

4 Add the tomatoes and season well. Cover and microwave on HIGH for 15 to 20 minutes, stirring twice during cooking, until the vegetables are soft but not too mushy. Remove the sprigs of herbs. Stir in the torn basil leaves and check the seasoning.

5 Leave to cool slightly and serve warm or cold, garnished with sprigs of parsley or basil.

Herby Baked Tomatoes

Dress up sliced, sweet tomatoes with fresh herbs and a crisp topping.

INGREDIENTS

Serves 4 to 6

$1\frac{1}{2}$ pounds large red and yellow tomatoes (about 8)

2 teaspoons red wine vinegar

$\frac{1}{2}$ teaspoon wholegrain mustard

1 garlic clove, crushed

2 teaspoons water

2 teaspoons chopped fresh parsley

2 teaspoons snipped fresh chives

$\frac{1}{2}$ cup fine fresh white bread crumbs

salt and ground black pepper

sprigs of flat leaf parsley, to garnish

1 Thickly slice the tomatoes and arrange half of them in a $3\frac{3}{4}$-cup microwaveproof dish that is suitable for broiling.

2 Mix the vinegar, mustard, garlic, seasoning, and water together. Sprinkle the tomatoes with half the parsley and chives. Drizzle over half the dressing.

3 Lay the remaining tomato slices on top, overlapping them slightly. Drizzle with the remaining dressing. Cover and microwave on HIGH for 6 minutes, rotating the dish twice during cooking.

4 Uncover and sprinkle the bread crumbs over. Cook under a heated hot broiler until the topping is crisp. Sprinkle with the remaining parsley and chives. Serve immediately, garnished with sprigs of flat leaf parsley.

COMBINATION MICROWAVE

This recipe is suitable for cooking in a combination microwave. Follow the oven manufacturer's timing guide for the best results.

Zucchini in Citrus Sauce

If baby zucchini are unavailable, use larger ones, but cook them whole. Then halve them lengthwise and cut into 4-inch pieces.

INGREDIENTS

Serves 4

12 ounces baby zucchini

2 tablespoons plus 2 teaspoons water

4 scallions, finely sliced

1-inch piece fresh gingerroot, grated

2 tablespoons apple cider vinegar

1 tablespoon soy sauce

1 teaspoon soft light brown sugar

3 tablespoons vegetable stock

finely grated peels and juices of $\frac{1}{2}$ lemon and $\frac{1}{2}$ orange

1 teaspoon cornstarch

1 Place the zucchini in a microwaveproof bowl with the 2 tablespoons water. Cover and microwave on HIGH for 5 minutes, stirring once or twice during cooking.

2 Meanwhile, put all the remaining ingredients, except the cornstarch, into a small microwaveproof pitcher. Microwave on HIGH for $1\frac{1}{2}$ minutes, stirring halfway through cooking.

3 Blend the cornstarch with the 2 teaspoons cold water and add to the sauce. Microwave on HIGH for 1 minute, stirring twice, until the sauce is thick.

4 Pour the sauce over the zucchini and stir lightly to coat evenly. Transfer to a warm serving dish and serve.

Red Cabbage in Port and Red Wine

A sweet-and-sour, spicy red cabbage dish, with the added crunch of pears and walnuts.

INGREDIENTS

Serves 6

1 tablespoon walnut oil

1 onion, sliced

2 whole star anise

1 teaspoon ground cinnamon

pinch of ground cloves

$6\frac{1}{2}$ cups finely shredded red cabbage

2 tablespoons dark brown sugar

1 tablespoon red-wine vinegar

4 tablespoons red wine

2 tablespoons port

2 pears, cut into $\frac{1}{2}$-inch cubes

$\frac{1}{4}$ cup raisins

salt and ground black pepper

$\frac{1}{2}$ cup walnut halves

1 Place the oil in a large microwaveproof bowl. Add the onion and microwave on HIGH for 3 minutes, stirring halfway through cooking.

2 Stir in the star anise, cinnamon, cloves, and cabbage.

3 Stir in the sugar, vinegar, red wine, and port. Cover and microwave on HIGH for 12 to 15 minutes, stirring twice during cooking, until the cabbage is almost tender.

4 Stir in the pears and raisins. Cover and microwave on HIGH for 5 minutes, or until the cabbage and pears are tender. Season to taste. Stir in the walnut halves and serve.

Spring Vegetable Medley

A colorful, dazzling medley of fresh and sweet young vegetables.

INGREDIENTS

Serves 4

1 tablespoon peanut oil

1 garlic clove, sliced

1-inch piece fresh gingerroot, finely chopped

4 ounces baby carrots

4 ounces patty pan squash

4 ounces baby corn cobs

4 ounces thin green beans, topped and tailed

4 ounces sugar snap peas, topped and tailed

4 ounces young asparagus, cut into 3-inch pieces

8 scallions, trimmed and cut into 2-inch pieces

4 ounces cherry tomatoes

For the dressing

juice of 2 limes

1 tablespoon honey

1 tablespoon soy sauce

1 teaspoon sesame oil

1 Place the peanut oil in a large microwaveproof bowl.

2 Add the garlic and ginger, and microwave on HIGH for 30 seconds.

3 Stir in the carrots, patty pan squash, corn, and beans. Cover and microwave on HIGH for 5 minutes, stirring halfway through cooking.

4 Add the sugar snap peas, asparagus, scallions, and cherry tomatoes. Cover and microwave on HIGH for 3 to 4 minutes, stirring halfway through cooking.

5 Mix the dressing ingredients together and add to the bowl.

6 Stir well, then cover again, and microwave on HIGH for 1 to 2 minutes until the vegetables are just tender but still crisp.

Mushroom and Fennel Stew

Dried shiitake mushrooms add a wonderfully rich flavor to this vegetarian hotpot.

INGREDIENTS

Serves 4

1 ounce dried shiitake mushrooms

1 small head of fennel or 4 celery stalks

2 tablespoons olive oil

12 shallots, peeled

3 cups trimmed and halved
  button mushrooms

⅔ cup hard cider

1 ounce sun-dried tomatoes

2 tablespoons sun-dried tomato paste

1 bay leaf

chopped fresh parsley, to garnish

1 Place the dried shiitake mushrooms in a bowl. Pour boiling water over to cover and set aside for 10 minutes.

2 Roughly chop the fennel or celery stalks. Place the oil in a microwaveproof bowl. Add the shallots and fennel or celery. Cover and microwave on HIGH for 5 to 6 minutes stirring halfway through cooking. Add the button mushrooms, cover, and microwave on HIGH for 1½ minutes.

3 Drain the shiitake mushrooms and reserve the liquid. Cut up any large pieces and add them to the fennel or celery.

4 Stir in the cider, sun-dried tomatoes, and sun-dried tomato paste. Add the bay leaf. Cover and microwave on HIGH for 2 minutes. Reduce the power setting to MEDIUM and microwave for 5 to 7 minutes longer, stirring halfway through cooking.

5 Stir in the reserved liquid from the soaked mushrooms. Cover and microwave on MEDIUM for 5 to 8 minutes until the mixture is very tender. Remove the bay leaf and serve, sprinkled with parsley.

COOK'S TIP

This makes an unusual vegetarian main course or accompaniment. Mushrooms provide useful amounts of vitamins, minerals, and fiber.

Potato, Leek, and Tomato Bake

This simple dish is delicious for lunch or supper—a real winner with all the family. Select the best tomatoes you can for a good flavor; if this means using small fruit, then add one or two extra.

INGREDIENTS

Serves 4

$1\frac{1}{2}$ pounds potatoes

2 leeks, trimmed and sliced

3 large tomatoes, sliced

a few fresh rosemary sprigs, crushed

1 garlic clove, crushed

$1\frac{1}{4}$ cups hot vegetable stock

1 tablespoon olive oil

salt and ground black pepper

1 Scrub and thinly slice the potatoes. Layer them with the leeks and tomatoes in a 5 cup microwaveproof dish that is suitable for broiling, scattering some rosemary between the layers and ending with a layer of potatoes.

2 Add the garlic to the stock, and stir in salt and pepper to taste. Pour over the vegetables. Brush the top layer of potatoes with the olive oil.

3 Cover and microwave on HIGH for 15 to 18 minutes or until the potatoes are tender. Leave to stand for 5 minutes, then remove the cover. Brown under a heated hot broiler, if liked, and serve hot.

COMBINATION MICROWAVE

This recipe is suitable for cooking in a combination microwave. Follow the oven manufacturer's timing guide for the best results.

Summer Vegetable Braise

Tender, young vegetables are ideal for speedy cooking methods and the microwave cooks them so they stay tender-crisp.

INGREDIENTS

Serves 4

6 ounces baby carrots

2 cups sugar snap peas or
   snow peas

$1\frac{1}{4}$ cups baby corn cobs

6 tablespoons vegetable stock

2 teaspoons lime juice

salt and black pepper

chopped fresh parsley and snipped
   fresh chives, to garnish

1 Place the carrots, peas, and baby corn cobs in a large microwaveproof bowl with the vegetable stock and lime juice.

2 Cover and microwave on HIGH for 7 to 9 minutes, stirring halfway through cooking, until the vegetables are just tender.

3 Season the vegetables to taste with salt and pepper and stir in the chopped fresh parsley and snipped chives. Microwave on HIGH for 1 minute until the vegetables are well flavored with the herbs. Serve at once.

VARIATION

To make a more substantial dish, tip the cooked vegetables into a gratin dish and top with a mixture of grated cheese and bread crumbs. Broil until golden and bubbling.

COOK'S TIP

You can make this dish in the winter, too, but cut larger, tougher root vegetables into chunks and cook them for slightly longer.

Mixed Pepper Pipérade

INGREDIENTS

Serves 4

2 tablespoons olive oil

1 onion, chopped

1 red bell pepper

1 green bell pepper

4 tomatoes, peeled and chopped

1 garlic clove, crushed

4 extra-large eggs, beaten with
   1 tablespoon water

ground black pepper

4 large, thick slices of whole wheat toast,
   to serve

1 Place the oil in a large microwaveproof bowl with the onion.

2 Remove the seeds from the red and green bell peppers and slice the peppers thinly. Stir the pepper slices into the onion, cover, and microwave on HIGH for 5 to 6 minutes, stirring halfway through cooking.

3 Add the tomatoes and garlic and season with black pepper. Cover again and microwave on HIGH for 6 minutes longer, stirring halfway through cooking, until pulpy.

4 Pour the egg mixture over the vegetables. Microwave on HIGH for 4 to $4\frac{1}{2}$ minutes, stirring twice during cooking, until the pipérade thickens to the consistency of lightly scrambled eggs. Serve immediately, with warm whole wheat toast.

COOK'S TIP

To rediscover the rich flavor of eggs, look for free-range varieties from an organic farm. Even if you do not use them in all your cooking, they are worth it for flavor in dishes of this type. Do not stir the pipérade too much or the eggs can become rubbery.

Middle Eastern Vegetable Stew

A spiced dish of mixed vegetables makes a delicious and filling vegetarian main course. Children may prefer less chili.

INGREDIENTS

Serves 4 to 6

3 tablespoons vegetable stock

1 green bell pepper, seeded and sliced

2 zucchini, sliced

2 carrots, sliced

2 celery stalks, sliced

2 potatoes, diced

14-ounce can crushed tomatoes

1 teaspoon chili powder

2 tablespoons chopped fresh mint

1 tablespoon ground cumin

14-ounce can garbanzo beans, drained

salt and ground black pepper

mint sprigs, to garnish

2 Add the potatoes, tomatoes, chili powder, fresh mint, ground cumin, and garbanzo beans to the vegetable dish and stir well. Cover the dish and microwave on HIGH for 15 to 20 minutes, remembering to stir twice during the cooking time.

3 Leave to stand, covered, for 5 minutes until all the vegetables are tender. Season to taste with salt and pepper. Serve hot, garnished with mint leaves.

VARIATION

Other vegetables can be substituted for those in the recipe. Use whatever you have to hand—try rutabaga, sweet potato, or parsnips.

1 Place the vegetable stock in a large microwaveproof casserole with the sliced bell pepper, zucchini, carrots, and celery. Cover and microwave on HIGH for 2 minutes.

COOK'S TIP

Garbanzo beans are traditional in this type of Middle Eastern dish, but if you prefer, red kidney or haricot beans can be used instead.

Zucchini and Potato Tortilla

INGREDIENTS

Serves 4

2 tablespoons chopped fresh tarragon

4 extra-large eggs, beaten

2 tablespoons olive oil

1 onion, finely chopped

3 cups diced potatoes

1 garlic clove, crushed

2 zucchini, thinly sliced

salt and ground black pepper

1 Stir the tarragon into the eggs and season with salt and pepper; set aside.

2 Place the oil and onion in a large, shallow microwaveproof dish that is suitable for broiling. Cover and microwave on HIGH for 3 minutes. Add the diced potatoes, garlic, and sliced zucchini, cover again, and microwave on HIGH for 10 minutes, stirring twice during cooking.

3 Pour the eggs over the vegetables, cover, and microwave on HIGH for 3 to 5 minutes, rotating the dish twice, until the eggs are beginning to set slightly. Meanwhile, heat the broiler.

4 Place the tortilla under the broiler and cook for a few minutes until the top is set and is tinged golden. Cut into wedges and serve from the dish.

COMBINATION MICROWAVE

This recipe is suitable for cooking in a combination microwave. Follow the oven manufacturer's timing guide for the best results.

Chicken and Pesto Baked Potatoes

Although it is usually served with pasta, pesto also gives a wonderful lift to rice, bread, and potato dishes— all good starchy carbohydrates. Here, it is combined with chicken and yogurt to make a low-fat topping for baked potatoes.

INGREDIENTS

Serves 4

4 baking potatoes, 6 ounces each, pricked

1 tablespoon pesto sauce

1 cup low-fat plain yogurt

2 chicken breast halves, cooked

1 Arrange the potatoes in a circle on double thick paper towels. Microwave on HIGH for 12 to 15 minutes, turning over once halfway during cooking. Leave to stand for 3 to 4 minutes.

2 Stir the pesto into the yogurt until well combined.

COOK'S TIP

The chicken can be cooked in the microwave, if you like. Microwave on HIGH for 3 to 4 minutes, turning over halfway through cooking.

3 Skin and slice the chicken. Cut the potatoes open and fill with the chicken slices. Top with the pesto-flavored yogurt and garnish with basil. Serve at once, while still hot.

Cauliflower with Three Cheeses

INGREDIENTS

Serves 4

4 baby cauliflowers

$\frac{1}{2}$ cup water

1 cup light cream

$\frac{3}{4}$ cup diced dolcelatte cheese

$\frac{3}{4}$ cup diced mozzarella cheese

3 tablespoons freshly grated
  Parmesan cheese

freshly grated nutmeg

ground black pepper

toasted bread crumbs, to garnish

1 Place the cauliflowers floret-side down in a microwaveproof dish. Add the water, cover and microwave on HIGH for 9 to 11 minutes, rearranging once. Leave to stand for 3 minutes.

2 Place the cream in a small microwaveproof bowl with the cheeses. Microwave on HIGH for 2 to 3 minutes, stirring three times, until the cheeses have melted. Season with nutmeg and freshly ground pepper.

3 Drain the cauliflowers thoroughly and place one on each of four warmed plates.

4 Spoon a little of the cheese sauce over each cauliflower and sprinkle with toasted bread crumbs. Serve at once.

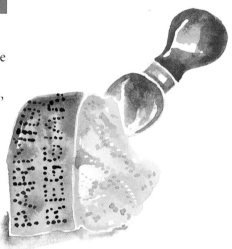

Winter Vegetable Stew

Use whatever vegetables you have to hand in this richly flavored and substantial one-pot meal.

INGREDIENTS

Serves 4

2 onions, sliced

4 carrots, sliced

1 small rutabaga, sliced

2 parsnips, sliced

3 small turnips, sliced

$\frac{1}{2}$ celery root, cut into matchstick strips

2 leeks, thinly sliced

1 garlic clove, chopped

1 bay leaf, crumbled

2 tablespoons chopped fresh mixed herbs,
  such as parsley and thyme

$1\frac{1}{4}$ cups vegetable stock

1 tablespoon all-purpose flour

$1\frac{1}{2}$ pounds red-skinned potatoes,
  scrubbed and thinly sliced

4 tablespoons butter

salt and ground black pepper

1 Arrange all the vegetables, except the potatoes, in layers in a large microwaveproof dish with a tight-fitting lid that is suitable for broiling.

2 Season the vegetable layers lightly with salt and pepper and sprinkle them with chopped garlic, crumbled bay leaf, and chopped herbs.

3 Blend the stock into the flour and pour over the vegetables. Arrange the potatoes in overlapping layers on top. Dot with butter and cover tightly.

4 Microwave on HIGH for 10 minutes. Reduce the power setting to MEDIUM and microwave for 25 to 30 minutes longer until the vegetables are tender. Remove the lid and cook under a heated hot broiler until golden and crisp. Serve hot.

COMBINATION MICROWAVE

This recipe is suitable for cooking in a combination microwave. Follow the oven manufacturer's timing guide for the best results.

Broccoli and Chestnut Terrine

Served hot or cold, this versatile terrine is equally suitable for a dinner party as for a picnic.

INGREDIENTS

Serves 4 to 6

$3\frac{1}{2}$ cups broccoli cut into small flowerets

4 tablespoons water

$1\frac{1}{2}$ cups roughly chopped cooked chestnuts

1 cup fresh whole wheat bread crumbs

4 tablespoons low-fat plain yogurt

2 tablespoons freshly grated Parmesan cheese

salt and ground black pepper

grated nutmeg

2 eggs, beaten

1 Line a 9- x 5-inch glass bread pan with plastic wrap.

2 Place the broccoli in a microwaveproof bowl with the water. Cover and microwave on HIGH for 6 minutes, stirring once; drain well. Reserve a quarter of the smallest flowerets and chop the rest finely.

3 Mix together the chestnuts, bread crumbs, yogurt, and Parmesan, adding seasoning and grated nutmeg to taste.

4 Fold in the chopped broccoli, reserved small flowerets, and the beaten eggs.

5 Spoon the broccoli mixture into the prepared container. Cover and microwave on HIGH for 3 minutes. Reduce the power setting to MEDIUM and microwave for 5 to 8 minutes longer, or until just firm and set. Leave to stand for 5 minutes.

6 Turn out the terrine onto a flat plate or tray. Serve cut into thick slices. New potatoes and salad are suitable accompaniments.

Mixed Mushroom Ragout

These mushrooms are delicious served hot or cold, and can be made up to two days in advance.

INGREDIENTS

Serves 4

1 small onion, finely chopped

1 garlic clove, crushed

1 teaspoon coriander seeds, crushed

2 tablespoons red-wine vinegar

1 tablespoon soy sauce

1 tablespoon dry sherry

2 teaspoons tomato paste

2 teaspoons soft light brown sugar

5 tablespoons hot vegetable stock

$1\frac{1}{2}$ cups baby button mushrooms

$1\frac{1}{2}$ cups quartered chestnut mushrooms

$1\frac{1}{2}$ cups sliced oyster mushrooms

salt and ground black pepper

sprig of fresh cilantro, to garnish

1 Mix the onion, garlic, coriander seeds, red-wine vinegar, soy sauce, sherry, tomato paste, sugar, and stock in a large microwaveproof bowl. Cover and microwave on HIGH for 3 minutes, stirring once. Uncover and microwave on HIGH for 2 to 3 minutes longer until the liquid reduces by half.

2 Add the mushrooms, stirring well. Cover and microwave on HIGH for 3 to 4 minutes, stirring once, until tender.

3 Remove the mushrooms with a perforated spoon and transfer them to a warm serving dish.

4 Microwave the juices on HIGH for 3 to 5 minutes until reduced to about 5 tablespoons. Season to taste with salt and ground black pepper.

COOK'S TIP

If coriander is a favorite spice of yours, it is worth buying a pepper mill and filling it with coriander seeds. This way, you can grind a little coriander into all sorts of savory dishes to add a hint of exotic seasoning.

5 Leave to cool for 2 to 3 minutes. Pour the liquid over the mushrooms. Serve hot or well chilled, garnished with a sprig of fresh cilantro.

Mushroom and Okra Curry

This simple but delicious curry, with its fresh gingery mango relish, is best served with plain basmati rice.

INGREDIENTS

Serves 4

4 garlic cloves, roughly chopped

1-inch piece fresh gingerroot, roughly chopped

1 or 2 fresh red chilies, seeded and chopped

$\frac{3}{4}$ cup water

1 tablespoon sunflower oil

1 teaspoon coriander seeds

1 teaspoon cumin seeds

1 teaspoon ground cumin

2 green cardamom pods, seeds removed and ground

pinch of ground turmeric

14-ounce can crushed tomatoes

1 pound mushrooms, quartered if large

1½ cups okra trimmed and cut into ½in slices

2 tablespoons chopped fresh cilantro

basmati rice, to serve

For the mango relish

1 large ripe mango, about 1¼ pounds in weight

1 small garlic clove, crushed

1 onion, finely chopped

2 teaspoons grated fresh gingerroot

1 fresh red chili, seeded and finely chopped

pinch each of salt and sugar

1 For the mango relish, peel the mango and cut the flesh from the seed.

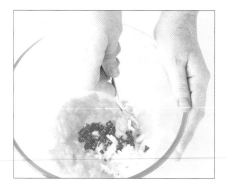

2 Mash the mango flesh with a fork or lightly process it in a blender or food processor, and mix in the rest of the relish ingredients; set aside.

3 Process the garlic, ginger, chilies, and 3 tablespoons of the water to a smooth paste in a blender or food processor.

4 Place the sunflower oil in a large microwaveproof bowl. Add the coriander and cumin seeds and microwave on HIGH for 30 seconds. Add the ground cumin, ground cardamom, and turmeric and microwave on HIGH for 30 seconds longer.

5 Stir in the spice paste, tomatoes, remaining water, mushrooms, and okra. Cover and microwave on HIGH for 10 to 12 minutes, stirring halfway through cooking.

6 Leave to stand, covered, for 5 minutes until the okra is tender. Stir in the fresh cilantro and serve with rice and the mango relish.

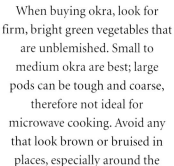

COOK'S TIP

When buying okra, look for firm, bright green vegetables that are unblemished. Small to medium okra are best; large pods can be tough and coarse, therefore not ideal for microwave cooking. Avoid any that look brown or bruised in places, especially around the stem end. As with most prepacked produce, reject sealed packages that look damp inside.

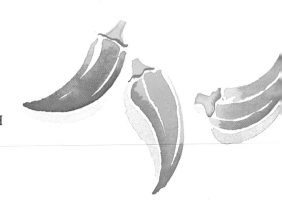

New Potato and Chive Salad

The secret of a good potato salad is to mix the potatoes with the dressing while they are still hot so they absorb the flavors.

INGREDIENTS

Serves 4 to 6

$1\frac{1}{2}$ pounds new potatoes (unpeeled)

4 tablespoons water

4 scallions

3 tablespoons olive oil

1 tablespoon white wine vinegar

$\frac{3}{4}$ teaspoon Dijon mustard

$\frac{3}{4}$ cup mayonnaise

3 tablespoons snipped fresh chives

salt and ground black pepper

1 Place the potatoes and water in a microwaveproof dish. Cover and microwave on HIGH for 9 to 12 minutes, stirring halfway through cooking. Leave to stand, covered, for 3 minutes. Meanwhile, finely chop the white parts of the scallions along with a little of the green parts.

2 Whisk together the oil, vinegar, and mustard. Drain the potatoes well, then immediately toss them lightly with the dressing, seasoning, and scallions; set aside to cool.

3 Stir the mayonnaise and chives into the potatoes. Cover and chill well until ready to serve. Potato salad is delicious with cooked sausages, chicken wings, or cold meats.

COOK'S TIP

Look for the small, waxy potatoes, sold especially for salads and cold dishes—they are particularly good in this recipe, because they don't fall apart like floury, older potatoes do.

Salade Niçoise

INGREDIENTS

Serves 4

6 tablespoons olive oil

2 tablespoons tarragon vinegar

1 teaspoon tarragon or Dijon mustard

1 small garlic clove, crushed

12 small new or salad potatoes

4 ounces thin green beans

3 or 4 hearts of lettuces, roughly chopped

7-ounce can tuna in oil, drained

6 anchovy fillets, halved lengthwise

12 ripe olives, pitted

4 tomatoes, chopped

4 scallions, finely chopped

2 teaspoons capers

2 tablespoons pine nuts

2 hard-cooked eggs, chopped

salt and ground black pepper

1 Mix the oil, vinegar, mustard, garlic, and seasoning in a large salad bowl.

2 Place the potatoes in a microwaveproof bowl with 2 tablespoons water. Cover and microwave on HIGH for 6 to 8 minutes, stirring halfway through cooking. Leave to stand, covered, for 3 minutes; drain thoroughly.

3 Place the beans in a microwaveproof bowl with 1 tablespoon water. Cover and microwave on HIGH for 3 minutes, stirring once. Leave to stand, covered, for 2 minutes; drain.

4 Stir the potatoes and beans with the lettuce, tuna, anchovies, olives, tomatoes, scallions, and capers.

5 Just before serving, place the pine nuts on a small microwaveproof plate and microwave on HIGH for 3 to 4 minutes, stirring once every minute, until brown.

6 Sprinkle the pine nuts over the salad while still hot. Add the eggs and toss all the ingredients together well. Serve with chunks of hot, crusty bread.

Watercress and Potato Salad

New potatoes are equally good hot or cold, and this colorful, nutritious salad is an ideal way of making the most of them.

INGREDIENTS

Serves 4

1 pound small new potatoes
   (unpeeled)
3 tablespoons water
1 bunch watercress
$1\frac{1}{2}$ cups halved cherry tomatoes
2 tablespoons pumpkin seeds
3 tablespoons low-fat fromage blanc
1 tablespoon apple cider vinegar
1 teaspoon brown sugar
salt
paprika

1 Place the potatoes and water in a microwaveproof bowl. Cover and microwave on HIGH for 7 to 10 minutes, stirring halfway through cooking. Leave to stand, covered, for 3 minutes; drain and leave to cool.

2 Toss the potatoes, watercress, tomatoes, and pumpkin seeds together.

3 Place the fromage blanc, vinegar, sugar, and salt and paprika to taste in a screw-top jar and shake well to mix. Pour over the salad just before serving.

VARIATION

To make Spinach and Potato Salad, substitute about 8 ounces fresh baby spinach leaves for the watercress.

COOK'S TIP

If you are preparing this salad in advance, mix the dressing in the jar and set aside. Shake the dressing again and toss it into the salad just before serving.

Fruity Brown Rice Salad

An Oriental-style dressing gives this colorful rice salad extra piquancy. Whole grains, like brown rice, are unrefined, so they retain their natural fiber, vitamins, and minerals.

Serves 4 to 6

4 scallions

⅔ cup long-grain brown rice

1¼ cups boiling water

1 small red bell pepper, seeded and diced

7-ounce can corn kernels, drained

3 tablespoons golden raisins

8-ounce can pineapple pieces in
    natural juice

1 tablespoon soy sauce

1 tablespoon sunflower oil

1 tablespoon hazelnut oil

1 garlic clove, crushed

1 teaspoon finely chopped fresh gingerroot

salt and ground black pepper

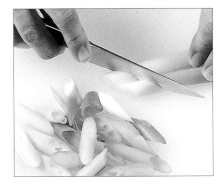

1 Slice the scallions on the diagonal; set them aside ready for garnishing the salad.

2 Place the rice in a large microwaveproof bowl with the boiling water and a little salt. Cover loosely and microwave on HIGH for 3 minutes. Reduce the power setting to MEDIUM and microwave for 25 minutes longer, stirring twice during cooking. Leave to stand, covered, for 5 minutes.

3 Tip the rice into a serving bowl and add the red pepper, corn, and golden raisins. Drain the canned pineapple pieces, reserving the juice, and toss them lightly into the rice mixture. Do not overmix or you will break the grains of rice.

4 Pour the reserved pineapple juice into a clean screw-top jar. Add the soy sauce, sunflower and hazelnut oils, garlic, and ginger with salt and pepper to taste. Shake well to combine.

5 Pour the dressing over the salad and toss well. Scatter the scallions over the top.

Mediterranean Salad with Basil

A variation of Salade Niçoise with pasta, conjuring up all the sunny flavors of the Mediterranean.

INGREDIENTS

Serves 4

1 pound chunky fresh pasta shapes

a little oil

$6\frac{1}{4}$ cups plus 2 tablespoons boiling water

6 ounces thin green beans

2 large ripe tomatoes

1 cup fresh basil leaves

7-ounce can tuna fish in oil, drained and roughly flaked

2 hard-cooked eggs, shelled and sliced or quartered

2-ounce can anchovy fillets, drained

1 tablespoon capers

about 4 ripe olives

For the dressing

6 tablespoons extra-virgin olive oil

2 tablespoons white-wine vinegar or lemon juice

2 garlic cloves, crushed

$\frac{1}{2}$ teaspoon Dijon mustard

2 tablespoons chopped fresh basil

salt and ground black pepper

1 Whisk all the ingredients for the dressing together and leave to infuse while you make the salad.

2 Place the fresh pasta in a large microwaveproof bowl with a little oil and the main quantity of boiling water. Cover and microwave on HIGH for 2 to 3 minutes, stirring halfway through cooking; drain well and cool.

3 Place the beans in a microwaveproof bowl with the 2 tablespoons boiling water. Cover and microwave on HIGH for 3 to 4 minutes; drain and refresh in cold water.

4 Slice or quarter the tomatoes and arrange on the bottom of a bowl. Moisten with a little dressing and cover with a quarter of the basil leaves. Add with the beans. Moisten with a little more dressing and cover with a third of the remaining basil.

5 Toss the pasta in a little more dressing and spoon it over the salad with half the remaining basil and the tuna.

6 Arrange the eggs on top. Finally, scatter the anchovy fillets, capers, and ripe olives over. Pour the remaining dressing over and garnish with the remaining basil. Serve immediately. Don't be tempted to chill this salad—all the flavors will be dulled.

 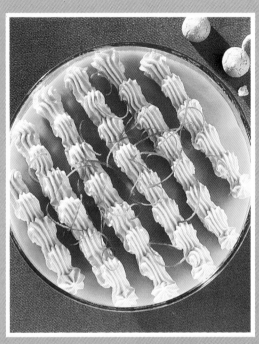 

DESSERTS

Chocolate-Amaretti Peaches

Quick and easy to prepare, this delicious dessert can also be made with fresh nectarines or apricots.

INGREDIENTS

Serves 4

1 cup amaretti cookies, crushed

2 ounces semi-sweet chocolate, chopped

grated peel of $\frac{1}{2}$ orange

1 tablespoon honey

$\frac{1}{4}$ teaspoon ground cinnamon

1 egg white, lightly whisked

4 firm ripe peaches

5 tablespoons white wine

1 tablespoon sugar

whipped cream, to serve

1 Mix together the amaretti cookies, chocolate, orange peel, honey, and cinnamon in a bowl. Stir in the egg white to bind the mixture.

2 Halve and pit the peaches and fill the cavities with the chocolate mixture, mounding it up slightly.

3 Arrange the stuffed peaches in a lightly buttered, shallow microwaveproof dish that will just hold them. Pour the wine into a cup and stir in the sugar.

4 Pour the sweetened wine around the peaches. Cover loosely and microwave on HIGH for 2 to 3 minutes until the peaches are tender. Serve at once with a little of the cooking juices spooned over and the whipped cream.

Plum and Walnut Crumble

Walnuts add a lovely crunch to the fruit layer in this crumble— almonds would be equally good.

INGREDIENTS

Serves 4 to 6

$2\frac{1}{4}$ pounds plums, halved
  and pitted

$\frac{3}{4}$ cup walnut pieces, toasted

scant 1 cup light brown sugar

6 tablespoons butter, diced

$1\frac{1}{2}$ cups all-purpose flour

1 Butter a 5-cup microwave-proof dish that is suitable for broiling. Put the plums in the dish, then stir in the nuts and half the light brown sugar.

2 Rub the butter or margarine into the flour until the mixture resembles coarse crumbs. Stir in the remaining sugar and continue to rub in the fat until fine crumbs are formed.

3 Cover the fruit with the crumb mixture and press it down lightly. Microwave the crumble on HIGH for 14 to 16 minutes, rotating the dish three times during cooking. Brown the top under a heated hot broiler until golden and crisp, if liked, before serving.

VARIATION

To make Oat and Cinnamon Crumble, substitute oatmeal for half the flour in the crumble mixture and add $\frac{1}{2}$ to 1 teaspoon ground cinnamon.

COMBINATION MICROWAVE

This recipe is suitable for cooking in a combination microwave. Follow your oven manufacturer's timing guide for the best results.

Rhubarb and Strawberry Crisp

Serves 4

8 ounces strawberries, hulled and cut in half if large

3 cups rhubarb cut into pieces

$\frac{1}{2}$ cup sugar

1 tablespoon cornstarch

$\frac{1}{3}$ cup fresh orange juice

1 cup all-purpose flour

1 cup oatmeal

$\frac{1}{2}$ cup soft light brown sugar

$\frac{1}{2}$ teaspoon ground cinnamon

$\frac{1}{2}$ cup blanched almonds, very finely ground

10 tablespoons butter, chilled

1 egg, lightly beaten

1 Mix the strawberries with the rhubarb and sugar in a $7\frac{1}{2}$-cup microwaveproof dish that is suitable for broiling.

2 Blend the cornstarch with the orange juice in a small bowl. Pour this mixture over the fruit and stir lightly to coat the pieces.

3 Mix the flour, oats, brown sugar, cinnamon, and almonds in a large bowl. Rub in the butter using your fingertips until the mixture resembles coarse bread crumbs. Stir in the beaten egg.

4 Spoon the oat mixture evenly over the fruit and press down gently. Microwave on HIGH for 12 to 14 minutes, rotating the dish twice during cooking. Brown under a heated hot broiler until golden and crisp, if liked.

COMBINATION MICROWAVE

This recipe is suitable for cooking in a combination microwave. Follow your oven manufacturer's timing guide for the best results.

Baked Apples with Apricots

Serves 6

$\frac{1}{2}$ cup chopped ready-to-eat
   dried apricots

$\frac{1}{2}$ cup walnuts, chopped

1 teaspoon grated lemon peel

$\frac{1}{2}$ teaspoon ground cinnamon

$\frac{1}{2}$ cup soft light brown sugar

2 tablespoons butter, at
   room temperature

6 large eating apples

1 tablespoon butter, melted

$\frac{1}{2}$ cup water or fruit juice

1 Place the apricots, walnuts, lemon peel, and cinnamon in a bowl. Add the sugar and butter and stir until thoroughly mixed.

2 Core the apples, without cutting all the way through to the base. Peel the top of each apple and slightly widen the top of each opening to make plenty of room for the filling.

3 Spoon the filling into the apples, packing it down lightly into their middles.

4 Place the stuffed apples in a microwaveproof dish large enough to hold them side by side.

5 Brush the apples with the melted butter and pour the water or fruit juice around them. Microwave on HIGH for 9 to 10 minutes, rearranging them halfway through cooking, until the apples are tender. Serve hot.

Creole Bread and Butter Pudding

Serves 4 to 6

4 ready-to-eat dried apricots, chopped

1 tablespoon raisins

2 tablespoons golden raisins

1 tablespoon chopped mixed peel

7 ounces French loaf, thinly sliced

4 tablespoons butter, melted

2 cups milk

$\frac{2}{3}$ cup heavy cream

$\frac{1}{2}$ cup superfine sugar

3 eggs

$\frac{1}{2}$ teaspoon vanilla extract

2 tablespoons whiskey

For the cream

$\frac{2}{3}$ cup heavy cream

2 tablespoons thick plain yogurt

1–2 tablespoons whiskey

1 tablespoon sugar

1 Lightly butter a deep $6\frac{1}{2}$ to $7\frac{1}{2}$ cup microwaveproof dish that is suitable for broiling. Mix the dried fruits and mixed peel, and sprinkle a little over the bottom of the dish. Brush both sides of the bread slices with melted butter.

2 Fill the dish with alternate layers of bread and dried fruit, finishing with a layer of bread.

3 Pour the milk and cream into a microwaveproof pitcher and microwave on HIGH for 3 to 4 minutes until just boiling. Meanwhile, whisk the sugar, eggs and vanilla extract together.

4 Whisk the hot milk and cream into the eggs and then strain the mixture over the bread and fruit. Sprinkle the whiskey over the top. Press the bread into the milk and egg mixture, cover, and leave to stand for 20 minutes.

5 Microwave on MEDIUM for 10 to 15 minutes until the mixture is almost set in the middle, rotating the dish four times during cooking. Brown under a heated hot broiler, if liked.

6 Just before serving, mix the cream, yogurt, whiskey, and sugar into a small microwaveproof bowl and microwave on HIGH for 1 to 2 minutes, stirring once. Serve with the hot pudding.

Castle Puddings with Custard

Serves 4 to 8

about 3 tablespoons black-currant,
    strawberry, or raspberry jelly

$\frac{1}{2}$ cup butter

generous $\frac{1}{2}$ cup superfine sugar

2 eggs, beaten

few drops of vanilla extract

generous 1 cup self-rising flour

For the custard

scant 2 cups milk

4 eggs

$1\frac{1}{2}$ to 2 tablespoons sugar

few drops of vanilla extract

1 Butter eight microwaveproof individual pudding bowls or large teacups and put about 2 teaspoons of the jam in the base.

2 Cream the butter and sugar together in a bowl until light and fluffy. Gradually beat in the eggs, beating well after each addition and adding the vanilla extract toward the end. Fold in the flour, then divide the batter among the bowls or cups.

3 Microwave on HIGH for 3 to 4 minutes until just set. Leave to stand for 3 minutes. Turn each out onto a warm serving plate; keep warm.

4 To make the custard, place the milk in a microwaveproof pitcher and microwave on HIGH for 4 minutes. Beat the eggs and sugar in a microwaveproof bowl. Gradually whisk in the hot milk.

5 Reduce the power setting to MEDIUM-HIGH and microwave for 5 to 6 minutes, stirring every 1 minute, until the custard is thick enough to coat the back of a spoon. Do not allow it to boil. Stir in the vanilla extract. Serve with the warm puddings.

Gingerbread Upside-Down Pudding

A proper dessert that goes down well on a cold winter's day.

Serves 4 to 6

sunflower oil for brushing

1 tablespoon soft brown sugar

8 walnut halves

4 peaches, halved and pitted, or canned peach halves

For the base

$\frac{1}{2}$ cup whole wheat flour

$\frac{1}{2}$ teaspoon baking soda

$1\frac{1}{2}$ teaspoon ground ginger

1 teaspoon ground cinnamon

$\frac{1}{2}$ cup molasses sugar

1 egg

$\frac{1}{2}$ cup skim milk

$\frac{1}{4}$ cup sunflower oil

1 For the topping, brush the bottom and sides of a 9-inch round, deep microwaveproof dish with oil. Line with waxed paper. Oil the paper and sprinkle the bottom with sugar.

2 Place a walnut half in each peach half. Arrange the peaches cut-side down in the dish.

3 For the cake, sift together the flour, baking soda, ginger, and cinnamon. Stir in the sugar. Beat together the egg, milk, and oil, then stir into the dry ingredients until smooth.

4 Pour the batter evenly over the peaches and microwave on MEDIUM for 6 to 8 minutes until the batter shrinks away from the sides of the dish, but the surface still looks wet. Leave to stand for 5 minutes. Turn out into a serving plate. Serve hot with yogurt or custard.

Sticky Toffee Pudding

Serves 6

1 cup walnuts, toasted
  and chopped

$\frac{1}{4}$ cup butter

scant 1 cup soft brown sugar

4 tablespoons light cream

2 tablespoons lemon juice

2 eggs, beaten

1 cup all-purpose flour

1 Grease a 1-quart microwave-proof bowl or pudding basin and add half the walnuts.

2 Beat 4 tablespoons of the butter with 4 tablespoons of the sugar, the cream, and 1 tablespoon of the lemon juice in a small microwaveproof bowl. Microwave on HIGH for $1\frac{1}{2}$ to 2 minutes, stirring once, until smooth. Pour half into the bowl and swirl to coat it a little way up the sides.

3 Beat the remaining butter and sugar until light. Gradually beat in the eggs. Fold in the flour, remaining nuts, and lemon juice; spoon into the bowl.

4 Three-quarters cover the bowl with plastic wrap and microwave on LOW for 7 to 10 minutes, until the batter is well-risen and has shrunk away from the sides of the bowl, but is still wet on the surface. Leave to stand for 5 minutes.

5 Just before serving, microwave the remaining sauce on HIGH for 1 to $1\frac{1}{2}$ minutes to reheat. Unmold the dessert onto a warm plate. Pour the warm sauce over.

COOK'S TIP

Substitute other nuts of your choice for the walnuts, if wished.

Austrian Nut Pudding

This is a perfect pudding to make in the microwave.

INGREDIENTS

Serves 4

butter for greasing

4 tablespoons superfine sugar, plus a little extra for sprinkling

1 cup hazelnuts, chopped

4 tablespoons butter, softened

2 eggs, separated

$\frac{1}{2}$ cup very fine fresh white bread crumbs

$1\frac{1}{4}$ cups fresh raspberries

confectioners' sugar, to taste

cream, to serve

1 Lightly grease a 1-quart microwaveproof bowl or pudding basin. Sprinkle it evenly with a little superfine sugar.

2 Spread the hazelnuts on a microwaveproof plate and microwave on HIGH for 5 to 6 minutes, until toasted and golden; leave to cool.

3 Meanwhile, place the butter and sugar in a bowl and beat until pale and creamy. Beat in the egg yolks.

4 Place the cooled nuts in a food processor and process until finely ground.

5 Mix 1 tablespoon water into the bread crumbs. Beat this into the creamed mixture with the hazelnuts.

6 Whisk the egg whites in a clean bowl until stiff. Beat about 2 tablespoons into the creamed mixture to loosen it slightly. Carefully fold in the remaining egg whites with a large metal spoon.

7 Spoon the batter into the prepared bowl or basin. Cover and microwave on HIGH for 4 to 6 minutes.

8 Meanwhile, press the raspberries through a strainer into a bowl. Add confectioners' sugar to sweeten the purée to taste. Unmold the cooked pudding and serve it hot, with the raspberry sauce and cream.

Cinnamon and Coconut Rice

Serves 4-6

$\frac{1}{4}$ cup raisins

2 cups boiling water

1 cup short-grain rice

1 cinnamon stick

2 tablespoons sugar

2 cups milk

1 cup canned sweetened
   coconut milk

$\frac{1}{2}$ teaspoon vanilla extract

1 tablespoon butter

$\frac{1}{3}$ cup shredded coconut

ground cinnamon for sprinkling

light or heavy cream, to serve (optional)

3 Meanwhile, blend the milk, coconut milk, and vanilla extract together in a bowl; drain the raisins.

4 Remove the cinnamon stick from the rice. Stir in the raisins and the milk mixture. Cover and microwave on MEDIUM for 15 to 20 minutes longer, until the mixture is just thick. Do not overcook the rice.

5 Heat the broiler. Transfer the rice to a serving dish that is suitable for broiling. Dot with the butter and sprinkle with coconut. Broil about 5 inches from the heat for 3 to 5 minutes until just brown. Sprinkle with cinnamon. Serve warm or cold, with cream if liked.

COOK'S TIP

Select large plump raisins for this creamy dessert.

1 Soak the raisins in a small bowl in enough water to cover.

2 Place the boiling water in a microwaveproof bowl. Stir in the rice, cinnamon stick, and sugar. Cover and microwave on HIGH for 3 minutes. Reduce the power setting to MEDIUM and microwave for 12 minutes longer, or until the liquid is absorbed.

Hot Bananas with Rum and Raisins

Choose almost-ripe bananas with evenly colored skins, either all yellow or just green at the tips. Black patches indicate that the fruit is overripe.

INGREDIENTS

Serves 4

¼ cup seedless raisins

5 tablespoons dark rum

4 tablespoons unsalted butter

4 tablespoons soft light brown sugar

4 ripe bananas, peeled and
   halved lengthwise

¼ teaspoon ground nutmeg

¼ teaspoon ground cinnamon

2 tablespoons slivered almonds, toasted

chilled cream or vanilla ice cream,
   to serve (optional)

1 Put the raisins in a bowl with the rum. Leave them to soak for about 30 minutes to plump up.

2 Place the butter in a shallow microwaveproof dish and microwave on HIGH for 1 minute, or until the butter melts.

3 Stir in the sugar and microwave on HIGH for 1 minute. Add the bananas to the dish and coat them with the sugar mixture. Microwave on HIGH for 4 minutes, turning the fruit over once.

4 Sprinkle the spices over the bananas. Stir the rum and raisins in a small cup.

5 Microwave on HIGH for 30 to 45 seconds. Pour them over the bananas. Carefully set alight using a long taper and stir gently to mix.

6 Scatter the slivered almonds over. Serve immediately with chilled cream or vanilla ice cream, if you like.

Spiced Pears in Cider

INGREDIENTS

Serves 4

1 oz/1 cup hard cider

thinly pared strip of lemon peel

1 cinnamon stick

2 tablespoons soft brown sugar

4 firm pears

1 teaspoon arrowroot

1 tablespoon water

ground cinnamon, to sprinkle

low-fat fromage blanc, to serve

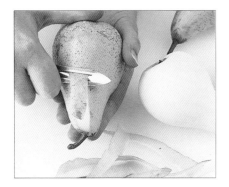

1 Place the cider, lemon peel, cinnamon stick, and sugar in a microwaveproof bowl. Microwave on HIGH for 3 to 5 minutes until boiling, stirring frequently to dissolve the sugar. Meanwhile, peel the pears thinly, leaving them whole with the stems on.

2 Add the pears to the cider syrup. Spoon the syrup over the pears. Three-quarters cover the dish with plastic wrap or with a lid. Microwave on HIGH for 5 to 6 minutes until the pears are just tender, turning and repositioning them in the bowl two or three times.

3 Carefully transfer the pears to another bowl using a perforated spoon. Microwave the cider syrup, uncovered, on HIGH for 15 to 17 minutes until it reduces by half.

4 Mix the arrowroot with the water in a small bowl until smooth, then stir it into the syrup. Microwave on HIGH for 1 minute, stirring twice, until clear and thick.

5 Pour the sauce over the pears and sprinkle with ground cinnamon. Leave to cool slightly. Serve warm with low-fat fromage blanc.

VARIATIONS

Other fruits can be poached in this spicy liquid. Try apples, peaches, or nectarines. Cook the fruit whole or cut in half or quarters. The apples are best peeled before poaching, but you can cook the peaches and nectarines with their skins on.

COOK'S TIP

Any variety of pear can be used, but it is best to choose firm pears, or they will break up easily— Conference are a good choice.

Honey-Fruit Yogurt Ice

INGREDIENTS

Serves 4 to 6

2 dessert apples, peeled, cored, and finely chopped

4 ripe bananas, roughly chopped

1 tablespoon lemon juice

2 tablespoons honey

1 cup thick plain yogurt

$\frac{1}{2}$ teaspoon ground cinnamon

crisp cookies, sliced hazelnuts, and banana slices, to serve

1 Place the apples in a small microwaveproof bowl, cover, and microwave on HIGH for 2 minutes, stirring once; leave to cool.

2 Place the bananas in a food processor or blender with the lemon juice, honey, yogurt, and cinnamon. Process until smooth and creamy. Add the cooked apples and process briefly to combine.

3 Pour the mixture into a freezer container and freeze until almost solid. Spoon back into the food processor and process again until smooth.

4 Return to the freezer until firm. Leave to soften at room temperature for 15 minutes. Serve in scoops, with crisp cookies, sliced hazelnuts, and banana slices.

Fall Pudding

INGREDIENTS

Serves 6

10 slices bread, at least one day old

1 tart cooking apple, peeled, cored and sliced

8 ounces ripe red plums, halved and pitted

8 ounces blackberries

4 tablespoons water

6 tablespoons superfine sugar

1 Remove the crusts from the bread and stamp out a 3-inch circle from one slice. Cut the remaining bread in half.

2 Place the bread circle in the bottom of a 5-cup bowl or pudding basin. Overlap the fingers around the sides, saving some for the top.

3 Mix the apple, plums, blackberries, water, and superfine sugar in a microwave-proof bowl. Cover and microwave on HIGH for 7 to 8 minutes until the sugar dissolves, the juices begin to flow and the fruit is soft. Stir twice during cooking.

4 Reserve the juice and spoon the fruit into the bread-lined bowl or basin. Top with the reserved bread, then spoon over the reserved fruit juices.

5 Cover the bowl or basin with a saucer and place weights on top. Chill the pudding overnight. Turn out onto a serving plate and serve with low-fat yogurt or fromage blanc.

Ruby Plum Mousse

INGREDIENTS

Serves 6

1 pound ripe red plums

3 tablespoons sugar

5 tablespoons water

4 tablespoons ruby port

1 tablespoon unflavored powdered gelatin

3 eggs, separated

$\frac{1}{2}$ cup superfine sugar

$\frac{2}{3}$ cup heavy cream

skinned and chopped pistachio nuts,
   to decorate

crisp cookies, to serve (optional)

1 Place the plums and sugar in a microwaveproof bowl. Add 2 tablespoons water. Cover and microwave on HIGH for 4 to 5 minutes, stirring once. Leave to stand for 3 minutes.

2 Press the fruit through a strainer to remove the pits and skins. Leave to cool, then stir in the port.

3 Pour the remaining 3 tablespoons water into a small bowl, sprinkle over the gelatin and leave to soften. Microwave on HIGH for 30 to 45 seconds until it is clear and dissolved. Stir into the plum purée.

4 Whisk the egg yolks and superfine sugar together until thick and mousse-like. Fold in the plum purée. Whip the cream until it stands in soft peaks and fold it in lightly using a large metal spoon.

5 Whisk the egg whites until they hold stiff peaks. Lightly fold them in using a metal spoon. Divide between six glasses and chill until set.

6 Decorate the mousses with chopped pistachio nuts and serve with crisp cookies, if liked.

Warm Fall Compote

A simple, yet very sophisticated, dessert using autumnal fruits.

INGREDIENTS

Serves 4

6 tablespoons superfine sugar

1 bottle red wine

1 vanilla bean, split

thinly pared strip of lemon peel

4 pears

2 purple figs, quartered

8 ounces raspberries

lemon juice, to taste

1 Put the sugar and wine in a large microwaveproof bowl. Stir in the vanilla bean and lemon peel. Microwave on HIGH for 4 to 6 minutes, stirring three times.

2 Peel and halve the pears, then scoop out the cores, using a melon baller. Add the pears to the syrup and stir well. Cover loosely and microwave on HIGH for 5 to 6 minutes, turning over two or three times during cooking so they color evenly.

3 Add the figs and microwave on HIGH for 2 minutes longer until the fruits are tender.

4 Transfer the poached pears and figs to a serving bowl using a perforated spoon, scatter the raspberries over.

5 Microwave the poaching liquid, uncovered, on HIGH for 5 to 7 minutes to reduce slightly and concentrate the flavor. Add a little lemon juice to taste. Strain the syrup over the fruits. Serve warm.

Tangerine Trifle

An unusual variation on a traditional trifle—add spirits, if you wish.

INGREDIENTS

Serves 4

5 trifle sponges, halved lengthwise

2 tablespoons apricot conserve

15 to 20 ratafia cookies

$4\frac{1}{2}$-ounce package tangerine-flavored
  jelly tablets

11-ounce can mandarin oranges, drained,
  juice reserved

$2\frac{1}{2}$ cups prepared custard

whipped cream and shreds of orange peel,
  to decorate

sugar for sprinkling

1 Spread the halved sponge cakes with apricot conserve. Arrange them in the bottom of a deep serving bowl or glass dish. Sprinkle the ratafia cookies over.

2 Break up the jelly into a microwaveproof pitcher. Add the juice from the canned mandarins and microwave on HIGH for 2 minutes; stir to dissolve the jelly.

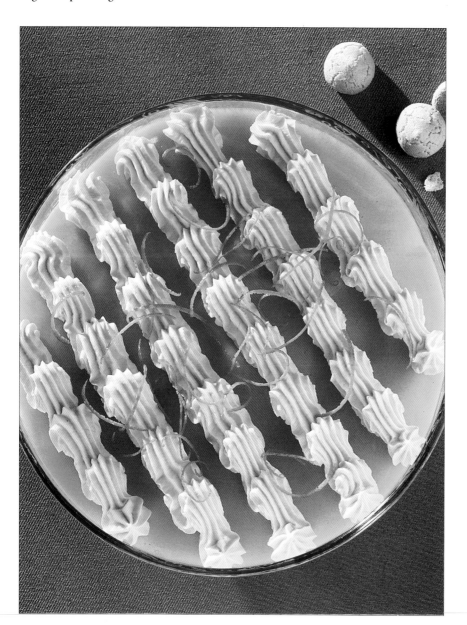

3 Make up the jelly to $2\frac{1}{2}$ cups with ice-cold water, stir well, and leave to cool for up to 30 minutes. Scatter the mandarin oranges over the cakes and ratafias.

4 Pour the jelly over the mandarin oranges, cake, and ratafias and chill for 1 hour, or until the jelly is set.

5 Pour the custard over the trifle and chill again. When ready to serve, pipe the whipped cream over the custard. Place the orange-peel shreds in a strainer and rinse under cold water. Sprinkle them with sugar and use to decorate the trifle.

Chocolate Fudge Sundaes

What better way is there to give everyone a weekend treat than to make these fabulous sundaes for Sunday tea?

INGREDIENTS

Serves 4

4 scoops each vanilla and coffee ice creams

2 small ripe bananas, sliced

whipped cream

toasted slivered almonds

For the sauce

$1/4$ cup soft light brown sugar

$1/2$ cup golden corn syrup

3 tablespoons strong black coffee

1 teaspoon ground cinnamon

5 ounces semi-sweet chocolate, chopped

$1/3$ cup whipping cream

3 tablespoons coffee liqueur (optional)

1 To make the sauce, place the sugar, syrup, coffee, and cinnamon in a large microwave-proof pitcher. Microwave on HIGH for 3 to 4 minutes, stirring once, until boiling and slightly thick.

2 Add the chocolate and stir until it melts. When smooth, stir in the cream and liqueur, if using. Leave the sauce to cool slightly.

3 Fill four serving glasses with a scoop each of vanilla and coffee ice creams.

4 Scatter the sliced bananas over the ice cream. Pour the warm fudge sauce over the bananas, then top each sundae with a generous swirl of whipped cream. Sprinkle with slivered almonds and serve at once before the ice cream melts.

VARIATION

Vary this endlessly by choosing other flavors of ice cream, such as strawberry, toffee, or chocolate. In the summer, substitute raspberries or strawberries for the bananas, and scatter chopped roasted hazelnuts on top in place of the slivered almonds.

Apricots with Orange Cream

Mascarpone is a very rich cream cheese made from thick Lombardy cream. It is delicious flavored with orange as a topping for these chilled, poached apricots.

INGREDIENTS

Serves 4

$2^1/_2$ cups ready-to-eat dried apricots

thinly pared strip of lemon peel

1 cinnamon stick

3 tablespoons sugar

$^2/_3$ cup sweet dessert wine (such as Muscat de Beaumes de Venise)

$^1/_2$ cup mascarpone cheese

3 tablespoons orange juice

pinch of ground cinnamon and fresh mint sprig, to decorate

1 Place the apricots, lemon peel, cinnamon stick, and 1 tablespoon of the sugar in a pan and cover with 2 cups cold water. Cover loosely and microwave on HIGH for 10 minutes. Leave to stand for about 5 minutes. Microwave on MEDIUM for 5 to 8 minutes until the fruit is tender.

2 Stir in the dessert wine. Leave until cold, then chill, for 3 to 4 hours, or overnight.

3 Mix together the mascarpone cheese, orange juice, and remaining sugar in a bowl and beat well until smooth. Chill until required.

4 Just before serving, remove the cinnamon stick and lemon peel from the apricots. Serve with a spoonful of the chilled mascarpone-orange cream, sprinkled with a little cinnamon and decorated with a sprig of fresh mint.

Rhubarb and Orange Fool

Perhaps this traditional English dessert got its name because it is so easy to make even a "fool" can attempt it.

INGREDIENTS

Serves 4

2 tablespoons orange juice

1 teaspoon finely shredded orange peel

$2^1/_4$ pounds (about 10 to 12 stems) rhubarb, chopped

1 tablespoon red-currant jelly

3 tablespoons sugar

$^2/_3$ cup prepared thick, creamy custard sauce

$^2/_3$ cup heavy cream, whipped

sweet cookies, to serve

1 Place the orange juice and peel, the rhubarb, red-currant jelly, and sugar in a microwave-proof bowl. Cover and microwave on HIGH for 8 to 10 minutes, stirring once, until the rhubarb is just tender but not mushy. Leave to cool completely.

2 Drain the cooled rhubarb to remove some of the liquid and reserve a few pieces with a little orange peel for decoration. Purée the remaining rhubarb in a food processor or blender, or press it through a strainer.

3 Stir the custard into the purée, then fold in the whipped cream. Spoon the fool into individual bowls, cover, and chill. Just before serving, top with the reserved fruit and peel. Serve with crisp, sweet cookies.

Fruit and Rice Ring

This unusual rice pudding looks beautiful turned out of a ring mold, but if you prefer, stir the fruit into the rice and serve it in individual dishes.

INGREDIENTS

Serves 4

5 tablespoons short-grain rice

$3\frac{1}{4}$ cups 2% milk

1 cinnamon stick

3 tablespoons sugar

finely grated peel of 1 small orange

$1\frac{1}{2}$ cups mixed dried fruit

$\frac{3}{4}$ cup orange juice

1 Place the rice, milk, and cinnamon stick in a large microwaveproof bowl. Cover and microwave on HIGH for 6 to 8 minutes, stirring two or three times, until boiling. Reduce the power setting to MEDIUM and microwave for 30 minutes longer, stirring twice, until no liquid remains. Remove the cinnamon stick and stir in the sugar and orange peel.

2 Place the fruit and orange juice in another microwaveproof bowl. Cover and microwave on HIGH for 6 minutes. Reduce the power setting to MEDIUM and microwave for 10 to 15 minutes until tender and no liquid remains.

3 Tip the fruit into the bottom of a lightly oiled $6\frac{1}{4}$-cup ring mold. Spoon the rice over, smoothing it down firmly. Cover and chill the pudding.

4 To serve, run a round-bladed knife around the edge of the mold and turn out the rice carefully onto a serving plate.

Lemon Soufflé with Blackberries

The simple fresh taste of the cold lemon mousse combines well with the rich blackberry sauce, and the color contrast looks wonderful, too. Blueberries or raspberries make equally delicious alternatives to blackberries.

INGREDIENTS

Serves 6

grated peel of 1 lemon and juice
   of 2 lemons

1 tablespoon unflavored powdered gelatin

5 extra-large eggs, separated

$\frac{3}{4}$ cup superfine sugar

few drops vanilla extract

$1\frac{2}{3}$ cups whipping cream

few fresh blackberries and blackberry
   leaves, to decorate

For the sauce

6 ounces blackberries (fresh or frozen)

2 to 3 tablespoons sugar

1 Place the lemon juice in a small microwaveproof bowl. Sprinkle the gelatin over and leave to soften. Microwave on HIGH for 30 to 45 seconds until it is clear and dissolves; leave to cool.

2 Put the lemon peel, egg yolks, sugar, and vanilla into a large bowl and whisk until the mixture is very thick, pale, and creamy.

3 Whisk the egg whites until stiff and almost peaky. Whip the cream until stiff and holding its shape.

4 Stir the gelatin mixture into the yolks. Fold in the whipped cream and lastly the egg whites. When lightly, but thoroughly, blended, pour into a $6\frac{1}{2}$ cup soufflé dish. Freeze for 2 hours.

5 To make the sauce, place the blackberries in a microwaveproof bowl with the sugar. Cover and microwave on HIGH for 2 to 3 minutes, stirring twice, until the juices begin to run and all the sugar dissolves. Pass through a fine strainer to remove the seeds. Cover and chill until ready to serve.

6 When the soufflé is almost frozen, but still spoonable, scoop or spoon onto individual plates and decorate with blackberries and blackberry leaves. Serve with the blackberry sauce.

Summer Berry Medley

Make the most of glorious seasonal fruits in this refreshing dessert. The sauce is also good swirled into plain or strawberry-flavored fromage blanc or yogurt.

INGREDIENTS

Serves 4 to 6

6 ounces redcurrants

6 ounces raspberries

$\frac{1}{4}$ cup sugar

2–3 tablespoons crème de framboise

1 to $1\frac{1}{2}$ pounds mixed soft summer fruits, such as strawberries, raspberries, blueberries, red currants, and black currants

vanilla ice cream, to serve

1 Strip the red currants from their stems using a fork and place in a bowl with the raspberries, sugar, and crème de framboise. Cover and leave to macerate for 1 to 2 hours.

2 Put the fruit with the macerating juices in a microwaveproof bowl. Cover and microwave on HIGH for 3 minutes, stirring once, until the fruit is just tender.

3 Pour the fruit into a blender or food processor and blend until smooth. Press through a nylon strainer to remove any seeds. Leave to cool, then chill.

4 Divide the mixed soft fruit between four glass serving dishes and pour the sauce over. Serve with scoops of good-quality vanilla ice cream.

Poached Pears in Red Wine

Serves 4

$1^{1}/_{4}$ cups red wine

6 tablespoons sugar

3 tablespoons honey

juice of $^{1}/_{2}$ lemon

1 cinnamon stick

1 vanilla bean, split open lengthwise

2-inch thinly pared strip of orange peel

1 clove

1 black peppercorn

4 firm, ripe pears

whipped cream or sour cream, to serve

1 Place the wine, sugar, honey, lemon juice, cinnamon stick, vanilla bean, orange peel, clove, and peppercorn in a microwaveproof bowl just large enough to hold the pears standing upright. Microwave on HIGH for 3 to 5 minutes, until boiling, stirring frequently to dissolve the sugar.

2 Meanwhile, peel the pears, leaving their stems intact. Take a thin slice off the bottom of each pear so it stands neatly square and upright.

COOK'S TIP

Remember that vanilla beans can be used more than once. Drain and dry a pod thoroughly, then store for future use.

3 Place the pears in the wine mixture, spooning it over them. Three-quarters cover the dish with plastic wrap or a lid. Microwave on HIGH for 5 to 6 minutes until the pears are just tender when pierced with the tip of a knife. Turn and reposition the pears in the bowl two or three times during cooking.

4 Carefully transfer the pears to another bowl using a perforated spoon. Microwave the poaching liquid, uncovered, on HIGH for 15 to 17 minutes until the syrup reduces by half; leave to cool. Strain the cooled liquid over the pears and chill them for at least 3 hours.

5 Place the pears in individual serving dishes and spoon a little of the red-wine syrup over. Serve with whipped or sour cream.

BAKING

Brown Soda Bread

Makes two 1-pound loaves

4 cups all-purpose flour

4 cups whole-wheat flour

2 teaspoons salt

1 tablespoon baking soda

4 teaspoons cream of tartar

2 teaspoons sugar

4 tablespoons butter

$3\frac{3}{4}$ cups buttermilk or skim milk

extra whole-wheat flour, to sprinkle

1 Sift all the dry ingredients into a large bowl, tipping any bran from the flour back into the bowl.

2 Rub the butter into the flour mixture. Add enough buttermilk or milk to make a soft dough; you may not need all of it, so add it cautiously.

3 Knead the dough lightly until smooth. Divide and shape it into two large balls and place on lightly oiled plates that are suitable for broiling. Cut a deep cross in the top of each loaf.

4 Sprinkle over a little extra wholemeal flour. Cook each loaf separately.

5 Microwave on MEDIUM for 5 minutes. Give the plate a half turn and microwave on HIGH for 3 minutes longer. Brown the top under a heated broiler if liked. Leave to stand for 10 minutes, then transfer to a wire rack to cool completely. Repeat with the second loaf. Best eaten on day of making.

COMBINATION MICROWAVE

This recipe is suitable for cooking in a combination microwave. Follow the oven manufacturer's timing guide for the best results.

Sage Soda Bread

This wonderful loaf, unlike bread made with yeast, has a velvety texture and a powerful sage aroma.

INGREDIENTS

Makes 1 loaf

3 cups whole-wheat flour

1 cup white bread flour

1 teaspoon salt

2 teaspoons baking soda

2 tablespoons shredded fresh sage

$1\frac{1}{4}$ to $1\frac{3}{4}$ cups buttermilk

1 Sift the dry ingredients into a large mixing bowl.

2 Stir in the sage and add enough buttermilk to make a soft dough.

COOK'S TIP

As an alternative to the sage, use finely chopped rosemary.

3 Shape the dough into a round loaf and place on a lightly oiled plate that is suitable for broiling. Cut a deep cross in the top.

4 Microwave on MEDIUM for 5 minutes. Give the plate a half turn and microwave on HIGH for 3 minutes longer. Brown the top under a heated hot broiler, if liked. Leave to stand for 10 minutes, then transfer to a wire rack to cool completely. Best eaten on the day of making.

COMBINATION MICROWAVE

This recipe is suitable for cooking in a combination microwave. Follow the oven manufacturer's timing guide for the best results.

Cheese and Marjoram Scones

Makes 18

1 cup whole-wheat flour

1 cup self-rising flour

pinch of salt

3 tablespoons butter

$\frac{1}{4}$ teaspoon dry mustard

2 teaspoons dried marjoram

$\frac{1}{2}$–$\frac{2}{3}$ cup finely grated
   cheddar cheese

about $\frac{1}{2}$ cup milk

$\frac{1}{3}$ cup pecans or walnuts,
   chopped

1 Sift the two types of flour into a bowl and add the salt. Cut the butter into small pieces, and rub it into the flour until the mixture resembles fine bread crumbs.

2 Add the mustard, marjoram, and grated cheese and stir in sufficient milk to make a soft dough. Knead the dough lightly.

3 Roll out the dough on a floured surface to about a $\frac{3}{4}$-inch thickness. Cut out about 18 scones, using a 2-inch square cookie cutter.

4 Brush the scones with a little milk and sprinkle the chopped pecans or walnuts over the top. Place the scones on a piece of nonstick parchment paper in the microwave, spacing them well apart. Microwave on HIGH for 3 to $3\frac{1}{2}$ minutes, repositioning the scones twice during cooking.

5 Insert a skewer into the middle of each scone: If it comes out clean, the scone is baked. Return any uncooked scones to the microwave and microwave on HIGH for 30 seconds longer. Brown under a heated hot broiler until golden, if liked. Serve warm, split and buttered.

VARIATION

For Herb and Mustard Scones, use 2 tablespoons chopped fresh parsley or chives instead of the dried marjoram and 1 teaspoon Dijon mustard instead of the dry mustard. Substitute $\frac{1}{2}$ cup chopped pistachio nuts for the pecans or walnuts.

Feta Cheese and Chive Scones

Makes 9

1 cup self-rising flour

$1\frac{1}{4}$ cups self-rising whole-wheat flour

$\frac{1}{2}$ teaspoon salt

3 ounces feta cheese

1 tablespoon snipped fresh chives

$\frac{2}{3}$ cup skim milk, plus extra for glazing

$\frac{1}{4}$ teaspoon cayenne pepper

3 Turn out the dough onto a floured surface and lightly knead until smooth. Roll out until $\frac{3}{4}$-inch thick and stamp out nine scones with a $2\frac{1}{2}$-inch cookie cutter. Brush with skim milk, then sprinkle the cayenne pepper over. Place the scones on a piece of nonstick parchment in the microwave, spacing them well apart.

4 Microwave on HIGH for 3 to $3\frac{1}{2}$ minutes, repositioning the scones twice during cooking. Insert a skewer into the middle of each scone; if it comes out clean, the scone is baked. Return any uncooked scones to the microwave and microwave for 30 seconds longer. Brown under a heated hot broiler until golden, if liked.

1 Sift the flours and salt into a mixing bowl, adding any bran left from the flour in the strainer.

2 Crumble the feta cheese and rub it into the dry ingredients. Stir in the chives. Add the milk and stir to make a soft dough.

Oat Tartlets with Minted Hummus

Serve these wholesome tartlets with a crisp salad of romaine lettuce.

INGREDIENTS

Serves 6

$1\frac{1}{2}$ cups medium steel-cut oats

$\frac{1}{2}$ teaspoon baking soda

1 teaspoon salt

2 tablespoons butter

1 egg yolk

2 tablespoons skim milk

14-ounce can garbanzo beans, rinsed and drained

juice of 1 or 2 lemons

$1\frac{1}{2}$ cups low-fat fromage blanc

4 tablespoons tahini

3 tablespoons chopped fresh mint

2 tablespoons pumpkin seeds

paprika for dusting

ground black pepper

1 Mix together the oats, baking soda, and salt in a large bowl. Rub in the butter until the mixture resembles fine bread crumbs. Stir in the egg yolk and add the milk if the mixture seems too dry.

2 Press the mixture into six $3\frac{1}{2}$-inch microwaveproof tartlet or mini quiche dishes and prick the bottoms and sides well with a fork. Microwave on HIGH for 4 to 6 minutes, repositioning twice during cooking, until cooked.

3 Purée the garbanzo beans, the juice of 1 lemon, fromage blanc, and tahini in a blender or food processor until smooth. Spoon into a bowl and season with black pepper and more lemon juice to taste. Stir in the chopped mint. Divide among the tartlet shells. Sprinkle with pumpkin seeds and dust with paprika.

Zucchini and Walnut Loaf

Cardamom seeds impart their distinctive aroma to this loaf. Serve this spread with ricotta and honey for a delicious snack.

INGREDIENTS

Makes 1 loaf

3 eggs

$\frac{1}{3}$ cup light muscovado sugar

$\frac{1}{2}$ cup sunflower oil

2 cups whole-wheat flour

1 teaspoon baking powder

1 teaspoon baking soda

1 teaspoon ground cinnamon

$\frac{3}{4}$ teaspoon ground allspice

$1\frac{1}{2}$ teaspoons green cardamom pods, seeds removed and crushed

1 cup zucchini coarsely grated

1 cup walnuts, chopped

$\frac{1}{4}$ cup sunflower seeds

1 Line the bottom and sides of a microwaveproof 9- x 5-inch bread pan with nonstick parchment paper.

2 Beat the eggs and sugar together in a large bowl and gradually add the oil.

3 Sift the flour into a separate bowl, adding the baking powder, baking soda, cinnamon, and allspice.

4 Mix the dry ingredients into the egg mixture, adding the cardamoms, zucchini, and walnuts. Reserve 1 tablespoon of the sunflower seeds, then add the remainder to the batter.

5 Spoon the batter into the bread pan. Level the top and sprinkle with the reserved sunflower seeds.

6 Shield each end of the dish with a smooth piece of foil, shiny side in. Cover with plastic wrap and microwave on HIGH for 8 to 9 minutes, giving the dish a quarter turn three or four times.

7 Remove the plastic wrap and foil for the last $1\frac{1}{2}$ minutes until the loaf is cooked, when a skewer inserted in the middle comes out clean. Leave to cool for 5 minutes before turning out onto a rack to cool completely. Brown under a heated hot broiler before serving, if liked.

COMBINATION MICROWAVE

This recipe is suitable for cooking in a combination microwave. Follow the oven manufacturer's timing guide for the best results.

Blueberry Crumble Quick Bread

Makes 8 pieces

4 tablespoons butter or margarine, at
    room temperature

$3/4$ cup superfine sugar

1 egg, at room temperature

$1/2$ cup milk

2 cups all-purpose flour

2 teaspoons baking powder

$1/2$ teaspoon salt

2 cups fresh blueberries or bilberries

For the topping

generous $1/2$ cup sugar

6 tablespoons all-purpose flour

$1/2$ teaspoon ground cinnamon

4 tablespoons butter, cut in pieces

1 Grease a 9- x 7-inch microwaveproof serving dish.

2 Cream the butter or margarine with the superfine sugar until light and fluffy. Beat in the egg, then stir in the milk.

3 Sift the flour, baking powder, and salt over and stir just enough to blend the ingredients.

4 Add the berries and stir them in lightly. Spoon the batter into the prepared dish.

5 For the topping, place the sugar, flour, ground cinnamon, and butter in a mixing bowl. Rub in the butter until the mixture resembles coarse bread crumbs; alternatively, cut in the butter with a pastry blender or two knives scissor-fashion.

6 Sprinkle the topping over the mixture in the baking dish. Microwave on MEDIUM for 12 minutes, rotating the dish twice during cooking. Brown under a heated hot broiler, if liked. Leave to stand for 5 minutes. Serve warm or cold.

Gingerbread

Serves 8 to 10

1 tablespoon vinegar

$\frac{3}{4}$ cup milk

$1\frac{1}{3}$ cups all-purpose flour

2 teaspoons baking powder

$\frac{1}{4}$ teaspoon baking soda

$\frac{1}{2}$ teaspoon salt

2 teaspoons ground ginger

1 teaspoon ground cinnamon

$\frac{1}{4}$ teaspoon ground cloves

$\frac{1}{2}$ cup butter, at room temperature

$\frac{1}{2}$ cup sugar

1 egg, at room temperature

$\frac{3}{4}$ cup molasses

whipped cream, to serve

chopped candied ginger, to decorate

1 Line the base of an 8-inch square shallow microwave-proof dish with waxed paper and grease the paper and sides of the dish.

2 Add the vinegar to the milk; set aside. The vinegar will curdle the milk.

3 Sift all the dry ingredients together three times in a mixing bowl; set aside.

4 Cream the butter and sugar until light and fluffy. Beat in the egg until well combined. Stir in the molasses.

5 Fold in the dry ingredients in four batches, alternately adding the curdled milk. Mix only enough to blend the ingredients.

6 Pour into the prepared dish and microwave on HIGH for 7 to 8 minutes until the cake is cooked and a skewer inserted into the middle of the cake comes out clean. Leave to cool in the dish until warm.

7 Cut into squares and serve warm, with whipped cream. Decorate with the candied ginger.

COMBINATION MICROWAVE

This recipe is suitable for cooking in a combination microwave. Follow the oven manufacturer's timing guide for the best results.

Spiced Banana Muffins

Whole-wheat muffins, with banana for added fiber, make a delicious, healthy treat at any time of the day. If liked, slice off the tops and fill with a teaspoon of jam or marmalade.

INGREDIENTS

Makes 12

$\frac{3}{4}$ cup whole-wheat flour

$\frac{1}{2}$ cup all-purpose flour

2 teaspoons baking powder

pinch of salt

1 teaspoon apple pie spice

$\frac{1}{4}$ cup soft light brown sugar

$\frac{1}{4}$ cup margarine, soft

1 egg, beaten

$\frac{2}{3}$ cup 2% milk

grated peel of 1 orange

1 ripe banana

$\frac{1}{4}$ cup oatmeal

scant $\frac{1}{4}$ cup chopped hazelnuts

1 Sift together both flours, the baking powder, salt, and apple pie spice into a bowl, then tip the bran remaining in the strainer into the bowl. Stir in the sugar.

2 Place the margarine in a microwaveproof bowl and microwave on HIGH for 1 minute until melted. Cool the margarine slightly, then beat in the egg, milk and grated orange peel.

3 Gently fold in the dry ingredients. Mash the banana with a fork, then stir it gently into the batter, being careful not to overmix.

4 Use the mixture to half-fill twelve double-thick paper cases. Cook six at a time, by placing them in a microwave muffin tray or in ramekin dishes. Combine the oatmeal and hazelnuts and sprinkle a little of the mixture over each muffin.

5 Place in the microwave, arranging the dishes in a circle. Microwave on HIGH for $2\frac{1}{2}$ to 3 minutes, rearranging once during cooking. Repeat with the remaining six muffins. Transfer to a wire rack and remove from their paper cases when cool enough to handle. Serve warm or cold.

Chocolate and Orange Angel Cake

This light-as-air cake with its fluffy frosting is virtually fat free, yet tastes heavenly. Make the frosting conventionally on the stovetop for best results.

INGREDIENTS

Serves 10

¼ cup all-purpose flour

2 tablespoons unsweetened cocoa powder

2 tablespoons cornstarch

pinch of salt

5 egg whites

½ teaspoon cream of tartar

½ cup superfine sugar

blanched and shredded peel of 1 orange, to decorate

For the frosting

1 cup superfine sugar

5 tablespoons water

1 egg white

1 Sift the flour, cocoa, cornstarch, and salt together three times. Whisk the egg whites in a large bowl until foamy. Add the cream of tartar and whisk again until soft peaks form.

2 Add the sugar to the egg whites, a spoonful at a time, whisking after each addition. Sift one-third of the flour and cocoa mixture over the meringue and gently fold in. Repeat, sifting and folding in the flour and cocoa mixture twice more.

3 Spoon the batter into a microwaveproof 8-inch ring mold and level the top. Microwave on MEDIUM for 10 to 12 minutes, rotating the dish twice. Leave to stand for 5 to 10 minutes. Turn upside-down on a wire rack and leave to cool in the dish. Carefully ease out of the dish.

4 Make the frosting conventionally: Put the sugar in a saucepan with the water and stir over low heat until it dissolves. Boil until the syrup reaches a temperature of 240°F on a candy thermometer, or when a drop of the syrup forms a soft ball when dropped into a cup of cold water. Remove from the heat.

5 Whisk the egg white until stiff. Add the syrup in a thin stream, whisking all the time. Continue to whisk until the frosting is very thick and fluffy.

6 Spread the frosting over the top and sides of the cooled cake. Sprinkle the orange peel over the top of the cake and serve.

Hot Chocolate Cake

This is wonderfully wicked, either hot as a pudding, to serve with a white chocolate sauce, or cold as a cake. The basic cake freezes well— thaw, then warm it in the microwave before serving.

INGREDIENTS

Makes 10 to 12 slices

$1\frac{3}{4}$ cups self-rising whole-wheat flour

$\frac{1}{4}$ cup unsweetened cocoa

pinch of salt

$\frac{3}{4}$ cup margarine, soft

$\frac{3}{4}$ cup soft light brown sugar

few drops vanilla extract

4 eggs

3 ounces white chocolate,
   roughly chopped

chocolate leaves and curls, to decorate

For the white chocolate sauce

3 ounces white chocolate

$\frac{2}{3}$ cup light cream

2 to 3 tablespoons milk

1 Sift the flour, cocoa, and salt into a bowl, adding the bran from the strainer.

2 Cream the margarine, sugar, and vanilla extract together until light and fluffy. Slowly beat in one egg.

3 Gradually stir in the remaining eggs, one at a time, alternately folding in some of the flour, until all the flour mixture is well blended.

4 Stir in the white chocolate and spoon the batter into a greased microwaveproof 9- x 5-inch bread pan. Shield each end of the dish with a small piece of smooth foil, shiny side in. Cover with plastic wrap and microwave on HIGH for 8 to 9 minutes, giving the dish a quarter turn three or four times during cooking. Remove the plastic wrap and foil for the last $1\frac{1}{2}$ minutes of the cooking time. The cake is cooked when a skewer inserted in the middle comes out clean. Leave to stand while making the sauce.

5 Place the chocolate and cream for the sauce in a microwave-proof bowl and microwave on MEDIUM for 2 to 3 minutes, until the chocolate melts. Add the milk and stir until cool.

6 Serve the cake sliced, in a pool of sauce, decorated with chocolate leaves and curls.

COMBINATION MICROWAVE

This recipe is suitable for cooking in a combination microwave. Follow your oven manufacturer's timing guide for the best results.

Apple and Hazelnut Shortcake

Serves 8 to 10

1 cup whole-wheat flour

4 tablespoons blanched hazelnuts,
 finely ground

4 tablespoons confectioners' sugar, sifted

10 tablespoons unsalted butter
 or margarine

3 sharp eating apples

1 teaspoon lemon juice

1 to 2 tablespoons sugar, or to taste

1 tablespoon chopped fresh mint, or
 1 teaspoon dried mint

1 cup whipping cream, crème fraîche, or
 sour cream

few drops vanilla extract

few mint leaves and whole hazelnuts,
 to decorate

1 Process the flour, ground hazelnuts, and confectioners' sugar with the butter in a food processor in short bursts. Alternatively, rub the butter into the dry ingredients until they come together. Do not overwork the mixture. Bring the dough together, adding a very little iced water, if necessary. Knead briefly, wrap in waxed paper and chill for 30 minutes.

2 Line the bottom of a 9-inch round shallow microwaveproof dish with waxed paper. Roll out the shortcake dough on a lightly floured surface to a round measuring about 9 inches in diameter.

3 Lift into the dish and press down well with the back of a spoon to level the surface and sides. Microwave on LOW for 8 minutes, or until a skewer, inserted into the middle of the shortcake, comes out clean. Give the dish a quarter turn every 2 minutes during cooking. Brown under a heated hot broiler until golden, if liked; leave to cool.

4 Meanwhile, peel, core, and chop the apples. Place in a microwaveproof bowl with the lemon juice. Add sugar to taste, cover, and microwave on HIGH for 5 to 7 minutes, stirring once, until tender. Mash the apple gently with the chopped fresh mint and leave to cool.

5 Whip the cream with the vanilla extract. Place the shortcake on a serving plate and top with the cooked apple.

6 Top the shortcake with the cream, swirling it into a decorative pattern. Decorate with a few mint leaves and whole hazelnuts. Serve at once.

COMBINATION MICROWAVE

This recipe is suitable for cooking in a combination microwave. Follow the oven manufacturer's timing guide for the best results.

Strawberry and Hazelnut Roulade

INGREDIENTS

Serves 6 to 8

2 large eggs

$\frac{1}{4}$ cup superfine sugar

$\frac{1}{2}$ cup all-purpose flour, sifted twice

3 tablespoons shelled hazelnuts, ground

$\frac{1}{2}$ cup heavy cream

1 egg white

$1\frac{1}{2}$ cups sliced strawberries

1 Line an 11- x 7-inch shallow rectangular microwaveproof dish with lightly greased waxed paper, leaving about 2 inches of the paper overlapping at the edges.

2 Whisk the eggs and sugar in a bowl until the mixture is very thick and has trebled in volume. Sift the flour over the egg mixture and fold it in with a large metal spoon. Pour the batter into the prepared dish, spreading it evenly.

3 Microwave on HIGH for $2\frac{1}{2}$ to 3 minutes until it is just firm in the middle, giving the dish a half turn once during the cooking time; leave to stand for 3 minutes.

4 Sprinkle a sheet of waxed paper with the ground hazelnuts. Turn the cake out onto the hazelnuts. Remove the lining paper. Hold another piece of waxed paper under a faucet for a few seconds to dampen it; crumple it up, spread it out again, and lay it on top of the cooked cake. Roll the cake up from one of the short edges, enclosing the paper. Let the cake cool completely on a wire rack.

5 Meanwhile, whip the cream until it stands in soft peaks. In another bowl, beat the egg white until stiff and fold it into the cream, mixing well.

6 Unroll the cake, remove the paper, spread the cream over the surface, and dot with the sliced strawberries. Roll up the cake again and place on a serving plate, seam side down. Chill the roulade for at least 1 hour until it becomes firm enough to slice. Just before serving, trim the ends to neaten.

Fruit-Topped Baked Cheesecake

Serves 6 to 8

4 tablespoons butter

2 cups crushed Graham crackers

$\frac{1}{2}$ cup ricotta cheese

1 cup quark

2 eggs, separated

1 tablespoon whole-wheat flour

3 tablespoons honey

2 teaspoons fresh orange juice

$\frac{2}{3}$ cup plain yogurt

$\frac{1}{3}$ cup golden raisins, chopped

about $1\frac{1}{4}$ cups mixed prepared fresh
   fruits, to decorate

1 Grease a 7-inch microwave-proof quiche dish. Line the bottom with waxed paper and grease the paper.

3 Place the ricotta in a bowl with the quark, egg yolks, flour, honey, orange juice, and yogurt and beat until smooth. Microwave the batter on MEDIUM for 7 to 8 minutes until thick, whisking every 2 minutes.

4 Stir in the golden raisins. Whisk the egg whites until they stand in stiff peaks and fold them into the cheesecake batter. Spoon over the prepared crumb crust.

5 Microwave on MEDIUM for 10 to 12 minutes until the cheesecake is just set in the middle, giving the dish a quarter turn every 3 minutes. Leave to stand until cool, then chill for 2 hours, or until firm enough to unmold, if liked. Alternatively, serve straight from the dish.

6 Top the cheesecake just before serving with the prepared fresh fruit or a favorite single fruit.

2 Place the butter in a microwaveproof bowl and microwave on HIGH for about 1 minute to melt. Add the Graham cracker crumbs and stir well. Use to line the bottom of the quiche dish, pressing the dough down flat with the back of a spoon.

Carrot and Pecan Cake

Fructose is used as the sweetening agent in this recipe. It has one and a half times the sweetening power as the same weight of sugar, but only has the same number of calories.

INGREDIENTS

Serves 6 to 8

$1\frac{1}{4}$ cups grated carrots

$\frac{1}{3}$ cup sunflower oil

2 tablespoons milk

2 eggs, beaten

6 tablespoons fructose

$\frac{2}{3}$ cup all-purpose flour

1 teaspoon baking powder

1 teaspoon baking soda

2 teaspoons ground cinnamon

$\frac{1}{2}$ cup raisins

$\frac{1}{4}$ cup shelled pecans, chopped

confectioners' sugar, to dust

1 Grease a 7-inch microwave-proof round cake dish and line it with waxed paper.

2 In a large bowl, beat the carrots with the oil, milk, eggs, and fructose, beating well.

3 Sift in the flour with the baking powder, baking soda, and cinnamon. Fold the dry mixture into the egg mixture, then stir in the raisins and pecans. Spoon the batter into the prepared cake dish and level the surface.

4 Place the cake dish on an inverted saucer in the microwave. Microwave on MEDIUM for 9 minutes, giving the dish a quarter turn every 3 minutes. Increase the power setting to HIGH and microwave for 2 to 3 minutes longer, giving the dish a quarter turn after $1\frac{1}{2}$ minutes.

5 The cake is cooked when it shrinks from the side of the dish. Leave the cake to stand for 10 minutes before turning it out of the dish to cool on a wire rack.

6 Sprinkle with sifted confectioners' sugar to serve.

Maple and Banana Quick Bread

INGREDIENTS

Serves 8 to 10

1 cup whole-wheat flour

1 teaspoon baking soda

2 bananas, mashed

4 tablespoons plain yogurt

4 tablespoons soft light brown sugar

5 tablespoons unsalted butter

1 egg, beaten

2 tablespoons maple syrup

$\frac{1}{2}$ cup dried dates, coarsely chopped

confectioners' sugar, to dust

1 Lightly grease a 9- x 5-inch microwaveproof bread pan and line the bottom with waxed paper.

2 Sift the whole-wheat flour with the baking soda, adding the bran left in the strainer.

3 Mix the bananas with the yogurt, brown sugar, butter, egg, and syrup, blending well. Add the flour mixture and dates and stir into a smooth batter. Spoon the batter into the bread pan and spread it out evenly.

4 To prevent the ends of the cake overcooking, wrap a 2-inch wide strip of smooth foil over each end of the dish. Place the dish on an inverted plate in the oven and microwave on MEDIUM for 10 minutes, giving the dish a quarter turn every $2\frac{1}{2}$ minutes.

5 Increase the power setting to HIGH and microwave for 2 minutes longer. Remove the foil, give the dish a quarter turn and microwave for 1 to 3 minutes longer until the quick bread shrinks from the sides of the dish. Leave to stand for 10 minutes before turning out to cool on a wire rack.

6 Sift a light coating of confectioners' sugar over the top of the cake before serving. Serve warm or cool.

Kugelhopf

Serves 10 to 12

1 cup crushed Graham crackers

15 blanched almonds

$1\frac{1}{4}$ cups milk

1 ounce fresh yeast, or $\frac{1}{2}$ ounce active-dry

2 tablespoons sugar

4 cups all-purpose flour

$\frac{3}{4}$ cup butter or margarine

3 large eggs, beaten

$\frac{1}{2}$ teaspoon salt

$\frac{1}{2}$ cup golden raisins

$\frac{1}{3}$ cup raisins

2 tablespoons currants

grated peel of 1 lemon

confectioners' sugar, to dust

strawberries, to serve

1 Grease a 9-inch microwave-proof ring mold and sprinkle the mold with the Graham cracker crumbs. Arrange the almonds on the bottom.

2 Pour the milk into a pitcher and microwave on HIGH for 1 minute, or until tepid. Stir in the fresh yeast; or reconstitute the active-dry yeast with the milk according to the package directions, adding 1 teaspoon of the sugar.

3 Place $1\frac{1}{2}$ cups of the flour in a microwaveproof bowl and gradually beat in the yeast mixture.

4 Cover loosely with plastic wrap and microwave on DEFROST for $1\frac{1}{2}$ to 2 minutes. Leave to stand until well risen and frothy, 10 to 15 minutes.

5 Place the butter or margarine in a microwaveproof bowl and microwave on HIGH for 1 to $1\frac{1}{2}$ minutes to melt. Add to the risen batter, together with the remaining sugar and flour, the eggs and salt. Beat the batter well with a wooden spoon. Stir in the golden raisins, raisins, currants, and lemon peel, mixing well. Spoon into the prepared mold and smooth the surface with a knife.

6 Cover the batter loosely with plastic wrap and microwave on DEFROST for 8 to 9 minutes until the batter rises to the top of the mold; leave to stand for 10 minutes. Microwave, uncovered, on HIGH for 6 minutes, giving the dish a quarter turn three times during cooking. Leave to stand for 5 minutes before turning out onto a wire rack.

7 When cool, dust the top with confectioners' sugar and fill the center with strawberries before serving.

Oat Florentines

These irresistible "bakes" make the best of familiar flapjacks and old-fashioned, chocolate-coated florentine cookies.

INGREDIENTS

Makes 16

6 tablespoons butter

3 tablespoons golden syrup or
   corn syrup

$1\frac{1}{4}$ cups oatmeal

2 tablespoons soft brown sugar

2 tablespoons chopped mixed candied peel

2 tablespoons candied cherries,
   coarsely chopped

$\frac{1}{4}$ cup hazelnuts, coarsely chopped

4 ounces semisweet chocolate

1 Lightly grease an 8-inch square microwaveproof shallow dish. Line the bottom with a sheet of rice paper.

2 Place the butter and syrup in a microwaveproof bowl and microwave on HIGH for $1\frac{1}{2}$ minutes to melt; stir well.

3 Add the oatmeal, sugar, peel, cherries, and hazelnuts, stirring well to blend.

COOK'S TIP

Rice paper is used for cooking in traditional recipes, as well as in microwave methods. It prevents doughs, such as this sweet oat base, from sticking by cooking onto them. When cooked, the rice paper can be eaten with the cookies or other items.

4 Spoon the dough into the dish and level the surface with the back of a spoon. Microwave on MEDIUM-HIGH for 6 minutes, giving the dish a half turn every 2 minutes; leave to cool slightly. Cut into 16 fingers and place them on a wire rack to cool.

5 Break the chocolate into pieces and place in a microwaveproof bowl. Microwave on HIGH for 2 to 3 minutes, stirring twice, until melted and smooth. Spread over the tops of the florentines and mark in a zigzag pattern with the prongs of a fork; leave to set.

Frosted Cupcakes

Makes about 24

1 cup self-rising flour

pinch of salt

4 tablespoons butter or margarine

4 tablespoons soft brown sugar

1 egg, beaten

milk, to mix

whipped cream or frosting, to top

candied cherries, angelica, candied orange
    slices, grated chocolate, chocolate
    vermicelli, or toasted coconut, to decorate

1 Sift the flour with the salt into a bowl. Rub in the butter or margarine until fine crumbs form. Stir in the sugar.

2 Mix in the beaten egg and sufficient milk to form a batter with a soft dropping consistency.

3 Place six paper cases in a six-hole microwaveproof muffin pan. Place spoonfuls of the prepared cake batter into each, filling them each about two-thirds full.

4 Microwave on HIGH for 2 minutes, giving the dish a half-turn after 1 minute. Transfer to a cooling rack. Repeat with the remaining batter, cooking in batches of six. Leave to cool completely before decorating.

5 To finish, pipe the tops of the cakes with swirls of whipped cream or coat with soft frosting. Decorate with an assortment of toppings. Serve on the same day of making.

COOK'S TIP

Make and eat microwave-cooked cupcakes on the same day. Alternatively, freeze them before adding any topping and decorations.

Chocolate Cupcakes Prepare the batter as shown, but add 1 tablespoon sifted unsweetened cocoa to the flour mixture.

Lemon Cupcakes Prepare the batter as shown, but add the grated peel of 1 lemon to the batter after mixing. Top with lemon-flavored frosting, if liked.

Coffee Cupcakes Prepare the batter as shown, but add 1 teaspoon coffee granules dissolved in a little boiling water to the batter with the eggs and milk. Top with coffee-flavored frosting, if liked.

Chocolate Chip Cupcakes Prepare the batter as shown, but add 1 ounce semisweet chocolate chips to the batter with the eggs and milk.

Fairy Cupcakes Prepare the batter as shown, but add 2 tablespoons currants to the batter with the eggs and milk.

Date-Filled Pastries

From Gibraltar to Baghdad, Jewish women traditionally get together to make hundreds of these labor-intensive pastries. Making a small quantity in the microwave is not so lengthy.

INGREDIENTS

Makes about 25

6 tablespoons margarine or butter, soft

$1\frac{1}{2}$ cups all-purpose flour

1 teaspoon rosewater

1 teaspoon orange-flower water

3 tablespoons water

4 teaspoons sifted confectioners' sugar, for sprinkling

For the filling

$\frac{2}{3}$ cup pitted dried dates

$\frac{1}{4}$ cup boiling water

$\frac{1}{2}$ teaspoon orange-flower water

1 To make the filling, chop the dates finely. Add the boiling water and orange-flower water and beat the mixture vigorously; leave to cool.

2 To make the pastries, rub the margarine or butter into the flour. Mix in the rose- and orange-flower waters and the water to make a firm dough.

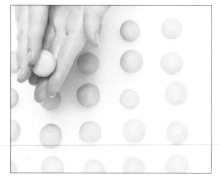

3 Shape the dough into about 25 small balls.

4 Press your finger into a ball of dough to make a small indentation, pressing the sides around and around to make the sides thinner. Put about $\frac{1}{4}$ teaspoon of the date mixture into the dough.

5 Seal by pressing the pastry together. Repeat with the remaining dough and filling.

6 Arrange the date pastries, seam side down, on parchment paper and prick each one with a fork. Microwave on HIGH for 3 to 5 minutes, rearranging twice during cooking. Leave to stand for 5 minutes before transferring to a rack to cool.

7 Put the cooled pastries on a plate and sprinkle the confectioners' sugar over. Shake lightly to make sure they are covered.

Coconut Pyramids

Without the danger of using a conventional oven, making a batch of these all-time favorites is an ideal wet-afternoon occupation for young children.

INGREDIENTS

Makes about 15

1 cup unsweetened shredded coconut

$\frac{1}{2}$ cup superfine sugar

2 egg whites

oil for greasing

1 Mix together the shredded coconut and sugar. Lightly whisk the egg whites. Fold enough egg white into the coconut to make a fairly firm dough. You may not need quite all the egg whites.

2 Form the dough into pyramid shapes by taking a teaspoonful and rolling it first into a ball. Flatten the base and press the top into a point. Arrange the pyramids on parchment paper, leaving space between them.

3 Microwave on HIGH for 2 to 3 minutes until the pyramids are just firm, but still soft inside. Transfer to a baking sheet and place under a heated hot broiler to tinge the tops golden, if liked.

COOK'S TIP

To freeze cookies, arrange in a single layer on a tray. When firm, pack in bags or boxes. Thaw for 1 hour before use.

4 Slide a metal spatula under the pyramids to loosen them. Leave to cool before removing from the baking sheet.

Cinnamon Balls

Ground almonds make these little cakes very moist. When cooked, they should be soft inside, with a pronounced cinnamon flavor. They harden, however, with keeping, so it is a good idea to freeze some—they can be defrosted quickly when required.

INGREDIENTS

Makes about 15

$1\frac{1}{2}$ cups blanched almonds, very finely ground

$\frac{1}{3}$ cup superfine sugar

1 tablespoon ground cinnamon

2 egg whites

oil for greasing

confectioners' sugar for dredging

1 Mix together the ground almonds, sugar, and cinnamon. Whisk the egg whites until they begin to stiffen. Fold enough egg whites into the almonds to make a fairly firm dough.

2 Wet your hands with cold water and roll small spoonfuls of the dough into smooth balls. Place these well apart on parchment paper.

3 Microwave on HIGH for $2\frac{1}{2}$ to $3\frac{1}{2}$ minutes, rearranging twice, until cooked but still slightly soft inside.

4 Slide a metal spatula under the balls to release them from the paper and leave to cool. Sift a few tablespoons of confectioners' sugar onto a plate. When the cinnamon balls are cold slide them onto the plate. Shake gently to completely cover the cinnamon balls in sugar.

COOK'S TIP

When completely cool, store the cinnamon balls in an airtight container. Alternatively, they keep well for up to about six months in the freezer.

Boston Banoffee Pie

INGREDIENTS

Makes an 8-inch pie

1 cup butter

$1\frac{1}{4}$ cups all-purpose flour

4 tablespoons sugar

7-ounce can skim, sweetened
  condensed milk

generous $\frac{1}{2}$ cup soft light brown sugar

2 tablespoons golden or corn syrup

2 small bananas, sliced

a little lemon juice

whipped cream, to decorate

1 teaspoon grated semisweet chocolate

1 Rub $\frac{1}{2}$ cup of the butter into the flour. Alternatively, process in a food processor until crumbled. Stir in the sugar.

2 Squeeze the mixture together with your hands until it forms a dough. Press into the bottom of an 8-inch microwaveproof quiche dish. Cut the dough away, leaving a $\frac{1}{4}$-inch overlap above the dish to allow for any shrinkage. Prick the bottom and side well with a fork.

3 Place a double-thick layer of paper towels over the bottom, easing it into position around the edges. Microwave on HIGH for $3\frac{1}{2}$ minutes, giving the dish a quarter turn every minute. Remove the paper and microwave on HIGH for $1\frac{1}{2}$ minutes longer; leave to cool.

4 Place the remaining $\frac{1}{2}$ cup butter in a large microwaveproof bowl or pitcher with the condensed milk, brown sugar, and golden syrup. Microwave on HIGH for 3 minutes, stirring well twice during cooking.

5 Microwave on HIGH for 3 to 5 minutes longer until the mixture thickens and turns a light caramel color, stirring three times. Pour into the cooked pastry shell and leave until cool.

6 Sprinkle the bananas with lemon juice and arrange on top of the caramel filling. Pipe a swirl of whipped cream in the center and sprinkle with the grated chocolate.

COOKING AND DEFROSTING CHARTS

~

Cooking Fish and Shellfish

COD steamed steaks and fillets	1 pound fillets 2 x 8-ounce steaks 4 x 8-ounce steaks	HIGH	Arrange fish fillets in a microwaveproof dish so the thin tail ends are to the center. Fold in any flaps of skin on steaks and secure with wooden toothpicks. Dot with a little butter, sprinkle with seasoning, and add a dash of lemon juice. Cover and microwave for 5 to 7 minutes for 1 pound fillets; 5 minutes for 2 x 8-ounce steaks; and 8 to 9 minutes for 4 x 8-ounce steaks, rearranging once halfway through cooking. Leave to stand, covered, for 3 minutes before serving.
FISH CAKES	4 x 3-ounces	HIGH	Place in a shallow microwaveproof dish and brush with a little melted butter, if liked. Microwave for 5 minutes, turning over once, halfway through cooking. Times refer to chilled or fresh fish cakes (thaw frozen fish cakes before cooking). Leave to stand for 2 to 3 minutes before serving. If liked, the fish cakes can be cooked in a heated browning dish.
FISHSTICKS	2 4 6 8 12	HIGH	For best results, cook in a heated browning dish. Microwave for 1½ minutes for 2; 2 minutes for 4; 3 minutes for 6; 4 minutes for 8; and 5 minutes for 12 fishsticks, turning over once, halfway through cooking. Times refer to frozen fishsticks. Leave to stand for 1 to 2 minutes before serving.
FISH ROES	4 ounces 8 ounces	LOW	Rinse the fish roes and place in a microwaveproof dish with a large knob of butter and seasoning to taste. Cover and microwave for 4 to 4½ minutes for 4 ounces; and 6 to 8 minutes for 8 ounces fish roes, stirring once halfway through cooking. Leave to stand, covered, for 2 minutes before serving.
FLOUNDER steamed fillets	1 pound fillets	HIGH	Arrange fish fillets in a microwaveproof dish so the thin tail ends are to the center of the dish. Dot with a little butter, sprinkle with seasoning, and add a dash of lemon juice. Cover and microwave for 4 to 6 minutes, rearranging once halfway through cooking. Leave to stand, covered, for 3 minutes before serving.
HADDOCK steamed steaks and fillets	1 pound fillets 2 x 8-ounce steaks 4 x 8-ounce steaks	HIGH	Arrange the fish fillets in a microwaveproof dish so the thin tail ends are to the center. Fold in any flaps of skin on steaks and secure with wooden toothpicks. Dot with a little butter, sprinkle with seasoning, and add a dash of lemon juice. Cover and microwave for 5 to 7 minutes for 1 pound fillets; 5 minutes for 2 x 8-ounce steaks; and 8 to 9 minutes for 4 x 8-ounce steaks, rearranging once halfway through cooking. Leave to stand, covered, for 3 minutes before serving.
HALIBUT steaks	2 x 8-ounce steaks	HIGH	Fold in any flaps of skin and secure with wooden toothpicks. Place in a shallow microwaveproof dish and dot with a little butter. Season with salt, pepper, and lemon juice. Cover and microwave for 4 to 5 minutes. Leave to stand, covered, for 2 to 3 minutes before serving.
HERRING fresh whole	per 1 pound	HIGH	Remove heads and clean and dress before cooking. Slash the skin in several places to prevent bursting during cooking. Place in a shallow microwaveproof dish and season to taste. Shield the tail ends of the fish if liked. Cover with paper towels and microwave for 3 to 4 minutes per 1 pound, turning over once halfway through cooking. Leave to stand, covered, for 2 to 3 minutes before serving.
KIPPERS fillets	2 4 8	HIGH	If buying whole fish, remove the heads and tails. Place skin-side down in a shallow microwaveproof cooking dish. Cover loosely and microwave for 1 to 2 minutes for 2 fillets; 3 to 4 minutes for 4 fillets; and 6 to 7 minutes for 8 fillets, rearranging once halfway through cooking. Leave to stand, covered, for 2 to 3 minutes before serving.

LOBSTER to reheat cooked whole lobster and tails	1 pound whole 1 pound tails	HIGH	Place in a shallow microwaveproof dish and cover loosely. Microwave for 6 to 8 minutes for 1 pound whole; and 5 to 6 minutes for 1 pound tails, turning over once halfway through cooking. Leave to stand, covered, for 5 minutes before serving.
MACKEREL fresh whole	per 1 pound	HIGH	Remove heads and clean and dress before cooking. Slash the skin in several places to prevent bursting during cooking. Place in a shallow microwave-proof dish and season to taste. Shield the tail ends of the fish if liked. Cover with paper towels and microwave for 3 to 4 minutes per 1 pound, turning over once halfway through cooking. Leave to stand, covered, for 2 to 3 minutes before serving.
MUSSELS fresh steamed	3 pints	HIGH	Discard any open mussels that do not close when sharply tapped. Sort the mussels and scrub thoroughly with cold running water. Place in a microwave-proof dish with 5 tablespoons water, fish stock, or dry white wine. Cover loosely and microwave for 5 minutes, stirring once halfway through cooking. Remove with a perforated spoon, discarding any mussels that do not open. Thicken the cooking juices with a little beurre manié (butter and flour paste), if liked, to serve with the mussels.
RED OR GRAY MULLET fresh whole	2 x 9 ounces 4 x 9 ounces	HIGH	Clean and dress before cooking. Place in a shallow microwaveproof dish and slash the skin in several places to prevent bursting during cooking. Cover and microwave for 4 to 5 minutes for 2 x 9-ounce mullet; and 8 to 9 minutes for 4 x 9-ounce mullet, turning over once halfway through cooking. Leave to stand, covered, for 5 minutes before serving.
SALMON steamed steaks	2 x 8 ounces 4 x 8 ounces	HIGH	Place in a shallow microwaveproof dish so the narrow ends are to the center of the dish. Dot with butter and sprinkle with lemon juice and salt and pepper. Cover with paper towels and microwave for $2\frac{1}{2}$ to 3 minutes for 2 x 8-ounce steaks; and $4\frac{1}{2}$ to $5\frac{3}{4}$ minutes for 4 x 8-ounce steaks, turning over once halfway through cooking. Leave to stand, covered, for 5 minutes before serving.
	4 x 6-ounce steaks	MEDIUM	Prepare and cook as above, but use MEDIUM power and allow $10\frac{1}{2}$ to $11\frac{1}{2}$ minutes.
whole salmon and salmon trout	1 pound 2 pounds 3 to $3\frac{1}{2}$ pounds 4 to $4\frac{1}{2}$ pounds	HIGH	Remove the head if liked. Slash or prick the skin in several places to prevent bursting during cooking. Place in a microwaveproof dish with $\frac{2}{3}$ cup boiling water and a dash of lemon juice. Cover and microwave for $4\frac{1}{2}$ to 5 minutes for a 1-pound fish, $8\frac{1}{2}$ to $10\frac{1}{2}$ minutes for a 2-pound fish; 11 to $14\frac{1}{2}$ minutes for a 3- to $3\frac{1}{2}$-pound fish; and $14\frac{1}{2}$ to $18\frac{1}{2}$ minutes for a 4- to $4\frac{1}{2}$-pound fish, rotating 3 times during cooking. Leave to stand, covered, for 5 minutes before serving.
SCALLOPS steamed fresh	1 pound	MEDIUM	Remove from their shells. Place in a shallow microwaveproof dish and cover with paper towels. Microwave for 8 to 12 minutes, rearranging once, halfway through cooking. Leave to stand, covered, for 3 minutes before serving.
SHRIMP to boil	1 pound 2 pounds	HIGH	Rinse and place in a microwaveproof dish with $2\frac{1}{2}$ cups water, a dash of vinegar or lemon juice, and a bay leaf if liked. Cover and microwave for 6 to 8 minutes for 1 pound; 8 to 10 minutes for 2 pounds, stirring once halfway through cooking. Leave to stand, covered, for 3 minutes before draining and shelling.

SOLE steamed fillets	1 pound	HIGH	Arrange fish fillets in a microwaveproof dish so the thin tail ends are to the center of the dish. Dot with a little butter, season, and add a dash of lemon juice. Cover and microwave for 4 to 6 minutes, rearranging once half-way through cooking. Leave to stand, covered, for 3 minutes before serving.
SMOKED HADDOCK steamed fillets	1 pound	HIGH	Arrange fish fillets in a microwaveproof dish so the thin tail ends are to the center of the dish. Dot with butter, sprinkle with seasoning, and add a dash of lemon juice. Cover and microwave for 5 to 6 minutes, rearranging once halfway through cooking. Leave the fish to stand, covered, for 3 minutes before serving.
poached fillets	1 pound	HIGH	Place the fillets in a shallow microwaveproof dish with the thin tail ends to the center. Pour $\frac{1}{2}$ cup milk over, dot with a little butter, and season to taste. Cover and microwave for 5 to 6 minutes, rearranging once halfway through cooking. Leave to stand, covered, for 3 minutes before serving.
TROUT whole	2 x 9 ounces 4 x 9 ounces	HIGH	Clean and gut before cooking. Place in a shallow microwaveproof dish. Slash the skin in several places to prevent bursting during cooking. Dot with butter if liked and season to taste. Cover and microwave for 4 to 5 minutes for 2 x 9-ounce trout; and 8 to 9 minutes for 4 x 9-ounce trout, turning over once halfway through cooking. Leave the fish to stand, covered, for 5 minutes before serving.
WHITING steamed fillets	1 pound	HIGH	Arrange fish fillets in a microwaveproof dish so the thin tail ends are to the center of the dish. Dot with a little butter, sprinkle with seasoning, and add a dash or two of lemon juice. Cover and microwave for 4 to 6 minutes, rearranging once halfway through cooking. Leave to stand, covered, for 3 minutes before serving.

Monkfish with Mexican Salsa

Cooking Poultry and Game

CHICKEN			
whole roast fresh chicken	2¼ pounds 3 to 3½ pounds 4 to 4½ pounds	HIGH	Rinse, dry, and truss the chicken into a neat shape. Season and calculate the cooking time after weighing (and stuffing). Cook breast-side down for half of the cooking time and breast-side up for the remaining cooking time. Brush with a browning agent, if liked, and shield the wingtips with foil if necessary. Microwave for 12 to 16 minutes for a 2¼-pound chicken; 18 to 24 minutes for a 3 to 3½-pound chicken; 25 to 36 minutes for a 4 to 4½-pound chicken. Cover with foil and leave to stand for 10 to 15 minutes before carving.
portions	1 x 8-ounce portion 2 x 8-ounce portions 4 x 8-ounce portions	HIGH	Prick with a fork and brush with a browning agent, if liked. Alternatively, crisp and brown under a heated hot broiler after cooking. Cover with buttered parchment paper to cook. Microwave for 5 to 7 minutes for an 8-ounce portion; 10 to 12 minutes for 2 x 8-ounce portions; 18 to 24 minutes for 4 x 8-ounce portions. Leave to stand, covered, for 5 to 10 minutes before serving.
drumsticks	2 4 8	HIGH	Prick with a fork and brush with a browning agent, if liked. Alternatively, crisp and brown under a heated hot broiler after cooking. Cover with buttered parchment paper to cook. Microwave for 3 to 5 minutes for 2 drumsticks; 8 to 9 minutes for 4 drumsticks; 16 to 19 minutes for 8 drumsticks. Leave to stand, covered, for 5 to 10 minutes before serving.
thighs	8	HIGH	Prick with a fork and brush with a browning agent, if liked. Alternatively, crisp and brown under a heated hot broiler after cooking. Cover with buttered parchment paper to cook. Microwave 8 thighs for 17 to 20 minutes. Leave to stand, covered, for 5 to 10 minutes before serving.
breast halves	2 4	HIGH	Prick with a fork and brush with a browning agent, if liked. Alternatively, crisp and brown under a heated hot broiler after cooking. Cover with buttered parchment paper to cook. Microwave for 2 to 3 minutes for 2 breasts; 3½ to 4 minutes for 4 breasts. Leave to stand, covered, for 5 to 10 minutes before serving.
livers, fresh or thawed frozen	8 ounces 1 pound	HIGH	Rinse well and prick to prevent bursting during cooking. Place in a microwaveproof dish with a knob of butter. Cover loosely and microwave for 2 to 3 minutes for 8 ounces; and 5 to 6 minutes for 1 pound, stirring twice during cooking. Leave to stand for 2 minutes before serving or using.
DUCK			
whole roast fresh duck	4 to 4½ pounds 5 to 5¼ pounds per 1 pound	HIGH	Rinse, dry, and truss the duck into a neat shape, securing any tail-end flaps of skin to the main body. Prick thoroughly and place on a rack or upturned saucer in a microwaveproof dish for cooking. Cook breast-side down for half of the cooking time, and breast-side up for the remaining cooking time. Microwave for 28 to 32 minutes for a 4- to 4½-pound duck; 35 to 40 minutes for a 5- to 5¼-pound duck; or calculate times at 7 to 8 minutes per 1 pound. Drain away excess fat 3 times during cooking and shield tips, tail end, and legs with foil if necessary. Cover with foil and leave to stand for 10 to 15 minutes before serving. Crisp the skin under a heated hot broiler if liked.
GAME BIRDS			
whole roast	1 x 1 pound 2 x 1 pound 1 x 2 pounds 2 x 2 pounds	HIGH	Rinse, dry, and truss the birds into a neat shape. Brush with a browning agent if liked. Cover with parchment paper to cook. Microwave for 9 to 10 minutes for a 1-pound bird; 18 to 22 minutes for 2 x 1-pound birds; 20 to 22 minutes for a 2-pound bird; and 35 to 40 minutes for 2 x 2-pound birds, turning over twice during cooking. Leave to stand, covered, for 5 minutes before serving.

TURKEY

whole roast fresh	6 pounds 9 pounds 12 pounds larger birds over 12 pounds *per* *1 pound*	HIGH	Rinse, dry, and stuff the turkey, if liked. Truss into a neat shape and weigh to calculate the cooking time. Brush with melted butter or browning agent, if liked. Divide the cooking time into quarters and cook breast-side down for the first quarter, on one side for the second quarter, on the remaining side for the third quarter, and breast-side up for the final quarter. Shield any parts that start to cook faster than others with small strips of foil. Microwave for 42 minutes for a 6-pound bird; 63 minutes for a 9-pound bird; 84 minutes for a 12-pound bird; or allow 7 minutes per 1 pound for larger birds. When cooked, cover with foil and leave to stand for 10 to 25 minutes (depending upon size of bird) before carving.
drumsticks	2 x 12 ounces	HIGH *then* MEDIUM	Place on a roasting rack, meaty sections downward. Baste with a browning agent, if liked. Cover and microwave on HIGH for 5 minutes, then on MEDIUM for 13 to 15 minutes, turning once. Leave to stand, covered, for 5 minutes before serving.
breast halves	2 x 8-ounce breast halves 4 x 8-ounce breast halves	MEDIUM	Beat out flat, if preferred, and place in a shallow dish. Baste with browning agent if liked. Microwave for 8 to 10 minutes for 2 x 8-ounce breast halves; and 16 to 18 minutes for 4 x 8-ounce breast halves, turning over once. Leave to stand for 2 to 3 minutes before serving.

Dijon Chicken Salad

Hot Chili Chicken

Cooking Meat

BACON back and slices	4 slices 1 pound	HIGH	Place small quantities between sheets of paper towels, larger quantities on a plate or microwaveproof bacon rack covered with paper towels. Microwave for $3\frac{1}{2}$ to 4 minutes for 4 slices; and 12 to 14 minutes for 1 pound, turning over once. Leave to stand for 1 to 2 minutes before serving.

BEEF
roast joint
	per 1 pound	HIGH *then*
		MEDIUM
			Ideally place the joint on a microwaveproof roasting rack or upturned saucer inside a roasting bag. Calculate the cooking time according to weight and microwave on HIGH for the first 5 minutes, then on MEDIUM for the remaining time. Turn the joint over halfway through the cooking time.
			
			per 1 pound
			topside or sirloin (boned and rolled)
			    rare 8 to 9 minutes
			    medium 11 to 12 minutes
			    well done 15 to 16 minutes
			forerib or back rib (on the bone)
			    rare 7 to 8 minutes
			    medium 13 to 14 minutes
			    well done 15 minutes
			rib roast (boned and rolled)
			    rare 11 to 12 minutes
			    medium 13 to 14 minutes
			    well done 15 to 16 minutes
			
			Cover with foil after cooking and leave to stand for 10 to 15 minutes before carving.

ground beef	1 pound	HIGH	Place in a microwaveproof dish, cover, and microwave for 10 to 12 minutes, breaking up and stirring twice.
hamburgers	1 x 4 ounces 2 x 4 ounces 3 x 4 ounces 4 x 4 ounces	HIGH	Ideally cook in a heated browning dish. If this isn't possible, cook on a roasting rack and increase the times slightly. Microwave for $2\frac{1}{2}$ to 3 minutes for 1; $3\frac{1}{2}$ to 4 minutes for 2; $4\frac{1}{2}$ to 5 minutes for 3; and 5 to $5\frac{1}{2}$ minutes for 4, turning over once halfway through the cooking time. Leave to stand for 2 to 3 minutes before serving.
meatloaf	1 pound loaf	HIGH	Place your favorite 1-pound seasoned beef mixture in a microwaveproof loaf dish, packing in firmly and leveling the surface. Microwave for 7 minutes, allow to stand for 5 minutes, then microwave for 5 minutes longer. Leave to stand, covered with foil, for 3 minutes before serving.
steaks	2 x 8-ounce rump, sirloin or tenderloin steaks 4 x 8-ounce sirloin or tenderloin steaks	HIGH	Cook with or without the use of a browning dish. If cooking without, brush with a browning agent, if liked, prior to cooking. Place in a lightly oiled microwaveproof dish and turn over halfway through the cooking time. Microwave for 5 to $5\frac{1}{2}$ minutes for 2 x 8-ounce steaks; and $7\frac{1}{2}$ to $8\frac{1}{2}$ minutes for 4 x 8-ounce steaks. If using a browning dish, heat first, add a little oil, and brush to coat the bottom. Add the steaks, pressing down well. Turn the steaks over halfway through the cooking time. Microwave for $2\frac{1}{4}$ to $2\frac{1}{2}$ minutes for 2 x 8-ounce steaks; and $3\frac{1}{2}$ to 4 minutes for 4 x 8-ounce steaks. Leave to stand for 1 to 2 minutes before serving.

HAM

braised steaks	4 x 4-ounce steaks	HIGH	Remove the rind and scissor-snip the fat off the ham steaks. Place in a large, shallow microwaveproof dish. Add $2/3$ cup wine, apple cider, or fruit juice (and marinate for 1 hour if liked). Microwave for 4 minutes, rearranging once. Leave to stand, covered, for 5 minutes before serving.
raw joint	per 1 pound	HIGH	Place in a pierced roasting bag in a microwaveproof dish. Microwave for 12 to 14 minutes per 1 pound, turning over halfway through the cooking time. Cover with foil and leave to stand for 10 minutes before carving.

KIDNEYS

fresh lamb, pig, or ox	4 ounces 8 ounces 1 pound	HIGH	Halve and core the kidneys. Heat a browning dish. Add 1 teaspoon oil and the kidneys. Microwave for 4 minutes for 4 ounces; 6 to 8 minutes for 8 ounces; and 12 to 15 minutes for 1 pound, turning and rearranging twice. Leave to stand, covered, for 3 minutes before serving.

LAMB

roast joint	per 1 pound	HIGH *then* MEDIUM	Place the joint on a microwaveproof roasting rack or upturned saucer inside a dish and shield any thin or vulnerable areas with a little foil. Calculate the cooking time according to weight and microwave on HIGH for the first 5 minutes, then on MEDIUM for the remaining time. Turn the joint over halfway through the cooking time.

per 1 pound

leg joint with bone		
	rare	8 to 10 minutes
	medium	10 to 12 minutes
	well done	12 to 14 minutes
boned leg joints		
	rare	10 to 12 minutes
	medium	13 to 15 minutes
	well done	16 to 18 minutes
shoulder joints		
	rare	7 to 9 minutes
	medium	9 to 11 minutes
	well done	11 to 13 minutes

chops and steaks	2 loin chops 4 loin chops 2 sirloin chops 4 sirloin chops	HIGH	Brush with a browning agent, if liked, or cook in a browning dish. Microwave for 6 to 7 minutes for 2 loin chops; 8 to 9 minutes for 4 loin chops; 6 to 8 minutes for 2 sirloin chops; and 8 to 10 minutes for 4 sirloin chops, turning over halfway through the cooking time. Leave to stand for 2 to 3 minutes before serving.
rack	2- to $2\frac{1}{2}$-pound rack with 7 ribs	HIGH	Chop rack in half and place both pieces together, bones interleaved guard-of-honor style, then tie in place. Place on a microwaveproof roasting rack. Microwave for 12 minutes for rare; 13 minutes for medium; and $14\frac{1}{2}$ to 15 minutes for well-done lamb, rotating the dish every 3 minutes. Cover with foil and leave to stand for 10 minutes before carving.

LIVER

fresh lamb liver	1 pound	HIGH	Heat a browning dish. Add 1 tablespoon oil and 1 tablespoon butter. Add sliced, washed, and dried liver, pressing down well. Microwave for 1 minute, turn over and microwave for 4 to 5 minutes longer, rearranging once. Leave to stand for 2 minutes before serving.

PORK

roast joint	per 1 pound	HIGH *or* MEDIUM	Place the joint in a microwaveproof dish on a rack if possible. Times are given for roasting on HIGH or MEDIUM. Both methods work well, but the latter tends to give a crisper crackling. Turn the joint over halfway through cooking. Brown and crisp under a heated hot grill after cooking, if liked, and before the standing time. Calculate the cooking time according to weight and microwave for: *per 1 pound* loin and leg, joints on bone HIGH 8 to 9 minutes *or* MEDIUM 12 to 14 minutes loin and leg joints (boned) HIGH 8 to 10 minutes *or* MEDIUM 13 to 15 minutes Cover with foil after cooking and leave to stand for 10 to 20 minutes before carving.
chops	2 loin chops 4 loin chops	HIGH	Brush with a browning agent, if liked, or cook in a browning dish. Microwave for 4 to 5 minutes for 2 loin chops; 6 to 8 minutes for 4 loin chops, turning over once halfway through cooking. Leave to stand for 5 minutes before serving.
pork tenderloin	12 ounces	HIGH *then* MEDIUM	Shield the narrow, thin ends of the tenderloin with a little foil. Place on a microwaveproof roasting rack or upturned saucer in a dish. Microwave on HIGH for 3 minutes, then on MEDIUM for 10 to 15 minutes, turning over once. Leave to stand, covered with foil, for 5 to 10 minutes before serving.
sausages, 2-ounce links	2 4 8	HIGH	Prick and place on a microwaveproof roasting rack in a dish if possible. Brush with a browning agent, if liked, or cook in a heated browning dish. Microwave for 2½ minutes for 2; 4 minutes for 4; and 5 minutes for 8 sausages, turning over once halfway through the cooking time. Leave to stand for 2 minutes before serving.

VEAL

roast joint	per 1 pound	HIGH *or* MEDIUM	Place the joint on a microwaveproof rack or upturned saucer in a dish. Times are given for cooking on HIGH *or* MEDIUM. Both methods work well, but the latter is ideal for less-tender cuts or large joints. Calculate the cooking time according to weight and microwave for: *per 1 pound* HIGH 8½ to 9 minutes *or* MEDIUM 11 to 12 minutes Turn the joint over halfway through the cooking time. Cover with foil after cooking and leave to stand for 15 to 20 minutes before carving.

Beef and Mushroom Burgers

Cooking Vegetables

ARTICHOKES			
globe	1 2 4	HIGH	Discard the tough, outer leaves. Snip the tops off the remaining leaves and trim the stems to the base. Wash and stand upright in a microwaveproof bowl. Pour the water and lemon juice over: use 6 tablespoons water and $1\frac{1}{2}$ teaspoons lemon juice for 1; $\frac{1}{2}$ cup water and 1 tablespoon lemon juice for 2; and $\frac{2}{3}$ cup water and 2 tablespoons lemon juice for 4. Cover and microwave for 5 to 6 minutes for 1; 10 to 11 minutes for 2; and 15 to 18 minutes for 4, basting and rearranging twice. Leave to stand for 5 minutes before serving.
Jerusalem	1 pound	HIGH	Peel and cut into even-size pieces. Place in a microwaveproof bowl with 4 tablespoons water or 2 tablespoons butter. Cover and microwave for 8 to 10 minutes, stirring once. Leave to stand, covered, for 3 to 5 minutes before serving.
ASPARAGUS			
fresh whole spears	1 pound	HIGH	Prepare and arrange in a shallow microwaveproof dish with pointed tops to the center. Add $\frac{1}{2}$ cup water. Cover and microwave for 12 to 14 minutes, rearranging the spears half way through the time but still keeping the tips to the center of the dish.
fresh-cut spears	1 pound	HIGH	Prepare and place in a large shallow microwaveproof dish. Add $\frac{1}{2}$ cup water. Cover and microwave for 9 to 11 minutes, rearranging once. Leave to stand, covered, for 5 minutes before serving.
BEANS			
fresh green	8 ounces whole 1 pound whole $1\frac{1}{2}$ cups cut 3 cups cut	HIGH	Place whole or cut beans in a microwaveproof bowl and add 2 tablespoons water. Cover and microwave for 8 to 10 minutes for 8 ounces whole beans; 15 to 18 minutes for 1 pound whole beans; 7 to 9 minutes for $1\frac{1}{2}$ cups cut beans; and 12 to 15 minutes for 3 cups cut beans, stirring once. Leave to stand, covered, for 2 to 3 minutes before serving.
fresh baby green whole or thin green whole beans	8 ounces 1 pound	HIGH	Place in a microwaveproof bowl with 2 tablespoons water. Cover and microwave for 7 to 9 minutes for 8 ounces; 12 to 15 minutes for 1 pound, stirring 3 times. Leave to stand, covered, for 2 to 3 minutes, before serving.
fresh sliced runner beans	$1\frac{1}{2}$ cups 3 cups	HIGH	Place in a microwaveproof bowl with 2 tablespoons water. Cover and microwave for 7 to 9 minutes for $1\frac{1}{2}$ cups; 12 to 15 minutes for 3 cups, stirring 3 or 4 times. Leave to stand, covered, for 2 to 3 minutes before serving.
fresh shelled fava beans	$1\frac{1}{2}$ cups 3 cups	HIGH	Place in a microwaveproof bowl and add the water: 5 tablespoons for 8 ounces beans; and $\frac{1}{2}$ cup for 1 pound beans. Cover and microwave for 5 to 7 minutes for 8 ounces; 6 to 10 minutes for 1 pound, stirring once. Leave to stand, covered, for 2 to 3 minutes before serving.
BEETS			
fresh	4 medium	HIGH	Wash the beets and pierce the skin with a fork, but do not peel. Place in a shallow microwaveproof dish with 4 tablespoons water. Cover loosely and microwave for 14 to 16 minutes, rearranging twice. Leave to stand, covered, for 5 minutes before removing skins to serve or use.
BROCCOLI			
fresh spears	8 ounces 1 pound	HIGH	Place spears in a large shallow microwaveproof dish with tender heads to center of dish. Add 4 tablespoons water. Cover and microwave for 4 to 5 minutes for 8 ounces; 8 to 9 minutes for 1 pound, rotating the dish once. Leave to stand, covered, for 2 to 4 minutes before serving.
fresh pieces	8 ounces 1 pound	HIGH	Cut into 1-inch pieces. Place in a microwaveproof bowl with 4 tablespoons water. Cover and microwave for $4\frac{1}{2}$ to 5 minutes for 8 ounces; $8\frac{1}{2}$ to $9\frac{1}{2}$ minutes for 1 pound, stirring once. Leave to stand, covered, for 3 to 5 minutes before serving.

BRUSSEL SPROUTS			
fresh	1 pound 2 pounds	HIGH	Remove outer leaves, trim, and cross-cut the bottoms. Place in a microwave-proof dish and add water: 4 tablespoons for 1 pound; ½ cup for 2 pounds. Cover and microwave for 6 to 7 minutes for 1 pound; 12 to 14 minutes for 2 pounds, stirring once. Leave to stand, covered, for 3 to 5 minutes before serving.
CABBAGE			
fresh	8 ounces 1 pound	HIGH	Core and shred, and place in a large microwaveproof dish. Add water: 4 tablespoons for 8 ounces; ½ cup for 1 pound. Cover and microwave for 7 to 9 minutes for 8 ounces; 9 to 11 minutes for 1 pound, stirring once. Leave to stand, covered, for 2 minutes before serving.
CARROTS			
fresh baby whole and sliced	1 pound whole 3 cups sliced	HIGH	Place in a microwaveproof dish with 4 tablespoons water. Cover and microwave for 12 to 14 minutes for whole; 10 to 12 minutes for sliced. Leave to stand, covered, for 3 to 5 minutes before serving.
CAULIFLOWER			
fresh whole	1½ pounds	MEDIUM	Trim but leave whole, and place floweret-side down in a microwaveproof dish with 1 cup water. Cover and microwave for 16 to 17 minutes, turning over once. Leave to stand for 3 to 5 minutes before serving.
fresh flowerets	1½ cups 3 cups	HIGH	Place in a microwaveproof dish with water: 3 tablespoons for 1½ cups; 4 tablespoons for 3 cups. Cover and microwave for 7 to 8 minutes for 1½ cups; 10 to 12 minutes for 3 cups, stirring once. Leave to stand for 3 minutes before serving.
CELERY			
fresh sliced	1 head (about 9 stalks)	HIGH	Slice into ¼-inch pieces and place in a shallow microwaveproof dish with 2 tablespoons water and 2 tablespoons butter. Cover and microwave for 5 to 6 minutes, stirring once. Leave to stand, covered, for 3 minutes before serving.
fresh celery hearts	4 hearts	HIGH	Halve each celery heart lengthwise and place in a shallow microwaveproof dish. Add 2 tablespoons water and a knob of butter if liked. Cover and microwave for 4½ to 5 minutes, turning once. Leave to stand, covered, for 3 minutes before serving.
CHARD			
fresh	1 pound	HIGH	Remove and discard the thick stem and shred the leaves. Place in a microwaveproof dish with ⅔ cup water. Cover and microwave for 5½ to 6½ minutes, stirring every 3 minutes. Leave to stand for 2 minutes before serving. Season after cooking.
CHINESE CABBAGE			
fresh	1 pound	HIGH	Slice and place in a large microwaveproof dish. Add 2 to 3 tablespoons water. Cover and microwave for 6 to 8 minutes, stirring once. Leave to stand, covered, for 3 to 5 minutes. Season after cooking.
CORN			
corn on the cob, fresh husked	1 x 6-ounce 2 x 6-ounce 3 x 6-ounce 4 x 6-ounce	HIGH	Wrap individually in plastic wrap or place in a microwaveproof dish with 4 tablespoons water and cover. Place or arrange evenly in the oven and microwave for 3 to 4 minutes for 1; 5 to 6 minutes for 2; 7 to 8 minutes for 3; and 9 to 10 minutes for 4, rotating and rearranging once. Leave to stand, covered, for 3 to 5 minutes before serving.
CURLY KALE			
fresh	1 pound	HIGH	Remove the thick stalk and stems, then shred. Place in a microwaveproof bowl with ⅔ cup water. Cover and microwave for 15 to 17 minutes, stirring every 5 minutes. Leave to stand for 2 minutes before serving.

EGGPLANT			
fresh cubes	2¼ cups	HIGH	Cut unpeeled eggplant into ¾-inch cubes. Place in a microwaveproof bowl with 2 tablespoons butter. Cover and microwave for 7 to 10 minutes, stirring every 3 minutes. Leave to stand, covered, for 4 minutes. Season *after* cooking.
fresh whole	8 ounces 2 x 8-ounces	HIGH	Peel off stems, rinse, and dry. Brush with a little oil and prick. Place on paper towels and microwave for 3 to 4 minutes for 1 eggplant; 4 to 6 minutes for 2, turning over once. Leave to stand for 4 minutes. Scoop out flesh and use as required.
ENGLISH MARROW			
fresh	1 pound	HIGH	Peel, remove seeds, and cut into small, neat dice. Place in a microwaveproof dish without water. Cover loosely and microwave for 7 to 10 minutes, stirring once. Leave to stand, covered, for 2 to 3 minutes before serving.
FENNEL			
fresh sliced	3 cups	HIGH	Place in a microwaveproof bowl with 3 tablespoons water. Cover and microwave for 9 to 10 minutes, stirring once. Leave to stand, covered, for 2 to 3 minutes before serving.
KOHLRABI			
fresh sliced	1 pound 2 pounds	HIGH	Trim away the root ends and stems, scrub and peel the bulb, and cut into ¼-inch slices. Place in a microwaveproof bowl with water: 3 tablespoons for 1 pound; and 5 tablespoons for 2 pounds. Cover and microwave for 5 to 6 minutes for 1 pound; 9 to 11 minutes for 2 pounds, stirring twice. Leave to stand, covered, for 3 to 4 minutes. Drain to serve.
LEEKS			
fresh whole	1 pound 2 pounds	HIGH	Trim and slice from the top of the white to the green leaves in 2 or 3 places. Wash thoroughly and place in a microwaveproof dish with water: 3 tablespoons for 1 pound; and 5 tablespoons for 2 pounds. Cover and microwave for 3 to 5 minutes for 1 pound; 6 to 8 minutes for 2 pounds, rearranging twice. Leave to stand, covered, for 3 to 5 minutes before serving.
fresh sliced	3 cups	HIGH	Place in a microwaveproof dish with 3 tablespoons water. Cover and microwave for 8 to 10 minutes, stirring once. Leave to stand, covered, for 2 to 3 minutes before serving.
MUSHROOMS			
fresh whole	8 ounces 1 pound	HIGH	Trim and wipe mushrooms. Place in a microwaveproof dish with water or butter: 2 tablespoons butter or 2 tablespoons water for 8 ounces mushrooms; and 3 tablespoons butter or 3 tablespoons water for 1 pound mushrooms. Cover and microwave for 3 to 4 minutes for 8 ounces; and 4 to 5 minutes for 1 pound, stirring twice. Leave to stand for 1 to 2 minutes before serving. Season after cooking.
fresh sliced	3 cups 6 cups	HIGH	As above, but microwave for 2 to 3 minutes for 3 cups mushrooms; and 3 to 4 minutes for 6 cups mushrooms.
OKRA			
fresh	1 pound	HIGH	Top and tail, and sprinkle lightly with salt. Leave to drain for 30 minutes. Rinse and place in a microwaveproof dish with 2 tablespoons water or 2 tablespoons butter. Cover and microwave for 8 to 10 minutes, stirring once. Leave to stand, covered, for 3 minutes before serving.
ONIONS			
fresh whole	4	HIGH	Peel and place in a microwaveproof dish. Cover and microwave for 10 to 12 minutes, rearranging and rotating once. Leave to stand, covered, for 2 minutes before serving.
fresh sliced	3 cups	HIGH	Peel and cut into thin wedges or slices. Place in a microwaveproof dish with 2 tablespoons butter and 2 tablespoons water. Cover loosely and microwave for 7 to 10 minutes, stirring once. Leave to stand, covered, for 5 minutes before serving.

PAK CHOI (or bok choy cabbage)	1 pound	HIGH	Slice stems and leaves and place in a large microwaveproof dish. Add 2 tablespoons water and microwave for 6 to 8 minutes, stirring once. Leave to stand for 3 to 5 minutes before serving.
PARSNIPS fresh whole	1 pound	HIGH	Peel and prick with a fork. Arrange in a microwaveproof dish with tapered ends to the center. Dot with 1 tablespoon butter and add 3 tablespoons water and 1 tablespoon lemon juice. Cover and microwave for 9 to 12 minutes, rearranging once. Leave to stand, covered, for 3 minutes before serving.
fresh slices	3 cups	HIGH	Peel and slice. Place in a microwaveproof dish with 1 tablespoon butter, 3 tablespoons water, and 1 tablespoon lemon juice. Cover and microwave for 9 to 12 minutes, stirring twice. Leave to stand, covered, for 3 minutes before serving.
PEAS fresh	$\frac{2}{3}$ cup $1\frac{1}{2}$ cups 3 cups	HIGH	Place shelled peas in a microwaveproof bowl with butter and water: 1 tablespoon butter and 2 teaspoons water for $\frac{2}{3}$ cup peas; 2 tablespoons butter and 1 tablespoon water for $1\frac{1}{2}$ cups peas; and 4 tablespoons butter and 2 tablespoons water for 3 cups peas. Cover and microwave for 3 minutes for $\frac{2}{3}$ cup; 4 to 5 minutes for $1\frac{1}{2}$ cups; and 6 to 8 minutes for 3 cups, stirring once. Leave to stand, covered, for 3 to 5 minutes before serving.
POTATOES whole potatoes to be mashed	2 pounds	HIGH	Peel and cut into $\frac{1}{2}$-inch cubes. Place in a microwaveproof bowl with 5 tablespoons water. Cover and microwave for 11 to 13 minutes, stirring once. Leave to stand, covered, for 5 minutes. Drain and mash with butter and seasoning to taste.
new potatoes or old, peeled and quartered	1 pound	HIGH	Scrub and scrape new potatoes, if liked. Peel and quarter old potatoes. Place in a microwaveproof dish with 4 tablespoons water. Cover and microwave for 7 to 10 minutes for new; and 6 to 8 minutes for old, stirring once. Leave to stand, covered, for 5 minutes before serving.
baked	6 ounces 2 x 6-ounce 3 x 6-ounce 4 x 6-ounce	HIGH	Scrub and prick the skin. Place on a double sheet of paper towels. Microwave for 4 to 6 minutes for 1; 6 to 8 minutes for 2; 8 to 12 minutes for 3; 12 to 15 minutes for 4, turning over once. If cooking more than 2 potatoes, arrange in a ring pattern. Leave to stand for 5 minutes, before serving.
PUMPKIN fresh	1 pound	HIGH	Remove the skin, seeds and membrane and cut into 1-inch cubes. Place in a microwaveproof dish with 1 tablespoon butter. Cover and microwave for 4 to 6 minutes, stirring twice. Leave to stand for 3 minutes, then season to serve plain, or mashed with cream and herbs.
RUTABAGAS fresh	1 pound	HIGH	Peel and cut into $\frac{1}{2}$-inch cubes. Place in a microwaveproof bowl with 1 tablespoon butter and 2 tablespoons water. Cover and microwave for 10 to 12 minutes, stirring twice. Leave to stand, covered, for 4 minutes. Drain to serve.
SNOW PEAS fresh	4 ounces 8 ounces	HIGH	Trim and place in a microwaveproof bowl with water: 1 tablespoon for 4 ounces; 2 tablespoons for 8 ounces. Cover and microwave for 3 to 4 minutes for 4 ounces; and 4 to 5 minutes for 8 ounces, stirring once. Leave to stand, covered, for 2 minutes before serving.
SPINACH fresh	1 pound	HIGH	Chop or shred and rinse. Place in a microwaveproof bowl without any extra water. Cover and microwave for 6 to 8 minutes, stirring once. Leave to stand for 2 minutes before serving. Season after cooking.

SQUASH fresh	1 pound	HIGH	Pierce whole squash with a knife several times. Microwave for 3 to 5 minutes per 1 pound until the flesh pierces easily with a skewer. Leave to stand for 5 minutes. Halve, scoop out the seeds and fibers and discard them. Serve fresh in chunks or mashed with butter.
SWEET POTATOES fresh	1 pound, whole 3 cups, cubed	HIGH	If cooking whole, prick the skins and place on paper towels. Microwave for 7 to 9 minutes, turning twice. Leave to cool for handling and peel away the skins to serve. To cook cubes, place in a microwaveproof bowl with 3 tablespoons water. Cover and microwave for 6 to 8 minutes, stirring twice. Drain and toss with butter and seasoning. Leave to stand for 2 minutes before serving.
TOMATOES whole and halves	1 medium 4 medium 4 large (beefsteak)	HIGH	Prick whole and/or halved tomatoes, arrange in a circle on a plate, cut-sides up. Dot with butter and season to taste. Microwave for 30 seconds for 1 medium; 2 to 2½ minutes for 4 medium; and 3½ to 4 minutes for 4 large (beefsteak) tomatoes, according to size and ripeness. Leave to stand for 1 to 2 minutes before serving.
TURNIPS whole	1 pound	HIGH	Choose only small to medium turnips. Peel and prick with a fork. Arrange in a ring pattern in a shallow microwaveproof dish. Dot with 1 tablespoon butter and add 3 tablespoons water. Cover and microwave for 14 to 16 minutes, rearranging once. Leave to stand, covered, for 3 minutes before serving.
sliced or cubed	3 cups	HIGH	Place slices or cubes in a microwaveproof dish with 1 tablespoon butter and 3 tablespoons water. Cover and microwave for 11 to 12 minutes for slices; and 12 to 14 minutes for cubes. Leave to stand, covered, for 3 minutes before serving.
ZUCCHINI fresh	8 ounces 1 pound	HIGH	Top and tail and slice thinly. Place in a microwaveproof dish with butter: 2 tablespoons for 8 ounces; 3 tablespoons for 1 pound. Cover loosely and microwave for 4 to 6½ minutes for 8 ounces; 6 to 8 minutes for 1 pound, stirring once. Leave to stand, covered, for 2 to 3 minutes before serving.

Broccoli and Chestnut Terrine

Middle Eastern Vegetable Stew

Cooking Frozen Vegetables

ASPARAGUS frozen whole spears	1 pound	HIGH	Place in a microwaveproof dish with ½ cup water. Cover and microwave for 9 to 12 minutes, rearranging once. Leave to stand for 5 minutes before serving.
BEANS frozen green beans	8 ounces whole 1 pound whole 1½ cups cut 3 cups cut	HIGH	Place in a microwaveproof bowl with water, cover, and microwave with 2 tablespoons water for 9 to 10 minutes for 8 ounces whole beans; 4 tablespoons water and 14 to 15 minutes for 1 pound whole beans; 2 tablespoons water and 6 to 7 minutes for 1½ cups cut beans; and 4 tablespoons water and 10 to 12 minutes for 3 cups cut beans, stirring once. Leave to stand, covered, for 2 to 3 minutes before serving.
frozen baby green or thin whole beans	8 ounces 1 pound	HIGH	Place in a microwaveproof bowl with water, cover, and microwave with 2 tablespoons water for 8 to 9 minutes for 8 ounces beans; and 4 tablespoons water and 13 to 15 minutes for 1 pound beans, stirring 3 times. Leave to stand, covered, for 2 to 3 minutes before serving.
frozen sliced runner beans	1½ cups 3 cups	HIGH	Place in a microwaveproof bowl with water, cover, and microwave with 2 tablespoons water for 6 to 7 minutes for 8 ounces beans; and 4 tablespoons water and 10 to 12 minutes for 1 pound beans, stirring twice. Leave to stand, covered, for 2 to 3 minutes before serving.
frozen shelled fava beans	8 ounces 1 pound	HIGH	Place in a microwaveproof bowl with water, cover and microwave with 4 tablespoons water for 6 to 7 minutes for 8 ounces beans; and ½ cup and 10 to 11 minutes for 1 pound beans, stirring twice. Leave to stand, covered, for 2 to 3 minutes before serving.
BROCCOLI frozen spears	1 pound	HIGH	Place in a microwaveproof dish with 4 tablespoons water. Cover and microwave for 13 to 14 minutes, stirring once. Leave to stand, covered, for 2 to 3 minutes before serving.
BRUSSEL SPROUTS frozen	1 pound	HIGH	Place in a microwaveproof dish with 2 tablespoons water. Cover and microwave for 10 to 11 minutes, stirring once. Leave to stand, covered, for 3 to 5 minutes before serving.
CABBAGE frozen	8 ounces 1 pound	HIGH	Place in a large microwaveproof dish with water, cover and microwave with 4 tablespoons water for 6 to 8 minutes for 8 ounces; and ½ cup water and 8 to 10 minutes for 1 pound, stirring once. Leave to stand, covered, for 2 minutes before serving.
CARROTS frozen whole and sliced	1 pound whole 3 cups sliced	HIGH	Place in a microwaveproof dish with water. Cover and microwave with 2 tablespoons water for 10 to 12 minutes for whole carrots; and 2 tablespoons water and 8 to 10 minutes for sliced carrots, stirring once. Leave to stand, covered, for 2 to 3 minutes before serving.
CAULIFLOWER frozen flowerets	1 pound	HIGH	Place in a microwaveproof dish with 4 tablespoons water. Cover and microwave for 8 to 9 minutes, stirring once. Leave to stand, covered, for 2 to 3 minutes before serving.
CORN frozen sweetcorn kernels	1 pound	HIGH	Place in a microwaveproof dish with 4 tablespoons water. Cover and microwave for 7 to 8 minutes, stirring once. Leave to stand, covered, for 2 to 3 minutes before serving.

LEEKS frozen sliced	1 pound	HIGH	Place in a microwaveproof dish with 3 tablespoons water. Cover and microwave for 11 to 12 minutes, stirring once. Leave to stand, covered, for 2 to 3 minutes before serving.
MIXED VEGETABLES frozen	8 ounces 1 pound	HIGH	Place in a microwaveproof dish with water. Cover and microwave with 2 tablespoons water for 4 to 5 minutes for 8 ounces; and 2 tablespoons water and 7 to 8 minutes for 1 pound, stirring once. Leave to stand, covered, for 2 minutes before serving.
MUSHROOMS frozen whole button	4 ounces 8 ounces	HIGH	Place in a shallow microwaveproof dish with a knob of butter. Cover and microwave for 3 to 4 minutes for 4 ounces; and 5 to 6 minutes for 8 ounces, stirring twice. Leave to stand, covered, for 1 to 2 minutes. Season to taste to serve.
PARSNIPS frozen whole	1 pound	HIGH	Arrange in a shallow microwaveproof dish with tapered ends to center. Cover and microwave for 9 to 10 minutes, rearranging once. Toss in butter and seasonings to serve. Leave to stand, covered, for 2 to 3 minutes before serving.
PEAS frozen	8 ounces 1 pound	HIGH	Place in a microwaveproof dish with water. Cover and microwave with 2 tablespoons water for 4 to 6 minutes for 8 ounces; and 4 tablespoons water and 6 to 8 minutes for 1 pound, stirring once. Leave to stand, covered, for 3 minutes.
RUTABAGA frozen cubed	1 pound	HIGH	Place in a microwaveproof dish, cover, and microwave for 8 to 10 minutes, stirring twice. Leave to stand, covered, for 2 to 3 minutes. Toss in butter and seasonings or mash with same to a purée.
SNOW PEAS frozen	8 ounces	HIGH	Place in a microwaveproof dish with 2 tablespoons water. Cover and microwave for 3 to 4 minutes, stirring once. Leave to stand, covered, for 2 to 3 minutes before serving.
SPINACH frozen	10-ounce package	HIGH	Place in a microwaveproof dish. Cover and microwave for 7 to 9 minutes, stirring twice to break up during cooking. Season *after* cooking.
ZUCCHINI frozen sliced	1 pound	HIGH	Place in a shallow microwaveproof dish with 3 tablespoons butter, if liked. Cover loosely and microwave for 7 to 8 minutes, stirring once. Leave to stand, covered, for 2 to 3 minutes before serving.

Summer Vegetable Braise

Mixed Mushroom Ragout

Cooking Pasta, Legumes, and Grains

BARLEY pot barley	heaping ¾ cup	HIGH *then* MEDIUM	Toast if liked before cooking. Place in a microwaveproof dish with 1 quart boiling water and a pinch of salt, if liked. Cover loosely and microwave on HIGH for 3 minutes, then on MEDIUM for 40 minutes. Leave to stand for 5 to 10 minutes before fluffing with a fork to serve.
BULGAR grains	1⅓ cups	HIGH *then* MEDIUM	Place in a microwaveproof dish with 2¼ cups boiling water and a pinch of salt, if liked. Cover loosely and microwave on HIGH for 3 minutes, then on MEDIUM for 9 to 12 minutes. Leave to stand for 5 to 10 minutes before fluffing with a fork to serve.
COUSCOUS precooked	2 cups	MEDIUM	Place in a microwaveproof dish with 1 cup boiling water and 4 tablespoons butter. Cover loosely and microwave for 15 minutes. Leave to stand for 5 to 10 minutes before fluffing with a fork to serve.
DRIED BEANS adzuki black black-eye peas borlotti broad cannellini fava flageolet haricot mung pinto red kidney soy	1½ cups	HIGH *then* MEDIUM	Soak dried beans overnight in cold water or hasten soaking by par-cooking in the microwave. Place the dried beans in a microwaveproof bowl with boiling water to cover. Cover and microwave on HIGH for 5 minutes. Leave to stand, covered, for 1½ hours before draining to cook. Place soaked or par-cooked beans in a microwaveproof dish and cover with boiling water. Cover and microwave all beans on HIGH for 10 minutes. Reduce the power to MEDIUM and microwave adzuki, black-eye peas, mung and pinto beans for 10 to 15 minutes; and black, borlotti, butter, cannellini, fava, flageolet, haricot, red kidney, and soy beans for 20 to 25 minutes, adding extra boiling water to cover if needed. Drain to use.
DRIED GARBANZO BEANS	1⅓ cups	HIGH *then* MEDIUM	Soak dried beans overnight, or according to package directions. Place soaked peas in a microwaveproof dish and cover with boiling water. Cover and microwave on HIGH for 10 minutes, then on MEDIUM for 20 to 25 minutes, adding extra boiling water to cover if needed. Drain to use.
DRIED WHOLE GREEN PEAS	1⅓ cups	HIGH *then* MEDIUM	Soak dried peas overnight, or according to package directions. Place soaked peas in a microwaveproof dish and cover with boiling water. Cover and microwave on HIGH for 10 minutes, then on MEDIUM for 10 to 15 minutes, adding extra boiling water to cover if needed. Drain to use.
DRIED SPLIT PEAS	heaping 1 cup	HIGH	Soak dried peas overnight, or according to package directions. Place soaked peas in a microwaveproof dish and cover with boiling water. Cover and microwave on HIGH for 10 minutes. Drain to use.
DRIED LENTILS	heaping 1 cup	HIGH	Place the lentils in a microwaveproof dish with a few seasoning vegetables, such as chopped onion, celery, carrot or bouquet garni and a squeeze of lemon juice. Add 3¾ cups boiling water or stock. Cover and microwave for 15 to 25 minutes, stirring once halfway through cooking. Cook for the shorter length of time if the lentils are to be served in a salad mixture or as a meal accompaniment, the longer time if the lentils are to be puréed for use.
MILLET	1⅓ cups	HIGH *then* MEDIUM	Toast if liked before cooking. Place in a microwaveproof dish with 2¾ cups boiling water and a pinch of salt, if liked. Cover loosely and microwave on HIGH for 3 minutes, then on MEDIUM for 12 minutes. Leave to stand for 5 to 10 minutes before fluffing with a fork to serve.

STEEL-CUT OATS grains	1 cup	HIGH *then* MEDIUM	Toast if liked before cooking. Place in a microwaveproof dish with 3 cups boiling water and a pinch of salt, if liked. Cover loosely and microwave on HIGH for 3 minutes, then on MEDIUM for 20 to 22 minutes. Leave to stand for 5 to 10 minutes before fluffing with a fork to serve.
PASTA fresh: egg noodles spaghetti tagliatelle ravioli	8 ounces	HIGH	Place the pasta in a large microwaveproof dish. Cover with 3 cups boiling water and add 1 teaspoon oil. Cover loosely and microwave for 2 to 2½ minutes for egg noodles; 4 to 6 minutes for spaghetti; 2 to 3 minutes for tagliatelle; and 6 to 8 minutes for ravioli, stirring once halfway through the cooking time. Leave to stand for 2 minutes before draining to serve.
dried: egg noodles spaghetti tagliatelle short-cut macaroni pasta shapes ravioli	8 ounces	HIGH	Place the pasta in a large microwaveproof dish. Add a generous 5 cups of boiling water and 1 teaspoon oil. Cover loosely and microwave: 6 minutes for egg noodles; 10 to 12 minutes for spaghetti; 6 minutes for tagliatelle; 10 minutes for short-cut macaroni; 10-12 minutes for pasta shapes; and 10 minutes for ravioli, stirring once halfway through the cooking time. Leave to stand for 3 to 5 minutes before draining to use.
RICE long-grain white	heaping ½ cup heaping 1 cup	HIGH *then* MEDIUM	Place the rice in a large microwaveproof dish. Add boiling water: 1¼ cups for a heaping ½ cup rice; and 2¼ cups for a heaping 1 cup rice with a pinch of salt and knob of butter, if liked. Cover loosely and microwave on HIGH for 3 minutes. Stir well, then re-cover and microwave on MEDIUM for 12 minutes. Leave to stand, covered, for 5 minutes before fluffing with a fork to serve.
long-grain brown	⅔ cup 1½ cups	HIGH *then* MEDIUM	Place the rice in a large microwaveproof dish. Add boiling water: 1¼ cups for ⅔ cup; 2¼ cups for 1½ cups rice with a pinch of salt and knob of butter, if liked. Cover loosely and microwave on HIGH for 3 minutes. Stir well, then re-cover and microwave on MEDIUM for 25 minutes. Leave to stand, covered, for 5 minutes before fluffing with a fork to serve.
long-grain and wild rice mix	14-ounce package	HIGH *then* MEDIUM	Place the rice mixture in a microwaveproof dish with 2¾ cups boiling water, a pinch of salt, and knob of butter, if liked. Cover loosely and microwave on HIGH for 3 minutes. Stir well, re-cover, and microwave on MEDIUM for 12 minutes, stirring once. Leave to stand, covered, for 5 minutes before fluffing with a fork to serve.
RYE grains	1 cup	HIGH *then* MEDIUM	Soak the rye grains for 6 to 8 hours in cold water, then drain. Place in a microwaveproof dish with 3 cups boiling water. Cover loosely and microwave on HIGH for 3 minutes, then on MEDIUM for 40 minutes. Leave to stand 5 to 10 minutes before fluffing with a fork to serve.
WHEAT berries	heaping 1 cup	HIGH *then* MEDIUM	Soak wheat berries for 6 to 8 hours in cold water, then drain. Place in a microwaveproof dish with 4 cups boiling water. Cover loosely and microwave on HIGH for 3 minutes, then on MEDIUM for 40 minutes. Leave to stand 5 to 10 minutes before fluffing with a fork to serve.

Cooking Fruit

APPLES poached in light syrup	1 pound	HIGH	Peel, core, and slice apples and place in a microwaveproof bowl with $1\frac{1}{4}$ cups hot sugar syrup. Cover loosely and microwave for 3 minutes, stirring once. Leave to stand, covered, for 5 minutes.
	2 pounds	HIGH	As above, but microwave for 5 to 6 minutes.
stewed	1 pound	HIGH	Peel, core, and slice apples and place in a microwaveproof bowl with $\frac{1}{2}$ cup sugar. Cover loosely and microwave for 6 to 8 minutes, stirring once. Leave to stand, covered, for 2 to 3 minutes.
baked	4 large	HIGH	Wash and remove cores from the apples and score around the middle to prevent bursting. Place in a microwaveproof dish, stuff with a little dried fruit if liked. Pour $\frac{1}{2}$ cup water around fruit and microwave for 9 to 10 minutes, rearranging once. Leave to stand, covered, for 3 to 4 minutes before serving.
APRICOTS poached in light syrup	6 to 8	HIGH	Skin, halve, and pit, slicing if preferred. Place in a microwaveproof bowl with $1\frac{1}{4}$ cups hot sugar syrup. Cover loosely and microwave for 3 to 4 minutes, stirring once. Leave to stand, covered, for 5 minutes.
stewed	6 to 8	HIGH	Pit and wash. Place in a microwaveproof bowl, sprinkle with $\frac{1}{2}$ cup sugar. Cover and microwave for 6 to 8 minutes, stirring once. Leave to stand, covered, for 5 minutes before serving.
BANANAS baked	2 large	HIGH	Peel and halve the bananas lengthwise. Place in a microwaveproof dish with a little sugar and fruit juice. Microwave for 3 to 4 minutes, stirring or rearranging twice.
BLACKBERRIES poached in light syrup	1 pint	HIGH	Hull and rinse. Place in a microwaveproof bowl with $1\frac{1}{4}$ cups hot sugar syrup. Cover loosely and microwave for 2 minutes, stirring once. Leave to stand, covered, for 5 minutes.
BLACK CURRANTS fresh	1 pound	HIGH	Top and tail and place in a microwaveproof dish with $\frac{1}{2}$ cup sugar and 2 tablespoons water. Cover loosely and microwave for 5 minutes, stirring once. Leave to stand, covered, for 5 minutes.
CHERRIES poached in light syrup	1 pound	HIGH	Prick and pit, if preferred. Place in a microwaveproof bowl with $1\frac{1}{4}$ cups of hot sugar syrup. Cover loosely and microwave for 2 to 3 minutes, stirring once. Leave to stand, covered, for 5 minutes.
stewed	1 pound	HIGH	Pit, wash, and place in a microwaveproof bowl with $\frac{1}{2}$ cup sugar and a little grated lemon peel, if liked. Cover and microwave for 4 to 5 minutes, stirring once. Leave to stand, covered, for 3 to 5 minutes.
CRANBERRIES cranberry sauce	$4\frac{1}{2}$ cups	HIGH	Place the cranberries, 6 tablespoons water, and $1\frac{3}{4}$ cups sugar in a large microwaveproof bowl. Cover with vented plastic wrap and microwave for 18 to 20 minutes, stirring every 6 minutes, until pulpy.
DAMSONS poached in light syrup	1 pound, whole or halved	HIGH	Prick whole damsons or halve and pit, if preferred. Place in a microwaveproof bowl with $1\frac{1}{4}$ cups hot sugar syrup. Cover loosely and microwave for 3 minutes for whole damsons; 2 minutes for halves, stirring once. Leave to stand, covered, for 5 minutes.

stewed	1 pound	HIGH	Pit and wash. Place in a microwaveproof bowl with $\frac{1}{2}$ cup sugar and a little grated lemon rind, if liked. Cover and microwave for 4 to 5 minutes, stirring once. Leave to stand, covered, for 3 to 5 minutes.
GOOSEBERRIES fresh	1 pound	HIGH	Top and tail and place in a microwaveproof bowl with 2 tablespoons water. Cover and microwave for 4 to 6 minutes. Stir in $\frac{1}{2}$ cup sugar and leave to stand, covered, for 5 minutes.
GREENGAGES poached in light syrup	1 pound whole or halved	HIGH	Prick whole greengages or halve and pit, if preferred. Place in a microwaveproof bowl with $1\frac{1}{4}$ cups hot sugar syrup. Cover loosely and microwave for 3 minutes for whole greengages; 2 minutes for halves, stirring once. Leave to stand, covered, for 5 minutes.
stewed	1 pound		Pit and wash. Place in a microwaveproof bowl with $\frac{1}{2}$ cup sugar and a little grated lemon peel, if liked. Cover and microwave for 4 to 5 minutes, stirring once. Leave to stand, covered, for 3 to 5 minutes.
NECTARINES poached in light syrup	8	HIGH	Skin and prick thoroughly. Place in a microwaveproof bowl with $1\frac{1}{4}$ cups hot sugar syrup and a dash of lemon juice. Cover loosely and microwave for 6 minutes, stirring once. Leave to stand, covered, for 5 minutes.
stewed	4	HIGH	Pit, wash and slice. Place in a microwaveproof bowl with $\frac{1}{2}$ cup sugar. Cover and microwave for 4 to 5 minutes, stirring once. Leave to stand, covered, for 5 minutes.
ORANGES poached in light syrup	4	HIGH	Peel if preferred, or scrub the skin, then slice finely. Place in a microwaveproof bowl with $1\frac{1}{4}$ cups hot sugar syrup. Cover loosely and microwave for 3 minutes, stirring once. Leave to stand, covered, for 5 minutes.
PEACHES poached in light syrup	4 whole or sliced	HIGH	Skin and prick thoroughly or skin, pit, and slice. Place in a microwaveproof bowl with $1\frac{1}{4}$ cups hot sugar syrup. Cover loosely and microwave for 4 minutes for whole peaches; 3 minutes for slices, stirring once. Leave to stand, covered, for 5 minutes.
stewed	4	HIGH	Pit, wash, and slice. Place in a microwaveproof bowl with $\frac{1}{2}$ cup sugar. Cover and microwave for 4 to 5 minutes, stirring once. Leave to stand, covered, for 5 minutes.
PEARS poached in light syrup	2 pounds whole dessert 2 pounds whole cooking 2 pounds halved dessert	HIGH	Peel and prick if kept whole, or halve and core. Place in a microwaveproof bowl with $1\frac{1}{4}$ cups hot sugar syrup. Cover loosely and microwave for 5 minutes for whole dessert pears; 10 minutes for whole cooking pears; and 3 minutes for halved dessert pears, stirring once. Leave to stand, covered, for 5 minutes.
stewed	6	HIGH	Peel, halve, and core. Dissolve $\frac{1}{3}$ cup sugar in a little water and pour over the pears. Cover loosely and microwave for 8 to 10 minutes, stirring once. Leave to stand, covered, for 5 minutes.
PINEAPPLE poached in light syrup	2 pounds	HIGH	Peel, core, and cut into bite-size pieces. Place in a microwaveproof bowl with $1\frac{1}{4}$ cups hot sugar syrup. Cover loosely and microwave for 5 minutes, stirring once. Leave to stand, covered, for 5 minutes.

PLUMS poached in light syrup	1 pound whole or halved	HIGH	Prick if kept whole or halve and pit. Place in a microwaveproof bowl with $1\frac{1}{4}$ cups hot sugar syrup. Cover loosely and microwave for 3 minutes for whole plums; 2 minutes for halved, stirring once. Leave to stand, covered, for 5 minutes.
stewed	1 pound	HIGH	Pit and wash. Place in a microwaveproof bowl with $\frac{1}{2}$ cup sugar and a little grated lemon peel if liked. Cover and microwave for 4 to 5 minutes, stirring once. Leave to stand, covered, for 3 to 5 minutes.
RASPBERRIES poached in light syrup	$3\frac{1}{2}$ cups	HIGH	Hull and rinse. Place in a microwaveproof bowl with $1\frac{1}{4}$ cups hot sugar syrup. Cover loosely and microwave for 2 minutes, stirring once. Leave to stand, covered, for 5 minutes.
RED CURRANTS fresh	1 pound	HIGH	Top and tail and place in a microwaveproof bowl with $\frac{1}{2}$ cup sugar and 2 tablespoons water. Cover loosely and microwave for 5 minutes, stirring once. Leave to stand for 5 minutes.
RHUBARB fresh	12 ounces	HIGH	Cut into 1-inch pieces. Place in a microwaveproof bowl with 2 tablespoons water. Cover loosely and microwave for 6 to 7 minutes, stirring once. Stir in $\frac{1}{2}$ cup sugar and 1 teaspoon lemon juice. Leave to stand, covered, for 2 to 3 minutes.
poached in light syrup	1 pound	HIGH	Cut into 1-inch pieces. Place in a microwaveproof bowl with $1\frac{1}{4}$ cups hot sugar syrup. Cover loosely and microwave for 4 minutes, stirring once. Leave to stand, covered, for 5 minutes.
STRAWBERRIES poached in light syrup	1 pound	HIGH	Hull and rinse. Place in a microwaveproof bowl with $1\frac{1}{4}$ cups hot sugar syrup. Cover loosely and microwave for 2 minutes, stirring once. Leave to stand, covered, for 5 minutes.

SUGAR SYRUP

To make sugar syrup for poaching fruits, place $\frac{1}{2}$ cup sugar and $1\frac{1}{4}$ cups water in a microwaveproof pitcher. Microwave on HIGH for 4 to 5 minutes, stirring 3 times. Use as required.
Makes about $1\frac{1}{4}$ cups.

Plum and Walnut Crumble

Baked Apples with Apricots

Defrosting Fish and Shellfish

COD			
frozen steaks	1 x 8 ounces 2 x 8 ounces 4 x 8 ounces	DEFROST	To defrost, place in a microwaveproof dish, cover and microwave for 2 to 2 $\frac{1}{2}$ minutes for 1 steak; 3 to 4 minutes for 2 steaks; and 6 to 7 minutes for 4 steaks, turning over or rearranging once. Leave to stand, covered, for 10 minutes before using.
frozen fillets	1 pound	DEFROST	To defrost, place in a microwaveproof dish with the thicker portions to the outer edge. Cover and microwave for 7 to 8 minutes, rearranging once. Leave to stand for 5 minutes before using.
CRABMEAT			
frozen	8 ounces	DEFROST	Leave in wrappings. Microwave for 4 minutes, turning over once. Leave to stand for 2 minutes, then flake to use.
FISH CAKES			
frozen	4 x 3 ounces	DEFROST	To defrost, unwrap and place in a shallow microwaveproof dish. Cover and microwave for 5 to 6½ minutes, rearranging once. Leave to stand for 2 minutes before cooking.
FLOUNDER			
frozen fillets	1 pound	DEFROST	To defrost, place in a microwaveproof dish with the thicker portions to the outer edge. Cover and microwave for 7 to 8 minutes, rearranging once. Leave to stand for 5 minutes before using.
frozen whole	1 x 10 ounces 2 x 10 ounces	DEFROST	To defrost, place on a plate, cover and microwave for 4 to 6 minutes for 1 flounder; and 10 to 12 minutes for 2 flounder, shielding the tail end with a little foil halfway through cooking if necessary. Leave to stand for 5 minutes before using.
HADDOCK			
frozen steaks	1 x 8 ounces 2 x 8 ounces 4 x 8 ounces	DEFROST	To defrost, place in a microwaveproof dish, cover, and microwave for 2 to 2½ minutes for 1 steak; 3 to 4 minutes for 2 steaks; and 6 to 7 minutes for 4 steaks, turning over or rearranging once. Leave to stand for 10 minutes before using.
frozen fillets	1 pound	DEFROST	To defrost, place in a microwaveproof dish with the thicker portions to the outer edge. Cover and microwave for 7 to 8 minutes, rearranging once. Leave to stand for 5 minutes before using.
HALIBUT			
frozen steaks	1 x 8 ounces 2 x 8 ounces 4 x 8 ounces	DEFROST	To defrost, place in a microwaveproof dish, cover, and microwave for 2 to 2½ minutes for 1 steak; 3 to 4 minutes for 2 steaks; and 6 to 7 minutes for 4 steaks, turning over or rearranging once. Leave to stand for 10 minutes before using.
HERRING			
frozen whole	per 1 pound	DEFROST	To defrost, place in a shallow microwaveproof dish and microwave for 5 to 7 minutes per 1 pound, turning over once. Leave to stand for 10 minutes before using.
KIPPERS			
frozen fillets	6 ounces boil-in-the-bag	HIGH	To defrost *and* cook, place the frozen boil-in-the-bag on a plate and snip a couple of vents in the bag. Microwave for 5 to 6 minutes, turning over once. Leave to stand for 2 to 3 minutes before serving.
LOBSTER			
frozen whole, cooked	per 1 pound	DEFROST	To defrost, place in a microwaveproof dish, cover, and microwave for 12 to 15 minutes per 1 pound, giving the dish a quarter turn every 2 minutes and turning over after 6 minutes. Leave to stand for 5 minutes before serving.
MACKEREL			
frozen whole	per 1 pound	DEFROST	To defrost, place in a shallow microwaveproof dish and microwave for 5 to 7 minutes per 1 pound, turning over once. Leave to stand for 10 minutes before using.

MUSSELS frozen cooked shelled	8 ounces	DEFROST	To defrost, spread the mussels on a plate in a single layer. Microwave for $3\frac{1}{2}$ to 4 minutes, stirring to rearrange once. Leave to stand for 2 minutes before using.
RED OR GRAY MULLET frozen whole	2 x 7 to 9 ounces 4 x 7 to 9 ounces	DEFROST	To defrost, place in a shallow microwaveproof dish and microwave for 9 to 11 minutes for 2 whole fish; and 19 to 21 minutes for 4 whole fish, turning or rearranging twice. Leave to stand for 5 minutes before using.
RED SNAPPER frozen whole	1 to $1\frac{1}{2}$ pounds	MEDIUM	To defrost individually (for best results), place in a shallow microwaveproof dish, cover, and microwave for $2\frac{1}{2}$ to $3\frac{1}{2}$ minutes, turning over once. Rinse in cold water then pat dry. Leave to stand for 2 to 3 minutes before using.
SALMON AND SALMON TROUT frozen steaks	2 x 8 ounces 4 x 8 ounces 4 x 6 ounces	DEFROST	To defrost, place in a shallow microwaveproof dish, cover, and microwave for 4 to 5 minutes for 2 x 8-ounce steaks; 10 to 12 minutes for 4 x 8-ounce steaks; and 10 minutes for 4 x 6-ounce steaks, turning over and rearranging once. Leave to stand, covered, for 5 to 10 minutes before using.
frozen whole salmon or salmon trout	1 pound 2 pounds 3 to $3\frac{1}{2}$ pounds 4 to $4\frac{1}{2}$ pounds	DEFROST	To defrost, place in a shallow microwaveproof dish, cover and microwave for 6 to 8 minutes for a 1-pound fish; 12 to 16 minutes for a 2-pound fish; 18 to 20 minutes for a 3- to $3\frac{1}{2}$-pound fish; and 22 to 24 minutes for a 4- to $4\frac{1}{2}$-pound fish, turning over and rotating the dish twice. Shield the head and tail with a little foil as necessary. Leave to stand, covered, for 5 to 10 minutes before using.
SCALLOPS frozen	12 ounces 1 pound	DEFROST	To defrost, place in a microwaveproof bowl, cover, and microwave for 6 to 8 minutes for 12 ounces; and $7\frac{1}{2}$ to 10 minutes for 1 pound, stirring and breaking apart twice. Leave to stand, covered, for 5 minutes before using.
SCAMPI frozen cooked	1 pound	DEFROST	To defrost, place in a shallow microwaveproof dish and microwave for 7 to 8 minutes, stirring twice. Leave to stand, covered, for 5 minutes before using.
SHRIMP frozen cooked	1 pound	DEFROST	To defrost, place in a microwaveproof dish and microwave for 7 to 8 minutes, stirring twice. Leave to stand for 2 to 3 minutes before using.
SMOKED HADDOCK frozen fillets	6 ounces boil-in- the-bag	HIGH	To defrost *and* cook, place bag on a plate and snip a couple of vent holes. Microwave for 5 to 6 minutes, turning over once. Leave to stand for 2 to 3 minutes before using.
SMOKED SALMON frozen sliced	3 to 4 ounces	DEFROST	To defrost, unwrap the salmon and separate the slices. Arrange evenly on a plate and microwave for $1\frac{1}{2}$ to 2 minutes, turning once.
SOLE frozen fillets	1 pound	DEFROST	To defrost, place in a microwaveproof dish with thicker portions to the outer edge. Cover and microwave for 7 to 8 minutes, rearranging once. Leave to stand for 5 minutes before using.
TROUT frozen whole	2 x 8 to 10 ounces 4 x 8 to 10 ounces	DEFROST	To defrost, place in a shallow microwaveproof dish and microwave for 9 to 11 minutes for 2 whole fish; and 19 to 21 minutes for 4 whole fish, turning or rearranging twice. Leave to stand for 5 minutes before using.
WHITING frozen fillets	1 pound	DEFROST	To defrost, place in a microwaveproof dish with thicker portions to the outer edge. Cover and microwave for 7 to 8 minutes, rearranging once. Leave to stand for 5 minutes before using.

Defrosting Poultry and Game

CHICKEN			
frozen quarters	2 x 8 ounces 4 x 8 ounces	LOW	To defrost, remove any wrappings and place in a microwaveproof dish so the meatiest parts are to the outer edge. Microwave for 7 to 9 minutes for 2 x 8-ounce quarters; and 15 minutes for 4 x 8-ounce quarters, turning over and rearranging once. Leave to stand for 10 minutes before using.
frozen drumsticks, about 4 ounces each	2 4 6	LOW	To defrost, remove any wrappings and place in a shallow microwaveproof dish so the meatiest parts are to the outer edge. Microwave for 4 to 5 minutes for 2; 7 to 8 minutes for 4; and 12 minutes for 6 drumsticks, turning over and rearranging once. Leave to stand for 10 minutes before using.
frozen thighs, about 4 ounces each	4 8	LOW	To defrost, remove any wrappings and place in a shallow microwaveproof dish so the meatiest parts are to the outer edge. Microwave for 8 minutes for 4 thighs; and 15 minutes for 8 thighs, turning over and rearranging once. Leave to stand for 10 minutes before using.
frozen wings	1 pound 2 pounds	LOW	To defrost, remove any wrappings and place in a shallow microwaveproof dish. Microwave for 8 minutes for 1 pound; and 15 minutes for 2 pounds wings, turning over and rearranging twice. Leave to stand for 10 minutes before using.
frozen boneless breast halves	2 x 8 ounces 4 x 8 ounces	LOW	To defrost, remove any wrappings and place in a shallow microwaveproof dish. Microwave for 8 minutes for 2 x 8-ounce breast halves; and 15 minutes for 4 x 8-ounce breast halves, turning over and rearranging once. Leave to stand for 10 minutes before using.
frozen whole chicken	2¼ pounds 3 to 3½ pounds 4 to 4½ pounds	DEFROST	To defrost, remove wrappings and place, breast-side down, on a microwaveproof rack or upturned saucer in a shallow dish. Microwave for 12 to 14 minutes for a 2¼-pound bird; 18 to 22 minutes for a 3- to 3½-pound bird; and 24 to 30 minutes for a 4- to 4½-pound bird, turning over halfway through the time and shielding legs, wingtips, or hot spots with foil if necessary. Leave to stand for 15 minutes before using. Remove any giblets at the end of the defrosting time.
frozen chicken livers	8 ounces	DEFROST	To defrost, remove from carton and place in a microwaveproof dish. Cover and microwave for 6 to 8 minutes, separating livers as they soften. Leave to stand, covered, for 5 minutes before using.
DUCK			
frozen whole	5 to 5½ pound per 1 pound	DEFROST	To defrost, shield the wingtips, tail end, and legs with foil as necessary for half of the time. Place breast-side down in a shallow microwaveproof dish and microwave for 10 minutes; turn breast-side up and microwave for 15 to 20 minutes longer, rotating twice. Stand, covered, for 15 minutes before using. Alternatively, defrost for 5 to 6 minutes per 1 pound.
frozen duck portions	4 x 12- to 14-ounce portions	HIGH *then* DEFROST	To defrost, place in a microwaveproof dish and microwave on HIGH for 7 minutes. Turn over, rearrange and microwave on DEFROST for 10 to 14 minutes. Leave to stand, covered, for 15 minutes before using.
GAME BIRDS			
frozen grouse, guinea fowl, partridge, pheasant, pigeon, quail, and woodcock	1 x 1 pound 2 x 1 pound 1 x 2 pounds 4 x 1 pound	DEFROST	To defrost, place on a plate or in a shallow microwaveproof dish, breast-side down. Cover loosely and microwave for half the recommended times: 6 to 7 minutes for 1-pound bird; 12 to 14 minutes for 2 x 1-pound birds; 12 to 14 minutes for 2-pound bird; and 24 to 28 minutes for 4 x 1-pound birds, turning breast-side up after half the time and rearranging if more than 1 bird. Allow to stand, covered, for 5 to 10 minutes before using.
GIBLETS			
frozen	1 bag from poultry bird	DEFROST	To defrost, place in a microwaveproof bowl, cover, and microwave for 2 to 3 minutes. Use as required.

TURKEY frozen whole	6 pounds 9 pounds 12 pounds 15 pounds	MEDIUM	To defrost, place the bird breast-side down in a shallow microwaveproof dish and microwave for a quarter of the time. Turn breast-side up and cook for additional quarter of the time. Shield wingtips and legs with small pieces of foil and turn turkey over, cook for the remaining time. Microwave for 21 to 33 minutes for a 6-pound bird; 32 to 50 minutes for a 9-pound bird; 42 to 66 minutes for a 12-pound bird; and 53 to 83 minutes for a 15-pound bird, checking for hot spots frequently. Leave to stand, covered, for 30 to 45 minutes, before using.
frozen drumsticks, 12 to 14 ounces each	2 4	LOW	To defrost, place in a microwaveproof dish with the meatiest parts to the outer edge. Microwave for 12 to 16 minutes for 2 drumsticks; and 24 to 26 minutes for 4 drumsticks, turning over and rearranging once. Leave to stand, covered, for 10 minutes before using.
frozen breast halves, about 8 ounces each	2 4	LOW	To defrost, place in a microwaveproof dish. Microwave for 5 to 7 minutes for 2 breast halves; 10 to 12 minutes for 4 breast halves, turning over and rearranging once. Leave to stand, covered, for 10 minutes before using.

Chicken and Fruit Salad

Defrosting Meat

BACON frozen slices	8 ounces	DEFROST	To defrost, place on a plate. Microwave for 2 to 3 minutes, turning over once.
frozen joint	1 pound 2 pounds	DEFROST	To defrost, if in vacuum pack, pierce and place on a plate. Microwave for 8 minutes for 1-pound joint; 15 to 17 minutes for 2-pound joint, turning over twice. Leave to stand, covered, for 20 to 30 minutes before using.
BEEF frozen uncooked joint	per 1 pound joints on bone per 1 pound boneless joints	DEFROST	To defrost, place joint on a microwaveproof roasting rack or upturned saucer in a dish. Microwave for 5 to 6 minutes per 1 pound for joints on bone; and 10 minutes per 1 pound for boneless joints, turning over once. Leave to stand, covered, for 30 to 45 minutes before using.
frozen ground beef	8 ounces 1 pound 2 pounds	DEFROST	To defrost, place in a microwaveproof bowl and microwave for 5 minutes for 8 ounces; 9 to 10 minutes for 1 pound; and 17 to 18 minutes for 2 pounds, breaking up twice during the cooking time. Leave to stand for 5 to 10 minutes before using.
frozen stewing or braising steak cubes	8 ounces 1 pound	DEFROST	To defrost, place in a shallow microwaveproof dish and microwave for 5 to 7 minutes for 8 ounces; 8 to 10 minutes for 1 pound, stirring twice. Leave to stand 5 to 10 minutes before using.
frozen hamburgers	4 x 4 ounces	DEFROST	To defrost, place on paper towels and microwave for 10 to 12 minutes, turning over and rearranging twice. Leave to stand 2 to 3 minutes before using.
frozen steaks	1 x 6 to 8 ounces 4 x 4 to 6 ounces 2 x 8 ounces	DEFROST	Place on a plate. Cover and microwave for 4 minutes for 1 x 6- to 8-ounce steak, 4 to 6 minutes for 4 x 4- to 6-ounce steaks; and 6 to 8 minutes for 2 x 8-ounce steaks, turning over once. Leave to stand, covered, for 5 to 10 minutes before using.
HAM frozen uncooked joint	1 pound 2 pounds	DEFROST	To defrost, place the joint on a plate and microwave for 4 to 5 minutes for a 1-pound joint; and 8 to 10 minutes for a 2-pound joint, turning over once. Leave to stand, covered, for 10 to 15 minutes before using.
frozen sliced cooked	4 ounces	DEFROST	To defrost, place on a plate and microwave for 3 to 4 minutes, turning over once. Leave to stand for 5 minutes before using.
KIDNEYS frozen lamb, pig, or ox	2 lamb 4 lamb 2 pig 4 pig 8 ounces ox 1 pound ox	DEFROST	To defrost, place in a microwaveproof bowl, cover and microwave for 1½ to 2 minutes for 2 lamb; 4 minutes for 4 lamb; 4 minutes for 2 pig; 7 to 8 minutes for 4 pig; 6 minutes for 8 ounces ox; and 9 to 10 minutes for 1 pound ox kidney, rearranging 3 times. Leave to stand, covered, for 5 minutes before using.
LAMB frozen chops	2 x 4- to 6-ounce loin chops 4 x 4- to 6-ounce loin chops 2 x 4- to 6-ounce sirloin chops 4 x 4- to 6-ounce sirloin chops	DEFROST	To defrost, place on a microwaveproof roasting rack and microwave for 3 to 4 minutes for 2 x 4- to 6-ounce loin chops; 6 to 8 minutes for 4 x 4- to 6-ounce loin chops; 3 to 4 minutes for 2 x 4- to 6-ounce sirloin chops; and 6 to 8 minutes for 4 x 4- to 6-ounce sirloin chops, turning over and rearranging once. Leave to stand, covered, for 10 minutes before using.
frozen uncooked joint	per 1 pound boned and rolled joint per 1 pound joints on bone	DEFROST	To defrost, place joint on a microwaveproof roasting rack or upturned saucer in a dish. Microwave both types of joint for 5 to 6 minutes per 1 pound, turning over once. Leave to stand, covered, for 30 to 45 minutes, before using.

LIVER frozen slices	8 ounces 1 pound	DEFROST	To defrost, spread slices on a plate. Cover and microwave for 4 to 5 minutes for 8 ounces; and 8 to 9 minutes for 1 pound, turning twice. Leave to stand, covered, for 5 minutes before using.
PORK frozen chops	2 x 4- to 6-ounce loin chops 4 x 4- to 6-ounce loin chops	DEFROST	To defrost, place on a microwaveproof roasting rack and microwave for 3 to 4 minutes for 2 x 4- to 6-ounce loin chops; 6 to 8 minutes for 4 x 4- to 6-ounce loin chops, turning and rearranging once. Leave to stand for 10 minutes before using.
frozen tenderloin	12 ounces per 1 pound	DEFROST	To defrost, place on a microwaveproof roasting rack and microwave for 3 to 4 minutes for a 12-ounce fillet or tenderloin; and 5 to 6 minutes per 1 pound, turning over once. Leave to stand for 10 minutes before using.
frozen uncooked joint	per 1 pound joint on bone per 1 pound boneless joints	DEFROST	To defrost, place joint on a microwaveproof roasting rack or upturned saucer in a dish. Microwave both types of joint for 7 to 8 minutes per 1 pound, turning over once. Leave to stand, covered, for 20 to 45 minutes before using.
SAUSAGEMEAT frozen links	1 pound	DEFROST	To defrost, remove any wrappings and place in a shallow microwaveproof dish. Cover and microwave for 6 to 8 minutes, breaking up twice. Leave to stand, covered, for 4 to 5 minutes before using.
SAUSAGES frozen links	4 standard 8 standard 8 cocktail 16 cocktail	DEFROST	To defrost separated or linked sausages, place on a plate, cover, and microwave for 3 to 4 minutes for 4 standard; 5 to 6 minutes for 8 standard; 3 minutes for 8 cocktail sausages; and 5 minutes for 16 cocktail sausages, separating, turning over and rearranging twice. Leave to stand, covered, for 2 to 5 minutes before using.
VEAL frozen chops	2 4 6	DEFROST	To defrost, arrange in a microwaveproof dish so the thicker portions are to the outer edge. Cover and microwave for 5 to 6 minutes for 2 chops; 8 to 10 minutes for 4 chops; and 12 to 15 minutes for 6 chops, turning and rearranging twice. Leave to stand, covered, for 5 to 10 minutes before using.
frozen roast	2 pounds 3 to 3½ pounds 4 to 4½ pounds 5 to 5¼ pounds	DEFROST	To defrost, place in a microwaveproof dish and microwave for 16 to 18 minutes for a 2-pound joint; 24 to 27 minutes for a 3- to 3½-pound joint; 32 to 36 minutes for a 4- to 4½-pound joint; and 40 to 45 minutes for a 5- to 5¼-pound joint, turning twice. Shield any thinner areas with foil as they defrost. Leave to stand, covered, for 10 to 20 minutes before using.

General Defrosting Chart

BREAD frozen large white or whole-wheat sliced or uncut loaf	1¾ pounds	DEFROST	Loosen wrapper but do not remove. Microwave for 4 minutes. Leave to stand for 5 minutes before slicing or removing precut slices. Leave 10 minutes longer before serving.
frozen individual bread slices and rolls	1 slice/1 roll 2 slices/2 rolls 4 slices/4 rolls	DEFROST	Wrap loosely in paper towels and microwave for 15 to 30 seconds for 1 slice/1 roll; 30 seconds to 1 minute for 2 slices/2 rolls; and 1½ to 2 minutes for 4 slices/4 rolls. Leave to stand for 2 minutes before serving.
frozen pita bread	2 4	DEFROST	Place on a double thickness of paper towels and microwave for 1½ to 2 minutes for 2 pitas; and 2 to 3 minutes for 4 pitas, turning once halfway through the cooking time.
frozen crumpets or English muffins	2 4	HIGH	To defrost *and* reheat, place on a double thickness of paper towels and microwave for 30 to 45 seconds for 2 crumpets or English muffins; 1 to 1½ minutes for 4 crumpets or English muffins, turning once.
CAKES frozen small light fruitcake	1 slice	DEFROST	To defrost, place on a microwaveproof rack and microwave, uncovered, for 5 minutes for a whole small cake; 30 to 45 seconds for 1 slice, rotating twice. Leave to stand for 10 minutes before serving.
frozen Black Forest gâteau	6-inch cake	DEFROST	To defrost, place on a serving plate and microwave, uncovered, for 4 to 6 minutes, checking constantly. Leave to stand for 30 minutes before serving.
frozen cake with cream filling	6-inch cake	HIGH	To defrost, place on a double thickness of paper towels and microwave for 45 seconds. Leave to stand for 10 to 15 minutes before serving.
frozen jam-filled cake	6- to 7-inch cake	DEFROST	To defrost, place on a double thickness of paper towels and microwave for 3 minutes. Leave to stand for 5 minutes before serving.
frozen cup cakes	2 4	DEFROST	To defrost, place on a rack and microwave for 1 to 1½ minutes for 2 cup cakes; and 1½ to 2 minutes for 4 cup cakes, checking frequently. Leave to stand for 5 minutes before serving.
frozen chocolate éclairs	2	DEFROST	To defrost, place on a double thickness of paper towels and microwave for 45 seconds to 1 minute. Leave to stand 5 to 10 minutes before serving.
frozen doughnuts	2 x cream-filled 2 x jam-filled	DEFROST	To defrost, place on a double thickness of paper towels and microwave for 1 to 1½ minutes for 2 cream-filled doughnuts; and 1½ to 2 minutes for 2 jam-filled doughnuts. Leave to stand 3 to 5 minutes before serving.
CASSEROLES frozen	2 servings 4 servings	HIGH	To defrost *and* reheat, place in a microwaveproof dish, cover, and microwave for 8 to 10 minutes for 2 servings; 14 to 16 minutes for 4 servings, breaking up and stirring twice as the casserole thaws. Leave to stand, covered, for 3 to 5 minutes before serving.
CHEESECAKE frozen	individual fruit-topped individual cream-topped family-size fruit-topped family-size cream-topped	DEFROST	To defrost, remove from container and place on a microwaveproof serving plate. Microwave for 1 to 1½ minutes for individual fruit-topped; 1 to 1¼ minutes for individual cream-topped; 5 to 6 minutes for family-size fruit-topped; and 1½ to 2 minutes for family-size cream-topped, rotating once and checking frequently. Leave to stand for 5 to 15 minutes before serving.
COOKIES frozen	8 ounces	DEFROST	Arrange in a circle around the edge of a plate. Microwave for 1 to 1½ minutes, turning over once halfway through cooking. Leave to stand for 5 minutes before serving.

CREPES frozen	8	MEDIUM	To defrost, place a stack of 8 crepes on a plate and microwave for $1\frac{1}{2}$ to 2 minutes, rotating once. Leave to stand for 5 minutes, then peel apart to use.
CROISSANTS frozen	2 4	DEFROST	To defrost, place on a double thickness of paper towels and microwave for 30 seconds to 1 minute for 2 croissants; and $1\frac{1}{2}$ to 2 minutes for 4 croissants.
FISH IN SAUCE frozen boil-in-the bag	1 x 6 ounces 2 x 6 ounces	DEFROST *or* MEDIUM	To defrost *and* cook, pierce the bag and place on a plate. Microwave for 11 to 12 minutes on DEFROST for 1 x 6-ounce bag; and 10 to 12 minutes on MEDIUM for 2 x 6-ounce bags. Shake gently to mix, leave to stand for 2 minutes then snip open to serve.
FRUIT CRUMBLE frozen cooked frozen uncooked	made with 4 cups prepared fruit and $1\frac{1}{2}$ cups crumble topping (to serve 4)	DEFROST *then* HIGH	To defrost *and* cook, microwave frozen cooked crumble for 15 minutes on DEFROST, then 5 minutes on HIGH; and frozen uncooked crumble for 15 minutes on DEFROST, then 10 to 14 minutes on HIGH, until cooked or reheated.
LASAGNE frozen prepared	1 pound	DEFROST *then* HIGH	To defrost *and* cook, remove any foil packaging and place in a microwave-proof dish. Cover and microwave on DEFROST for 8 minutes. Leave to stand for 5 minutes, then microwave on HIGH for 8 to 9 minutes. Brown under a heated hot broiler if liked.
ORANGE JUICE frozen concentrated	6 ounces	HIGH	To defrost, remove lid and place in a microwaveproof pitcher. Microwave for 1 to $1\frac{1}{2}$ minutes, stirring once. Add water to dilute and serve.
PASTA frozen cooked	10 ounces	DEFROST	To defrost *and* reheat, place in a microwaveproof dish, cover, and microwave for 10 minutes, stirring twice. Leave to stand, covered, for 2 to 3 minutes before serving.
PASTRY frozen piecrust and puff pastry dough	7 ounces 14 ounces	DEFROST	Do not remove from wrappings unless unsuitable for microwave. Microwave for $2\frac{1}{2}$ to 3 minutes for 7 ounces; and 4 minutes for 14 ounces. Leave to stand for 3 minutes before using.
PATE frozen	4 ounces 7 ounces 10 ounces	DEFROST	Unwrap and place on a plate or leave in dish if suitable for microwave. Cover and microwave for 1 minute for 4 ounces; 3 to 4 minutes for 7 ounces; and 3 to 4 minutes for 10 ounces, rotating 2 to 3 times. Leave to stand for 15 to 20 minutes before serving.
PIZZA frozen	12 inches 5 inches	HIGH	To defrost *and* cook, place on a plate and microwave for 3 to 5 minutes for a 12-inch pizza; and $1\frac{1}{2}$ to 2 minutes for a 5-inch pizza, rotating the dish twice.
QUICHES frozen unfilled cooked quiches	6 to 7 inches	DEFROST	To defrost, place on a plate and microwave for 1 to $1\frac{1}{2}$ minutes. Leave to stand for 5 minutes before using.
frozen filled cooked quiches	4 inches 8 inches	HIGH	To defrost *and* cook, place on a plate and microwave for 1 to $1\frac{1}{2}$ minutes for a 4-inch quiche; and $2\frac{1}{2}$ to $3\frac{1}{2}$ minutes for an 8-inch quiche. Leave to stand for 5 minutes before serving or using.
RICE frozen cooked	$1\frac{1}{2}$ cups 3 cups	HIGH	To defrost *and* reheat, place in a microwaveproof dish, cover, and microwave for 5 to 6 minutes for $1\frac{1}{2}$ cups; and 7 to 8 minutes for 3 cups, stirring twice. Leave to stand, covered, for 2 minutes before using.

SCONES OR BISCUITS			
frozen	2	DEFROST	To defrost, place on a double thickness of paper towels. Microwave for
	4		$1\frac{1}{4}$ to $1\frac{1}{2}$ minutes for 2 scones or biscuits; 3 minutes for 4 scones or biscuits, rearranging once.
SOUPS			
frozen	$1\frac{1}{4}$ cups	HIGH	To defrost *and* reheat, place in a bowl, cover, and microwave for
	$2\frac{1}{2}$ cups		4 to $4\frac{1}{2}$ minutes for $1\frac{1}{4}$ cups; and 7 to $7\frac{1}{2}$ minutes for $2\frac{1}{2}$ cups, breaking up and stirring 2 to 3 times.
STOCKS			
frozen	$1\frac{1}{4}$ cups	HIGH	Place in a pitcher or bowl, microwave, uncovered: $2\frac{1}{2}$ to 3 minutes for
	$2\frac{1}{2}$ cups		$1\frac{1}{4}$ cups; and 5 to 6 minutes for $2\frac{1}{2}$ cups, stirring and breaking up 2 to 3 times.
WHITE SAUCE			
frozen and variations (such as cheese, parsley, or mustard)	$1\frac{1}{4}$ cups	HIGH	To defrost *and* reheat, place in a microwaveproof dish and microwave for 4 to 5 minutes, stirring twice. Whisk to serve.
YOGURT			
frozen	5-ounce carton	HIGH	To defrost, remove lid and microwave for 1 minute. Stir well and leave to stand for 1 to 2 minutes before serving.

Maple and Banana Quick Bread

Index

A

alcohol, flambéing with, 30
almonds:
  blanching, 27
  cinnamon balls, 218
angel cake, chocolate and
  orange, 205
apples, cooking, 239
  apple and hazelnut
    shortcake, 207
  baked apples with
    apricots, 173
  honey-fruit yogurt
    ice, 182
apricots, cooking, 239
  apricots with orange
    cream, 188
  baked apples with
    apricots, 173
  golden pork and apricot
    casserole, 100
  peeling, 27
  Turkish lamb and apricot
    stew, 96
arranging food, 17
artichokes *see* globe
  artichokes; Jerusalem
  artichokes
asparagus, cooking,
  230, 235
  creamy risotto with
    asparagus, 140
Austrian nut pudding, 178

B

baby food, freezing and
  defrosting, 23
baby's bottles,
  warming, 30
bacon, 8, 227, 246
  pasta with tomato and
    smoky bacon sauce, 129
baked potatoes, 25
bananas, cooking, 239
  Boston banoffee pie, 219
  hot bananas with rum and
    raisins, 180
  maple and banana quick
    bread, 211
  spiced banana
    muffins, 204
banoffee pie, Boston, 219
barley, cooking, 237
batters, 31
beans, dried, 237
  borlotti beans with
    mushrooms, 117

chili con carne, 93
chunky bean and vegetable
  soup, 37
lemon and ginger spicy
  beans, 116
mung beans with
  potatoes, 118
soaking, 26

beef, 227, 246
  beef and lentil pie, 91
  beef and mushroom
    burgers, 88
  beef casserole and
    dumplings, 90
  beef chili soup, 36
  chili con carne, 93
  spicy spaghetti sauce, 92
  Stilton burgers, 86
  stuffed tomatoes, 89
beets, 230
black currants, 239
blackberries, 239
  lemon soufflé with black-
    berries, 191
blueberry crumble quick
  bread, 202
bones, 11
Boston banoffee pie, 219
bread:
  brown soda bread, 196
  Creole bread-and-butter
    pudding, 174

croutons, 28
fall pudding, 182
garlic or herb bread, 26
Melba toast, 50
proving yeast dough, 28
sage soda bread, 197
zucchini and walnut
  loaf, 201

bread crumbs, 28
broccoli, 231, 235
  broccoli and chestnut
    terrine, 158
  broccoli and Stilton
    soup, 42
browning, 20
browning dishes, 14-15
Brussel sprouts, 231, 235
bulgar wheat, 237
burgers:
  beef and mushroom
    burgers, 88
  Stilton burgers, 86
butter, softening, 27
butterflied lamb with
  cumin and garlic, 94

C

cabbage, 231, 235
cakes, 248
  carrot and pecan
    cake, 210

chocolate and orange
  angel cake, 205
cinnamon
  balls, 218
coconut pyramids, 217
frosted cupcakes, 214
gingerbread, 203
hot chocolate
  cake, 206
kugelhopf, 212
strawberry and hazelnut
  roulade, 208
cannelloni al forno, 120
caper sauce, 24
carbonara, pasta, 30
carrots, 231, 235
  carrot and pecan
    cake, 210
  curried carrot and apple
    soup, 40
casseroles, defrosting, 248
  beef casserole and
    dumplings, 90
  fisherman's casserole, 60
  golden pork and apricot
    casserole, 100
  Middle Eastern vegetable
    stew, 153
  mushroom and fennel
    stew, 149
  winter vegetable stew, 156
castle puddings with
  custard, 175
cauliflower and walnut
  cream soup, 40
cauliflower with three
  cheeses, 156
chard, 234
celery, 231
cheese:
  baked macaroni and
    cheese, 130
  broccoli and Stilton
    soup, 42
  cauliflower with three
    cheeses, 156
  cheese and marjoram
    scones, 198
  cheese sauce, 24
  feta cheese and chive
    scones, 199
  ravioli with four cheese
    sauce, 122
  softening and ripening, 27
  Stilton burgers, 86
cheesecake, 248
  fruit-topped baked
    cheesecake, 209

cherries, 239
chestnuts: broccoli and
    chestnut terrine, 158
chicken, 225, 244
    cannelloni al forno, 120
    chicken and fruit
        salad, 112
    chicken and pesto baked
        potatoes, 154
    chicken and vegetable
        risotto, 138
    chicken roll, 106
    Dijon chicken salad, 110
    hot chili chicken, 109
    spiced chicken with
        spinach, 108
    see also liver
chilies:
    beef chili soup, 36
    chili con carne, 93
    chili shrimp, 48
    hot chili chicken, 109
china containers, 13
Chinese cabbage, 231
chocolate:
    chocolate-amaretti
        peaches, 170
    chocolate and orange
        angel cake, 205
    chocolate fudge
        sundaes, 187
    hot chocolate cake, 206
    melting, 30
    oat florentines, 213
chow mein, 103
chowder, creamy
    cod, 35
cider, spiced pears
    in, 181
cinnamon and coconut
    rice, 179
cinnamon balls, 218
citrus juice, squeezing, 28
citrus peels, drying, 27
clams: spaghetti with
    tomato and clam
    sauce, 127
cleaning microwave
    cookers, 12
coconut:
    coconut pyramids, 217
    toasting, 27
coconut milk:
    cinnamon and coconut
        rice, 179
    coconut salmon, 75
cod, 222, 242
    cod Creole, 62
    green fish curry, 76
    see also smoked cod
coffee, reheating, 30
combination ovens, 11
containers, 13-15
cookies, 248

cookie cups, 29
    oat florentines, 213
corn, 235
    corn-on-the-cob, 25, 231
    corn soup, 46
couscous, sweet
    vegetable, 141
covering food, 18-19
crabmeat, 242
cranberries, 239
creamy cauliflower and
    walnut soup, 40
Creole bread-and-butter
    pudding, 174

crepes, 249
croissants, 249
croutons, 28
crumble, plum and
    walnut, 171
cucumber sauce, salmon
    with, 68
cupcakes, frosted, 214
curly kale, 232
curries:
    curried carrot and apple
        soup, 40
    curried lamb and
        lentils, 100
    curried parsnip
        soup, 38
    garbanzo bean
        curry, 119
    green fish curry, 76
    mushroom and okra
        curry, 160
    prawn curry, 77
    rogan josh, 98
    spicy lamb curry, 99

custard, castle puddings
    with, 175

D
damsons, 239
date-filled pastries, 216
deep-fat frying, 31
desserts, 168-93
defrosting, 21, 248-50
    fish and shellfish, 242-3
    meat, 246-7
    poultry and game, 244-5
desserts, 168-93

Dijon chicken
    salad, 110
dishes, 13-15
dried fruit: fruit and rice
    ring, 190
duck, 225, 244
dumplings, beef casserole
    and, 90

E
eggplants, 230
eggs, 31
    eggs en cocotte, 52
    mixed pepper
        pipérade, 152
    pasta carbonara, 130
    scrambled eggs, 24
    zucchini and potato
        tortilla, 154
English marrow, 232
equipment, 13-15

F
fall compote, warm, 184
fall pudding, 182
fennel, 232
    halibut with fennel and
        orange, 68
    mushroom and fennel
        stew, 149
feta cheese and chive
    scones, 199
fish and seafood, 58-83,
    222-4
fish and shellfish, 7
    defrosting, 242-3
    fish cakes, defrosting, 242
    fisherman's casserole, 60
    five-spice fish, 62
    Italian fish soup, 34
    Mediterranean fish
        cutlets, 80
    Seafood Pilaf, 78
    see also cod; haddock, etc.
five-spice fish, 62
flambéing with alcohol, 30
florentines, oat, 213
flounder, 223, 242–3
    Mediterranean flounder, 67
    stuffed flounder rolls, 66
fool, rhubarb and
    orange, 188
freezers, 21-3
frozen vegetables, 235-6
fruit, 9, 239-41
    fall pudding, 182
    fruit-topped baked
        cheesecake, 209
    fruity brown rice
        salad, 165
    summer berry
        medley, 192
    warm fall compôte, 184
    see also apples;
        strawberries, etc.
fruit and rice ring, 190

G
game, 8, 225-6
    defrosting, 244-5
garbanzo beans, 237
    garbanzo bean curry, 119
    oat tartlets with minted
        hummus, 200
garlic bread, 26
gelatin, dissolving, 29
giblets, 244
    giblet stock, 24
ginger:
    ginger and lime
        shrimp, 80
    gingerbread, 203
    gingerbread upside-down
        pudding, 176
glass containers, 13

globe artichokes, 230
golden pork and apricot
  casserole, 100
golden vegetable paella, 135
gooseberries, 240
grains, 9, 237-8
grape leaves, stuffed, 56
gray mullet, 223, 243
green beans, 230, 235
green fish curry, 76
greengages, 240

H
haddock, 222, 242
  herby fish cakes with
    lemon-chive sauce, 70
  potato-topped fish
    pie, 60
  sweet-and-sour fish, 72
  see also smoked haddock
halibut, 222, 242
  halibut with fennel and
    orange, 68
ham, 228, 246
  defrosting, 246
  pasta carbonara, 130
hazelnuts:
  apple and hazelnut
    shortcake, 207
  Austrian nut
    pudding, 178
  strawberry and hazelnut
    roulade, 208
herbs:
  drying, 27
  herb bread, 26
  herby fish cakes with
    lemon-chive
    sauce, 70
herring, 222, 242
hollandaise sauce, 25
honey:
  clarifying, 29
  honey-fruit yogurt ice, 182
hot-and-sour pork, 102
hot chili chicken, 109
hummus: oat tartlets with
  minted hummus, 200

I
ice cream:
  chocolate fudge
    sundaes, 187
  honey-fruit yogurt ice, 182
  softening, 30
Italian fish soup, 34

J
jams, softening, 29
jelly, dissolving, 29
Jerusalem artichokes, 230

artichoke and mushroom
  soup, 44
Jerusalem artichoke
  soup, 42
juices, removing excess, 20

K
kabobs, 8
  mackerel kabobs with
    parsley dressing, 71
kidney beans: chili con
  carne, 93
kidneys, defrosting, 246

kippers, 222, 242
kohlrabi, 232
kugelhopf, 212

L
lamb, 228, 247
  butterflied with cumin
    and garlic, 94
  curried lamb and
    lentils, 100
  lamb pie with a potato
    crust, 97
  rack of lamb with red
    currant bunches, 95
  rogan josh, 98
  spicy lamb curry, 99
  Turkish lamb and apricot
    stew, 96
lasagne, defrosting, 249
  turkey lasagne, 123
leeks, 232, 236
  chilled leek and potato
    soup, 38

leek terrine with deli
  meats, 54
leeks with mustard
  dressing, 53
potato, leek, and tomato
  bake, 150
legumes, 9, 237–8
lemon:
  lemon and ginger spicy
    beans, 116
  lemon soufflé with black-
    berries, 191
lentils, cooking, 237
  beef and lentil pie, 91

curried lamb and
  lentils, 100
red lentils, 26
spiced lentils and
  rice, 136
linen containers, 14
liver, 228, 247
  chicken liver pâté with
    Marsala, 50
  chicken liver salad, 113
lobster, 222, 242

M
macaroni and cheese,
  baked, 130
mackerel, 223, 242
  mackerel kabobs with
    parsley dressing, 71
maple and banana quick
  bread, 211
mascarpone: apricots with
  orange cream, 188
meat and poultry, 8, 84-113

meat, cooking, 227-9
  defrosting, 246-7
  leek terrine with deli
    meats, 54
Mediterranean fish
  cutlets, 80
Mediterranean flounder, 67
Mediterranean salad with
  basil, 166
Melba toast, 50
meringues, 31
metal containers, 15
Mexican salsa, monkfish
  with, 64
microwave cooking, 10-12
Middle Eastern vegetable
  stew, 153
milk, heating, 30
millet, cooking, 237
monkfish:
  monkfish with Mexican
    salsa, 64
  spiced fish with
    okra, 74
mousse, ruby plum, 184
muffins, spiced
  banana, 204
mulled wine, 30
mung beans with
  potatoes, 118
mushrooms, 232, 236
  artichoke and mushroom
    soup, 44
  beef and mushroom
    burgers, 88
  borlotti beans with
    mushrooms, 117
  mixed mushroom
    ragout, 159
  mushroom and fennel
    stew, 149
  mushroom and okra
    curry, 160
  mushroom, leek and
    cashew nut
    risotto, 137
  mushroom pâté, 51
mussels, 223, 242
mustard dressing, leeks
  with, 53

N
nectarines, cooking, 240
noodles: chow mein, 103
nuts:
  toasting, 27
  see also almonds;
    walnuts, etc.

O
oatmeal, 26
  cooking, 238

oat florentines, 213
oat tartlets with minted
  hummus, 200
oatmeal, 26
okra, cooking, 232
  mushroom and okra
    curry, 160
  spiced fish with okra, 74
one-stage sauce, 24
onions, 232
oranges, 240, 249
  apricots with orange
    cream, 188
  chocolate and orange
    angel cake, 205
  rhubarb and orange
    fool, 188

P
paella, golden vegetable, 135
pak soi, cooking, 233
paper containers, 13
parsley sauce, 24
parsnips, 233, 236
  curried parsnip soup, 38
pasta, 9, 238, 249
  arugula, snow peas, and
    pine nut pasta, 133
  Mediterranean salad with
    basil, 166
  pasta bows with smoked
    salmon and dill, 125
  pasta carbonara, 130
  pasta shells with smoked
    haddock, 124
  pasta with tomato and
    smoky bacon sauce, 129
  pasta with tuna, capers
    and anchovies, 126
  salmon pasta with parsley
    sauce, 78
  tuna and mixed vegetable
    pasta, 72
  see also lasagne;
    spaghetti, etc.
pastries, date-filled, 216
pastry, defrosting, 28, 249
pâté, defrosting, 249
  chicken liver pâté with
    Marsala, 50
  mushroom pâté, 51
peaches, cooking, 240
  chocolate-amaretti
    peaches, 170
  peeling, 27
pears, cooking, 240
  poached pears in red
    wine, 193
  spiced pears in cider, 181
peas, 233, 236
peas, split, 237
pecans: carrot and pecan
  cake, 210

peppers, bell:
  mixed pepper
    pipérade, 152
  tomato and red pepper
    soup, 44
pilaf, seafood, 78
pineapple, cooking, 240
  fruity brown rice
    salad, 165
pipérade, mixed
  pepper, 152
pizzas, defrosting, 249
plastic containers, 13-14
plums, cooking, 241

plum and walnut
  crumble, 171
ruby plum mousse, 184
popcorn, 31
poppadoms, 29
pork, 229, 247
  chicken roll, 106
  chow mein, 103
  golden pork and apricot
    casserole, 100
  hot-and-sour
    pork, 102
  pork crumble, 104
portable microwave
  ovens, 11
potatoes, cooking, 233
  baked potatoes, 25, 154
  beef and lentil pie, 91
  chicken and pesto baked
    potatoes, 154
  chilled leek and potato
    soup, 38
  herby fish cakes with
    lemon-chive sauce, 70

lamb pie with a potato
  crust, 97
mung beans with
  potatoes, 118
new potato and chive
  salad, 162
potato, leek, and tomato
  bake, 150
potato-topped fish pie, 60
watercress and potato
  salad, 164
zucchini and potato
  tortilla, 154
pottery containers, 13

poultry, 8, 85-113, 225-6
  defrosting, 244-5
  see also chicken; duck, etc.
power, microwave, 31
pumpkin, 233

Q
quiches, defrosting, 249
quick breads:
  blueberry crumble, 202
  maple and banana, 211

R
raspberries, 241
ratatouille, 144
  eggs en cocotte, 52
ravioli with four cheese
  sauce, 122
rearranging food, 17
red cabbage in port and red
  wine, 147
red currants, 241

rack of lamb with red
  currant bunches, 95
red mullet, 223, 243
red snapper,
  defrosting, 243
reheating food, 23
rhubarb, cooking, 241
  rhubarb and orange
    fool, 188
  rhubarb and strawberry
    crisp, 172
rice, 9, 238, 249
  cinnamon and coconut
    rice, 179
  fruit and rice ring, 190
  fruity brown rice
    salad, 165
  golden vegetable
    paella, 135
  seafood pilaf, 78
  spiced lentils and
    rice, 136
  stuffed grape leaves, 56
  Thai fragrant rice, 134
  vegetable rice, 26
  see also risotto
rigatoni with spicy sausage
  and tomato, 128
risotto:
  chicken and vegetable
    risotto, 138
  creamy risotto with
    asparagus, 140
  mushroom, leek, and
    cashew nut risotto, 137
rogan josh, 98
rotating food, 16
roulade, strawberry and
  hazelnut, 208
ruby plum mousse, 184
rutabagas, 233, 236
rye, cooking, 238

S
sage soda bread, 197
salads:
  chicken and fruit, 112
  chicken liver, 113
  Dijon chicken, 110
  fruity brown rice, 165
  Mediterranean salad with
    basil, 166
  new potato and
    chive, 162
  salade Niçoise, 163
  watercress and
    potato, 164
salmon, 223, 243
  coconut salmon, 75
  salmon pasta with parsley
    sauce, 78
  salmon with cucumber
    sauce, 68

whole cooked salmon, 82
see also smoked salmon
salmon trout, 243
sauces:
  caper, 24
  cheese, 24
  hollandaise, 25
  one-stage, 24
  parsley, 24
  white, defrosting, 250
  white pouring, 24
sausages, 8, 229, 247
  rigatoni with spicy sausage
    and tomato, 128
scallops, 223, 243
  scallops with
    ginger, 48
scampi, defrosting, 243
scones, defrosting, 250
  cheese and
    marjoram, 198
  feta cheese and chive, 199
scoring foods, 16
shellfish, 7, 59-82, 222-3
  defrosting, 242-3
  seafood pilaf, 78
  spaghetti with seafood
    sauce, 65
  see also scallops;
    shrimp, etc.
shielding food, 18
shortcake, apple and
  hazelnut, 207
shrimp, 223, 243
  chili shrimp, 48
  ginger and lime
    shrimp, 80
  shrimp curry, 77
smoked cod: creamy cod
  chowder, 35
smoked haddock, 224, 243
  pasta shells with smoked
    haddock, 124
smoked salmon,
  defrosting, 243
  pasta bows with smoked
    salmon and dill, 125
snow peas, 232, 236
  arugula, snow peas and
    pine nut pasta, 133
soda bread:
  brown, 196
  sage, 197
sole, 223, 243
soufflé, lemon with
  blackberries, 191
soups, 32-47, 250
  artichoke and
    mushroom, 44
  beef chili, 36
  broccoli and Stilton, 42
  cauliflower and walnut
    cream, 40
  chilled leek and potato, 38

chunky bean and
  vegetable, 37
corn, 46
creamy cod chowder, 35
curried carrot and
  apple, 40
curried parsnip, 38
Italian fish, 34
Jerusalem artichoke, 42
tomato and red pepper, 44
zucchini, 46
spaghetti:
  spaghetti with seafood
    sauce, 65

spaghetti with tomato and
  clam sauce, 127
spicy Bolognese, 92
spicy lamb curry, 99
spinach, 233, 236
  spiced chicken with
    spinach, 108
spring vegetable
  medley, 148
squash, cooking, 233
standing times, 20
sticky toffee
  pudding, 177
Stilton burgers, 86
stirring, 16
stocks, defrosting, 250
  giblet, 24
strawberries,
  defrosting, 241
  rhubarb and strawberry
    crisp, 172
  strawberry and hazelnut
    roulade, 208
summer berry medley, 192

summer vegetable
  braise, 151
sundaes, chocolate
  fudge, 187
sweet-and-sour fish, 72
sweet potatoes, 234
sweet vegetable
  couscous, 141

T
tagliatelle:
  pasta carbonara, 130
  tagliatelle with tomatoes

and zucchini, 132
tangerine trifle, 186
tartlets, oat with minted
  hummus, 200
techniques, 16-20
terrines:
  broccoli and
    chestnut, 158
  leek terrine with deli
    meats, 54
Thai fragrant rice, 134
thermometers, 14
toast, Melba, 50
toffee pudding,
  sticky, 177
tomatoes, 234
  cod Creole, 62
  herby baked
    tomatoes, 145
  pasta with tomato and
    smoky bacon sauce, 129
  peeling, 27
  potato, leek, and tomato
    bake, 150

spaghetti with tomato and
  clam sauce, 127
stuffed tomatoes, 89
tagliatelle with tomatoes
  and zucchini, 132
tomato and red pepper
  soup, 44
tortilla, zucchini, and
  potato, 154
trifle, tangerine, 186
trout, 224, 243
tuna:
  Mediterranean salad with
    basil, 166
  pasta with tuna, capers,
    and anchovies, 126
  salade Niçoise, 163
  tuna and mixed vegetable
    pasta, 72
turkey, 226, 245
  turkey lasagne, 123
Turkish lamb and apricot
  stew, 96
turning over, 16
turnips, cooking, 234

U
upside-down pudding,
  gingerbread, 176
utensils, 13-15

V
veal, 229, 247
vegetables, 9, 230-6
  chicken and vegetable
    risotto, 138
  chunky bean and vegetable
    soup, 37
  golden vegetable
    paella, 135
  Middle Eastern vegetable
    stew, 153
  ratatouille, 144
  spring vegetable
    medley, 148
  summer vegetable
    braise, 151
  sweet vegetable
    couscous, 141
  tuna and mixed vegetable
    pasta, 72
  vegetable rice, 26
  winter vegetable
    stew, 156

W
walnuts:
  plum and walnut
    crumble, 171
  sticky toffee
    pudding, 177

Acknowledgements

For their assistance in the production of this book the
publishers would like to thank:

Panasonic Consumer Electronics
Panasonic House
Willoughby Road
Bracknell
Berks RG12 8FP

Photography by:
James Duncan
Steve Baxter
Karl Adamson
Amanda Heywood
Edward Allwright
David Jordan
David Armstrong

Prop styling for
photography:
Judy Williams
Kirsty Rawlings
Blake Minton
Madeleine Brehaut
Claire Louise Hunt

Preparation of food for
photography:
Wendy Lee
Jane Stevenson
Katherine Hawkins
Judy Williams
Christine France
Elizabeth Wolf-Cohen
Sue Maggs
Janet Brinkworth
Annie Nichols
Jenny Stacey
Elizabeth Martin

Original recipe writing:
Sarah Gates
Christine France
Maggie Pannell
Catherine Atkinson
Judy Jackson
Elizabeth Lambert-Ortiz
Janet Brinkworth
Annie Nichols
Jenny Stacey
Maxine Clark
Shirley Gill
Hilaire Walden
Elizabeth Wolf-Cohen
Sue Maggs
Manisha Kanani
Shehzad Husain
Elizabeth Martin
Carol Bowen

Microwave recipe
consultant:
Carol Bowen